DOMINATRIX ON TRIAL

Bedford vs. Canada

TERRI-JEAN BEDFORD

iUniverse, Inc.
Bloomington

Dominatrix on Trial
Bedford vs. Canada

Copyright © 2011 Terri-Jean Bedford

All rights reserved. No part of this book may be used or reproduced by any means, graphic, electronic, or mechanical, including photocopying, recording, taping or by any information storage retrieval system without the written permission of the publisher except in the case of brief quotations embodied in critical articles and reviews.

iUniverse books may be ordered through booksellers or by contacting:

iUniverse
1663 Liberty Drive
Bloomington, IN 47403
www.iuniverse.com
1-800-Authors (1-800-288-4677)

Because of the dynamic nature of the Internet, any Web addresses or links contained in this book may have changed since publication and may no longer be valid. The views expressed in this work are solely those of the author and do not necessarily reflect the views of the publisher, and the publisher hereby disclaims any responsibility for them.

ISBN: 978-1-4620-2676-0 (sc)
ISBN: 978-1-4620-2677-7 (hc)
ISBN: 978-1-4620-2678-4 (e)

Library of Congress Control Number: 2011909965

Printed in the United States of America

iUniverse rev. date: 6/17/2011

Chapter 1.	The Raid	1
Chapter 2.	Bad Little Girl	8
Chapter 3.	Jail and Bail	21
Chapter 4.	Bad Big Girl	33
Chapter 5.	My Trials Begin	44
Chapter 6.	The Bondage Bungalow	58
Chapter 7.	My Trials Continue	74
Chapter 8.	Running the Bondage Bungalow	85
Chapter 9.	The Big Trial: Getting Ready	96
Chapter 10.	Sessions in the Bondage Bungalow	109
Chapter 11.	The Big Trial: What a Spectacle!	150
Chapter 12.	Clients of the Dominatrix	161
Chapter 13.	The Big Trial: What a Result!	170
Chapter 14.	Back in Business	183
Chapter 15.	Higher Courts	193
Chapter 16.	Dominatrix Lineup	208
Chapter 17.	Staying Alive	220
Chapter 18.	Constitutional Challenge	237
Chapter 19.	Constitutional Decision	249
Chapter 20.	Final Words	260

Acknowledgments

I would like to thank from the bottom of my heart the many lawyers, students, experts, and activists who have stood with me during many years of legal battles and personal struggles. They are too numerous to name here, but you will read about them.

However, it is my special privilege to dedicate this book to nine men and three women you will also read about, none of them lawyers, whom I call The Dozen. Their courage, generosity, hard work, encouragement, loyalty, and support of every kind have not only made it possible for me to keep fighting, survive economically, and tell my story, but, I believe, have saved my life and that of my child. They are citizens of the highest caliber. You should thank them for some of the freedoms you enjoy today, whatever your lifestyle. Some have consented to be named, but most of them wish to remain anonymous and thus have been given pseudonyms, and I have told my story in a manner that ensures their privacy.

When authorities are corrupt or incompetent, when nobody seems to care about victims, and when injustice and hypocrisy seem the rule, don't lose hope. Heroes walk among us.

Preface

Let's start with a confession, or rather two. A few times, I yawned when whipping men in chains. I also confess to nodding off in court when they were trying to jail me. But what's a girl to do? Maybe if I tell you my story, you'll understand why I was so tired.

I am Terri-Jean Bedford, Canada's most famous dominatrix. This is the story of my personal and professional life. My story tells how a future mother and grandmother was neglected and abused as a child and became a prostitute, dominatrix, defendant, and, finally, plaintiff in a constitutional challenge to Canada's prostitution laws.

For almost two years, I was a top dominatrix in the Toronto region. My facility was one of the best. Several such facilities existed in the area at the time, but rarely did police bother to investigate such establishments. These facilities catered to men and women who wished to act out adult fantasies of fetishism, transvestism, infantilism, and masochism. No sex or sexual acts happened in mine. Nothing occurred there that fit the description of "indecent." Everything was consensual and aboveboard. To be on the safe side, I ran my house with the assumption that every client was an investigating police officer.

Yet in September 1994, I was arrested on charges of keeping a common bawdy house. The charges were not even fit for trial, according to the first judge. But for years, the authorities appealed while refusing to drop the charges, apologize, or return my personal belongings. At first nobody could understand why they had called press conferences to publicize the raid. It was a front-page story in one of Toronto's daily newspapers, and the lead story on local television news the day after the raid. In the ensuing years, there were appeals by both prosecutors and defence, and then, in 2007, I joined with two other courageous women in challenging the constitutionality of Canada's prostitution and bawdy-house laws. Over the years, I have been interviewed and profiled extensively in the media. The issues raised by my trials have resulted in much discussion in the media; in the academic and legal communities; and on the streets. My trials have affected subsequent court decisions. And, of course, in 2010, the country's prostitution laws were struck down as a result of the constitutional challenge. Now, in 2011, the battle rages on in the courts, with many parties seeking to join the fray and large numbers of judges involved as well.

A few years after the famous raid, I opened another facility, but only three years later, I had to close it as my health deteriorated. Today I am disabled by a chronic liver disease and spinal deterioration. Over the years, I have written my memoirs, and only now do I feel that the time is right to publish them. I have continually been astonished at how much people know and remember about me and my court battles. When I've spoken about what I might put in a book, they have always been fascinated. They invariably said that not only would people be titillated by the private practices of some of our leading citizens and others, but they would also be intrigued by the many psychological and civil-liberty issues that have come to light.

So in this book, I will tell you all about my personal life, the goings-on in my houses, and my legal battles. But I also want to give you some insights into why clients visited me; what kind of woman becomes a dominatrix and why; and what such a career choice does to her. I will also introduce you to a great number of people who figure in this story as neither doms nor clients. They are friends, police officers, lawyers, judges, reporters, and concerned citizens.

You will read about my battles with authorities to determine what activities are legal between consenting adults in private; who decides what is legal; and who is accountable for those decisions. There is also the ongoing battle to make our laws, and how they are enforced, clear, consistent, and logical. If it is legal to put women's clothes on your boyfriend, tie him up, and tickle him for free, why might—I repeat, *might*—it be against the law to be paid for it?

As you read my story, you will be surprised by many other examples of our society's moral and legal hypocrisy. But you will also see the changes achieved in how society does or does not regulate our private relationships. These changes have enhanced our freedoms, and I am proud to say that I played a part in bringing them about. And finally, as you read my story, you will see that more such changes are needed, more are possible, and more are coming.

It became apparent to me as I wrote that the best way to tell you my story was to move each aspect of it along a bit at a time. That is why most chapters address a different aspect of my story than the one before, and the aspect discontinued is picked up in a later chapter.

One of my many supporters said that above all else, mine is really a story about citizenship. He said it was a story of what can be achieved when an ordinary or even disadvantaged individual advocates a cause and then *becomes* that cause. The cause to which he referred, in my case, is freedom. Freedom is not a gift. Our freedoms oblige us to act when they are challenged. Those who are able to fight for freedom must do so, or lose their self-respect.

My hope is that my efforts and my story will help all Canadians and others to enjoy their freedom of self-expression, and that it will enable the true professionals whose livelihoods extend from offering fantasy role-play or sex to be free to do so openly and safely. The dangers faced by women who provide these services are terrible. The current legal battle is seeking to change this. Right now we are winning, but the old laws remain for now, pending appeal. The hypocrisy of the position now being taken by many authorities against change is a national embarrassment. Nothing can be worse than what we have now. Canada can do better. I believe it will.

Chapter 1

The Raid

Thursday, September 15, 1994, was sunny, warm, and dry, so I had my morning coffee on the back patio. A couple of the staff sat with me for a few minutes. I tossed some crumbs to the squirrels and looked out over the huge yard. The garden I had planted was colorful in its late summer bloom. Life was good. I was a successful dominatrix (and you'll hear plenty about that later, and about all the eight rooms of the house outfitted for role-playing and dungeon play). I had a loyal staff: Judy, my receptionist, and Princess and Mistress Morgan, the two full-time dominatrices besides me. Edward was my hired security guard.

That era was one of the few times that my life was not a living hell. I was able to send money back home to my daughter and her guardians. I had a roof over my head, and I felt safe.

After coffee, Morgan, Edward, and I began cleaning the house, a task usually performed by our slave clients, if any were available on the given day. Princess arrived at eleven thirty and joined us for lunch. Judy was off that day. Three appointments had been scheduled: The first, a cross-dresser Princess was to supervise, was due to arrive at noon. The second was to be a show with me and Princess at one. The third was a tour of the house scheduled for two thirty.

The show was a scenario in which one woman dominated another while the client watched. I would put Princess in bondage and discipline her in a teacher-student scenario. The client, Tim, had seen Morgan and Princess act out this scenario once before. This time, he had requested me to be dominant with Princess. This did not strike us as odd, since some clients liked to watch such shows again and again with different women acting the roles.

Princess was on her monthly cycle and unable to concentrate on her role as a submissive, so I apologized and told Tim that the show was canceled. Tim said that he wanted a consultation with me instead of the show, even though he'd had three previous consultations. I didn't think this was odd, because many clients asked for such sessions to discuss their needs and wants in detail even after visiting many times. He mentioned a number of other scenarios and asked about hygiene and safety, which I took to mean that he was considering not just watching anymore, but being dominated himself. I told him to fill out a questionnaire or write out his fantasies, but he declined. He thanked me and left.

Of course, we found out later that day that Tim was an undercover police officer and that he had apparently made these requests so that we would be in full costume and Princess in bondage when they raided us and took their pictures.

Half an hour later, the doorbell rang, and I answered it, thinking that it was the two-thirty tour appointment arriving early. The cross-dresser was downstairs, having a shower before getting dressed to leave. I opened the door to a young man dressed casually and holding a piece of paper. He handed me the paper and said he was told to write some things down before he came back.

He reached into his back pocket and showed me his police badge, saying, "I'm with the York Regional Police. You are being served with a search warrant and are being charged with keeping a common bawdy house."

I was amazed. "You're out of your mind," I replied. "I don't offer sex here—it's strictly domination and cross-dressing, and that's legal."

He said, "No, you're charging money for it, and you can't do that."

As we spoke, about fifteen men lined up behind him at the door. The officer with the badge pushed me aside, and the men rushed into the house. These plainclothes detectives, uniformed constables, and emergency task-force team all acted as if they believed they were capturing terrorists or hijackers.

The bungalow consisted of one ground floor and a basement, where the dungeon, examination room, throne room, and shower were. The parlor, the classroom, the living room, office, bedroom, washroom, and the kitchen were upstairs. I ran to the foot of the stairs to yell downstairs to Edward that the police were here, and it was not a break-in. A massive officer grabbed me and told me to sit on one of the couches in the living room. I hesitated a second, and he grabbed me around my chest and punched me several times on the side of the head. I fought back, but he was huge. The blows were full punches and made me see stars, but I did not bleed. There was some bruising days later, but I did not think to report it. Then he held me down on a couch. I started to cry. He eventually let me go and went to look around the house.

Some officers brought Morgan into the room, and she sat across from me on another couch. We could hear people going through the house. Downstairs, the raid team was greeted by Edward, who had not heard my warning and thought they were intruders. He threw two officers down the stairs, but when they shouted, "Police! Lie down on the floor!" he became peaceful. Princess opened the door of the shower-room area and threw up her hands. The police pushed her down onto the floor beside Edward. They also pulled our client out of the shower and handed him a towel. The client, an elderly man, was shaking in terror.

Upstairs, Morgan and I sat on the couch, upset and yelling to the officers that they had no right or reason to be there.

I said to the officer who hit me, "I want your badge number. I'm charging you with assault."

He laughed and said, "Call me master."

Edward was brought into the living room and sat down beside me. Some of the officers searched Morgan's purse, and they asked her questions about her identity.

In the days and weeks ahead, Edward, Morgan, and Princess told me much of what I am now to tell you.

Princess was taken upstairs into my office and questioned by two officers. The police took $50 from our money box and handed it to her when she told them she had not been paid that day. They told her that she would have nothing to worry about, and they would not tell her family, provided she didn't call a lawyer and did what they said. They said a lawyer could not help her.

The cross-dresser client was ticketed as a "found-in" and told he would have to appear in court. He was allowed to leave a few minutes later.

The raid had now been under way for about thirty minutes. A plainclothes officer walked up to me with a female and told his colleague, "Search her in the bathroom." She led me to the bathroom and closed the door on us, out of the view of any other officer. I was wearing a simple, casual and somewhat skimpy outfit, which she told me to remove and drop to my ankles. She then ordered me to lower my panties. I was completely naked. She looked me over carefully for a few seconds and then told me to turn around. She told me to bend over. I heard her giggle, but when I turned around, she was not smiling, although she did have a very pleased look on her face. She told me to get dressed and patted the pockets of my clothes before taking me back to the couch. She told Morgan to stand up and took her to the bathroom, where the strip-search procedure was repeated.

Sitting on the couch, we could hear furniture being moved downstairs. We heard laughing and shouting. Princess saw the officers playing with my equipment and jokingly threatening each other with whips. The police wandered around the house and the grounds, talking to one another and taking pictures. I heard one of them say to another officer, "But there isn't anything illegal."

Morgan and I were told we would be taken to the police station and held overnight for bail. We asked if we could call our lawyer and were told we could call from the police station. We also asked if we could change our clothes before we left. Remember, I was wearing that skimpy outfit, and Morgan just had a turtleneck and jeans on, and we were going to appear in court. They refused to let us change. I started to beg.

They seemed to enjoy my begging, especially one female officer, but they stopped laughing when I said I would not go if I were not allowed to change. This started another of their numerous whispering conferences. But finally the woman officer, accompanied by one of the male officers, told me to get up and go get the clothes I needed. I went with them into a couple of rooms and got things suitable for court. I had to change in front of them, male officer included. They returned me to the couch and took Morgan to her clothes, which were downstairs, where the dungeon was.

Morgan was appalled when she saw what was going on downstairs. She saw officers playing with the whips while wearing the wigs. The raid had become a party for them. She went into the burlesque parlor, which was in a closed-off room on the opposite side of the basement from the dungeon and other rooms. This was where most of her clothes were stored and where she slept on a foldout couch. When she came out to go upstairs after she had changed clothes, she got angry with the officers playing with the whips and wigs.

She said, "Do you want to see what we do here?"

They said they did, so Morgan sat on the throne and told one of the officers to kiss her foot. He went down on all fours and kissed it. The other officers whooped with laughter, the female officer included. I could hear the laughing upstairs but did not know what was so funny.

Morgan said, "Kiss it again—this time with feeling," and the scene repeated itself.

Later, Morgan would tell me that what most struck her during this time was the look on the faces of the officers. The laughs coming from a few of them seemed forced to her, and she thought they were amazed by my establishment. "You could tell by the way they looked at me that they wanted to be spanked, and that they were turned on by the restraints and equipment."

The officers escorted Morgan back upstairs, and she sat down across from me. There was little more to say. Four of us were sitting there: Edward, the client, Morgan, and me. I could hear Princess talking with a couple of officers in my study. Finally one of the female officers, accompanied by two male officers in plain clothes and one uniformed male officer, came up to us and told us we were under arrest for running a bawdy house, or words to that effect. She told Morgan and me to stand up, which we did, at which point she quickly handcuffed us together with one pair of handcuffs. We were marched out of the house and into a police car. Many police cars lined the street, as well as forensic vans and moving vans. A crowd of people stood around, watching. The police took pictures of us leaving the house. We were driven to the police station in Richmond Hill, a small town north of Toronto, and placed in adjoining holding cells.

Edward was told to leave and come back in two hours. He walked to a nearby friend's house, where he called my lawyer's office, who said a lawyer would be at the bail hearing in the morning. Edward then phoned the landlord and said he should come to the bungalow in the evening, as there had been a problem at the house.

The client went home. Princess was also allowed to go home, after promising she would cooperate. She did, as it turned out, cooperate fully: she told the police everything right then and there, and it was always the truth. They were infuriated, because she told them no sex or indecent acts had occurred. She answered their subsequent lengthy interrogations in such detail and with such consistency that she said the officers questioning her (without a lawyer present) could not hide their frustration and anger. In fact, when the details of her interviews were disclosed prior to the trial, I could not find anything of significance that I disagreed with or that I wouldn't have said myself.

When the police looked into the backgrounds of Princess, Morgan, and Judy (my receptionist and assistant, who was off that day), they surely realized that these were just about the last women in the world who would be prostitutes. None of them were criminals, substance abusers, or even the type of women who would be "easy scores" in normal relationships. They all came from reputable families. One of them had a university degree; another was studying toward a college degree. And one of them was Edward's sister, and I can assure you that Edward would have had a fit if his sister were committing acts of prostitution and he had found out about it. All the women who worked for me had been hired as interactive actresses or administrative employees.

Early in the evening, Edward returned to the house, and shortly thereafter, the landlord arrived. The cars and people had left, and from the outside, the house looked no different than it had the day before. When the landlord came in, he asked why it looked so empty. The police had taken not only my bondage equipment and fixtures, but also everyday clothing and furniture. That included my television set, my bed, and many items so commonplace that it was inconceivable that these things could be evidence of any sort. I still can't believe the things they seized. They seized ladies' hats. They seized things from the schoolroom, like a blackboard and a small school desk. They also took large items, such as the living-room set, lounge chairs, and numerous other personal items that had no bearing on the business. They even seized Edward's tools and renovation supplies.

The police told the media in the days after the raid, that no further charges would be laid. However, a week later, they tracked down Judy and served her with a summons like the ones they had given Morgan and Princess. Judy remembered one of the officers as a client. She recalled that he had repeatedly asked for sex and wanted to watch lesbian shows; she had refused all of these requests. All staff were instructed to tell everyone on the phone and in person that we did not offer sex acts in our business. The police investigation verified this, but conveniently it failed to mention to the media that one of their officers had asked for a wide range of sex acts but had been consistently refused.

I'm glad that Judy was spared the trauma of the raid itself, and I'm glad that the police did not raid us when we were in session—one of the many ways they miscalculated. Looking back on the raid, it is clear that the police used excessive force, but why? What was the crime? Why my facility and not the others? And above all, what was I going to do about it?

Chapter 2

BAD LITTLE GIRL

Beginnings

The place and the life I came from were about as far you can imagine from my later life as a dominatrix in a big city. I was born in 1959 in Collingwood, a small town about a hundred miles north of Toronto. My parents were poor, and there were four of us children: my older sister, me, and my younger twin sisters. We lived on a farm just outside town. My father, Morley Miller, was black, of Kenyan ancestry; my mother, Marjorie Johnson, was white, with a French, Dutch, and English background. As a mixed couple, they were social outcasts, and life was difficult for children of a mixed marriage in a small Ontario town.

We lived in abject poverty. Many times, Mother couldn't even afford to buy milk and bread. Twice I was hospitalized for malnutrition. We suffered constantly from the cold, since the house was poorly insulated and we only had a small woodstove. We drew water from a well that would often freeze in the winter, so we had to melt snow for drinking water. We had an outhouse in the back, and the children were bathed in the kitchen sink. Our little farmhouse had only two rooms, so everyone had to cram into one bedroom. The twins slept in a crib; my older sister and I shared a bunk bed; and my parents shared a small bed in the corner of the room.

But in other ways, it was a wonderful place for a child to grow up. We had the advantages of a rural setting. A horse and buggy would deliver milk when we could afford it. Church bells could be heard in the distance on Sunday mornings. Big, sweeping willows in the yard offered shade from the summer sun. We had a large barn, and I would often spend hours jumping from the rafters into bales of hay below. I fondly remember the sun coming through the cracks in the roof of the barn while I lay in the hay, listening to the birds busy in their nests in the rafters.

When I was six, the authorities took me away. I was too young to remember how this happened, but I know that before they took me, I was always hungry and was not going to school. I will never forget waving good-bye to my parents from the social worker's car as it drove away. I was crying because I was scared and angry. I couldn't understand why they were letting this strange woman take me away, or why they were not coming along. Nobody had ever taken me away like this before. I only understood why many years later. I pieced together the story when I met my relatives many years later.

Today I remember my natural parents as kindly and loving, but very poor, and as outcasts from society. I never saw or heard from them after that day. When I became famous in the 1990s, my siblings and I were reunited, and it was only then that I found out that my mother had died in 1966 in a car accident, and my father had died about ten years later of natural causes.

My adoptive parents were the Bedfords. My new father, James, had seen a picture of me in the local paper's "Today's Child," a section devoted to children available for adoption. He was a big man, with one of the kindest faces I have ever seen. We became the best of friends right away. He was a World War II veteran and a devout Baptist; he saw to it that I received a full religious education in addition to my regular schooling. At eight I was baptized, and by the time I was nine, I was singing solos in the local Baptist church on Sunday mornings. I could sing hymns so movingly that the old ladies would cry. I even became the first child to sing in the church's adult choir.

The Bedfords lived in Windsor; James worked for the city of Detroit. He came home late at night from work, and I loved to wait for him on the porch. He did many special things for me; he took a direct involvement in my religious studies, helping me to memorize the scriptures. On Saturdays we went to the movies, and in the summer months, we would go to our cottage on Lake Erie.

My adoptive mother, Mary-Ellen, was a short, stout, matronly woman. The opposite of my new father, as I sensed from the first, she was cruel, taking every opportunity to demonstrate that there was no love between us, and expressing her hatred through continuous physical assaults and verbal humiliations. On my first day alone with her, she slapped and scolded me. She was obsessed with cleanliness, and I had chores to do from sunup to sundown: washing dishes and floors; weeding the garden; and doing the laundry. She would tell me that I had been "sent by the devil" to make her life miserable and that I was truly a sinner. As time went by, the punishments became more painful, and her behavior became more intense. I had to mold myself into the perfect daughter—or else. She was also very strict, reminding me constantly to speak up and to perform my chores to perfection. She enrolled me in piano lessons and enforced a strict practice schedule. I was also in the Girl Guides and Brownies, where my parents monitored my achievements closely.

James and Mary-Ellen adopted four children in all. They had none of their own. Mary-Ellen gave the other children preferential treatment. The youngest girl was very pretty; Mary-Ellen took her to the beauty salon to get her hair styled and dressed her in dainty clothes. She kept me far away from her "precious little baby doll," and she even took away my favorite dolls and gave them to that youngest sister. Mary-Ellen also was partial to my older brother, who could easily talk himself out of spankings, which he usually deserved. I think she was jealous of the affection my father showed me.

I was usually confined to my room when I was not with my foster parents. I wasn't allowed to eat at the same table with the other children when we came home from school for lunch; I had to eat in the laundry room. Then, when the dishes needed to be washed, it was almost always me who did it. Because of that and other chores, I was always the last to leave for school, so I never had much opportunity to play in the schoolyard before afternoon classes began.

I did not enter puberty early, but I did become sexually aware and began experimenting at the age of eight. I was continually discovering ways to attract potential partners. Sometimes I would be caught by teachers fondling my nipples or swinging my hips to tantalize the boys. My mother decided that I was mentally disturbed and complained to our doctor, but he told her that I was normal. The fact that my behavior disturbed Mary-Ellen made me even more determined to pursue it.

I began having sex with playmates, and sometimes I would get caught. A number of young men in Windsor lost their virginity to me. I also experimented with role-playing, even at that early age. I enjoyed playing games such as cops and robbers, cowboys and Indians, mother and child, and doctor and patient with both boys and girls. I would even tie up my partners or spank them at times. Looking back, I now see that I enjoyed being in control of these games and the participants. I also began to steal jewelry and undergarments from stores and to play hooky from school. I was truly becoming a bad girl. I don't think these early activities contributed directly to my becoming a dominatrix in later life. I will deal with that later.

One girl in my grade school shared some of my fantasies. For two years, we would get together on weekends and play with each other's bodies, exploring the wonders of female love and reaching incredible heights of passion. We were caught in the act quite often, to my family's great shame. The neighbors were talking, and they did not allow their children to play with me. I was scorned socially as well as being ostracized within my own family. Even the boys in the schoolyard (who previously had delighted in my company) shunned me. I think that my growing reputation as a lesbian was what most offended or intimidated people. The fact was, for a time, I was not a lesbian, but more of what we might now call bisexual. Or you might also say that the two of us were experimenting.

I was twelve when I left the Bedford household. When they became alarmed about my behavior, my parents sought help from Children's Aid. For two or three years, I saw psychiatrists and social workers. Mary-Ellen wanted to give me up for adoption, so a couple of times, I even found myself in family court for placement. The professionals concluded that I had no mental problems, but that I was hard to handle. James had taken a kindly rather than strict approach to me, but he saw how I enraged Mary-Ellen and realized that it would be best for both of us, and the other kids, if I were to go.

Not all my experiences in the Bedford household were bad. We had wonderful Christmases and Easters. We went to church regularly, and for at least that time, we were a happy family. Sometimes my mother's good side showed itself and gave me some sense of what being loved might feel like.

Maryvale School for Girls

It took some months for Children's Aid to find me a new home. I remember it as a happy day when I finally left the Bedfords—a sort of liberation. They dropped me off at the Maryvale School for Girls, on the outskirts of Windsor, with a few suitcases of clothing and some money in my bank account. The Bedfords took me inside and left me with one of the staff, kissed me good-bye, and said I should be good and take care of myself.

I only went back to visit the Bedfords on a few occasions when I was at Maryvale, for Christmas and other holiday weekends. The atmosphere at the Bedfords' when I visited was always very tense and rigid, with my siblings barely speaking to me. I was glad to go back to Maryvale each time.

The school was also a large convent, over a hundred years old. It was like an ominous stone cathedral, in the middle of which stood a chapel with a domed stained-glass ceiling. My initial reaction was one of amazement and curiosity. Although I had not been raised a Catholic, I now wondered if I were to be converted to Catholicism. Attached to the chapel were administration buildings with a school, a gymnasium, and a swimming pool. Farther back on the property were four cottages, each large enough to house about twenty girls. The cottages' ceilings were very high and the decor sparse and neat. Each cottage had a tiny kitchen, a dining room, and a large living room with a television and a record player. Also on the main floor were staff rooms and a telephone room, where the girls were allowed to make private calls (some of which were monitored by staff).

Upstairs in the cottages were the dormitories, divided so that four girls slept in one room. Other rooms had only two beds, and as girls progressed in the program, they would eventually get their own rooms as they graduated from one cottage to the next. Each cottage had its own purpose. Upon arrival, girls were sent to Cottage One for assessment and transition. At various stages, it was decided whether they moved up, stayed put, or needed special attention. I stayed in Cottage One for a long time before moving to Cottage Four, where there was more freedom and little supervision. I endured many trials and a few tribulations in Maryvale.

Soon after I arrived, I made an enemy of the school bully. She was an overweight loudmouth with flaming red hair, a perpetual frown, and a big belly that made her look pregnant. She had a very tough exterior for a young girl. I was in the doctor's waiting room one day soon after my arrival when she walked in.

I should mention here that I initially had no idea what kind of place my parents had left me in to live. I hadn't been there one day when my imagination took the better of me and I decided the place was a home for unwed mothers and wayward girls. That's why I asked this girl whether she wanted a boy or a girl. She didn't have a clue what I was talking about and asked me what I meant.

I replied, "Aren't you pregnant?"

In a rage, she told me to "shut my fucking mouth" and raved on and on about how insulted she was. She told me to stay out of her way, or I would get my face punched. Since I had never been confronted this way at school, I was devastated and couldn't get her threats out of my mind.

I was given basic items such as toothpaste and soap and told that when I ran out of things, I must ask for more. I was given a five-dollar weekly allowance. There was also a canteen in the basement. The cottage was run somewhat like a prison or training school: you earned privileges and canteen money by keeping the place clean and doing other assigned chores. If you misbehaved, started a fight, or were insubordinate, you were sent to segregation in the administration building. So I tried to keep my nose clean and stay out of trouble.

The schedule often included activities such as horseback riding, swimming, canoeing, sewing, and music. We had the normal school classes. We also went on shopping trips, which I could join when my parents had sent me some money. We were also taken to shows, circuses, and fairs. I fondly remember our camping trips, during which we got a chance to be close to some boys.

I started to get restless and horny. I was doing kinky things with my roomies. One special friend and I ran away together and hitchhiked to Northern Ontario twice before they separated us for good. She was sent away, and I was put in segregation. I was there for some weeks before being released to Cottage Four again.

It was at this time that I became confused about my sexuality. I didn't really think I was a lesbian, because I liked being intimate with boys as well as girls. But because of my promiscuous nature, I once again became an outcast. I was becoming too mature (in years and behavior) to remain at Maryvale, so the school administrators and Children's Aid sought a more suitable environment for me. Thus began my journey through the group-home system.

Toronto Group Home

I was transferred to a group home in Toronto when I was 14. I began my stay on a high note and did all I could to overcome my past, making new friends while attending high school. Excited and anxious to explore the city, I was allowed to go out after dinner, provided I kept my curfew.

Things went well for a while, but once again I became restless. I went off in search of some kind of love, missing the kind that is shared between family members. I had a fantasy that I would meet someone special if I hitchhiked around. I wanted adventure. I wanted to be free, so one night, I ran away from the home.

So much happened over the next few months, and I was so drunk and stoned and tired much of the time that my recollection of them and exactly when they happened is fuzzy. During my time on the run, I met many interesting people and had lots of sex with some of them, including a couple with whom I stayed for about two weeks before moving along. Through them I met a man who took me to a motel for a week. I hadn't acquired a taste for needles yet, so I declined to get high. Besides, he knew that I was jailbait and was scared as hell to be caught with a runaway in a motel room doing drugs. He dropped me off on the side of a road somewhere, and I stuck out my thumb.

I was gone for some time before the police picked me up and brought me back to the group home, where I became even more unmanageable. My social worker was called in to take me away.

From Toronto I was taken to group homes in two rural locations, where my reputation and case file preceded me. Every day spent in Maryvale had been documented in the case history that each group home received. By the time I arrived, my accommodations were already deemed only temporary. I stayed one week at the first rural group home and maybe a month at the other. It was a confusing time for me. The second rural group home was a farm just outside of Peterborough, which is a medium-sized city northeast of Toronto. The farm was a group home for girls like me. Here I found some peace from the roller-coaster ride of the previous year.

I was allowed to attend classes at the local high school. I had always wondered what it would be like to be in a loving family, so I took every chance I got to get out of the house and meet people who had real families. I was the only black student in the entire school and received special treatment from some of the teachers. When I was asked to perform in school plays, I learned to express myself in a creative manner and became very interested in learning more about theater and the fine arts. I also joined the track team. It seemed as if I were now becoming a normal teenager.

This relatively happy period ended when I had a falling-out with one of my housemates/lovers. A house meeting was called, and I was exposed as a lesbian. The staff at the house were brutal toward me. They had a severe punishment for such situations: they would sit on my back and wrap their arms around my chest. Then they would lift my torso off the floor until I cried in pain. The intent of this punishment was said to be to coerce someone to confess or to express feelings and emotions, but in my case, it was my "reward" for my lesbian behavior. I was removed from the home and taken back to Windsor by my social worker.

YWCA

The Children's Aid Society could do nothing more with me. Now sixteen years old, I was put up at the YWCA and given a living allowance. It was 1975. My social worker eventually acquired a room for me in an old Victorian house in Windsor's downtown core. I was on my own to do as I wished without answering to anyone. I usually stayed out late at night in a coffee shop on the city's main drag. The people I met there were from all walks of life. I was fascinated by the bikers and others who hung out at all hours of the night, talking about their exciting lifestyles. I became a regular at the café and became known by everyone. I was invited to parties and peoples' homes.

Sometimes I went to Detroit with some bikers. I wanted to be rough and tough, just like the biker babes. I was green and asked questions about everything. I met a girl who had tattoos all over her body; I just *had* to be her friend. I needed a partner, someone to watch my back, so we became buddies. One of the many people she introduced me to became a kind of father figure to me. He was an older man, a drug dealer and an ex-con. I went to live with him.

He gave me my first hit of speed and taught me things about sex I had never experienced before. I became a drug addict in no time, and at first he wanted to throw me out. Briefly he turned me out on the streets as a prostitute, but he became angry with me when I charged my customers too little. Then he got me fake identification, and I became an exotic dancer. When I wasn't doing that, I was working in a massage parlor. I was a very busy young lady, trying to keep him satisfied. I saw very little of the money I earned, as he was paid directly for my work.

He must have had many enemies, because one day someone fired five shots at his house. Luckily, I was not hit. I called the police, who soon swarmed the house and arrested him on charges of first-degree murder. I was then alone to face the hounds. People were coming to the house looking for him, and I began to fear for my life. I had nowhere to go and nobody to turn to. I had a bad addiction, so I checked myself into a hospital and tried to get clean.

While I was in the hospital, I discovered that James, my adoptive father, was a patient on the very same floor, almost across the hall from me. He was dying of cancer. When Mary-Ellen found out that I had been visiting him, singing to him, and playing my guitar for him, she forbade my visits. The minute before he died, I stood over his bed and became so overcome with grief that I passed out. When I came to, my father had passed on. My mother also forbade my presence at the funeral, but I got a day pass and went anyway.

After my hospital stay, I tried to stay clean and find a real job; I was determined to make a go of it. I was seventeen. I knew a woman named Mary who rented rooms in her house in downtown Windsor; I felt she was the only person I could turn to. She had often been arrested for bootlegging and running a bawdy house, but she was like a mother to me, very gracious and kind. To me she was a wise older woman who had seen much in her day.

I became friends with another boarder, an older Greek woman with a lot of class and style. She often took me over to Detroit. We became lovers and moved into our own apartment. With her help, I went back to school. A dominatrix by trade, she began to instruct me in the art. She specialized in men who wanted to be treated like babies. She had cross-dressing clients whom she played with and spanked. I learned quite a bit from her, but I didn't enjoy it to the point where it occurred to me to go out on my own as a dominatrix. I did not see it as my destiny at that time. Her physical and mental health were deteriorating because of menopause and diabetes. We parted company one day after a huge fight. Although I loved her, I couldn't handle the way she was always complaining and ordering me about without any consideration of how I felt.

I moved in with a slightly older man I'd recently met. He seemed gentle and generous, at least at the start. For some months, we were happy; I kept house for him while he worked at an auto plant in Windsor. Then I became pregnant and, beginning late in my pregnancy, he started abusing drugs and alcohol. He also became violent; he bought guns and large quantities of drugs, and he ran up big debts. Eventually he was fired from his job.

I gave birth to a baby girl. I was twenty years old. It was 1980. He became enraged whenever the baby cried. When I went to work in a massage parlor to support us, I hired a babysitter for when I was at work, because I knew this man couldn't take care of a child on his own. He had an affair with the babysitter, giving me an excuse to leave. I put my daughter in the care of her elderly godparents until I could get on my feet again. Her godparents were a couple I had lived beside and was good friends with. I had one of the lawyers I knew take care of the arrangements and get the court order. Their many children were now grown and on their own, and taking in my daughter entitled them to receive an allowance from the government, so taking my daughter in was also an advantage to them. My daughter was only five months old.

To numb the pain of this man's betrayal, a lost home, and having to give up my daughter, I drank and sometimes used cocaine. Looking back, I don't know how I managed to keep my sanity, given all the grief I suffered.

Calgary

At about this time, some friends told me about all the money they were making in the escort-service business in Calgary. It seemed to me that everyone was going west, so I did, too. The first service to which I applied hired me right away; later I was promoted to manager because of my business savvy and enthusiasm.

A few months after I started working there, I met a neurosurgeon while walking the streets. His wife had died just over a year before. He took me to his home, and in time I moved in with him. He gave me a car and a weekly allowance of $1,000. He had me to play the role of a dominant and sadistic wife, which he said was always his fantasy.

It was all too good to be true. He was very old and ugly, but the idea of becoming a doctor's wife and having such power was irresistible. In his basement, we built a dungeon equipped with bondage devices, including an examination table. I would dress in a nurse's uniform with leather underneath and chastise him for his lusty looks at his nurses. Sometimes I would make him sleep in restraints or wrapped in a sheet. Unlike practicing dominatrices, I had a full dungeon tailored to the whims of one individual. We were never pressed for time, and there were none of the inconveniences of running a business. My day was centered on preparing for his return from his medical practice.

However, our personalities were less compatible when we were not role-playing. He was highly educated, while I lacked his learning and was more artistically inclined. Perhaps it would have been better if he had just kept me in a home of my own and visited when he wanted. One day he came home very distraught and told me of the little boy he had lost on the operating table. I wasn't sympathetic and told him we should go out and party to take his mind off the incident. He threw me out of the house that night. I never went back, but I heard he tried to reach me through my girlfriends. I was with him for almost two years.

A few weeks after I left him, I was told that my daughter, who was two at that time, had fallen ill with the flu and been hospitalized. I caught the next plane to Windsor and arrived as she was being released from the hospital. Shaken, I made arrangements to give legal guardianship to her godparents; I didn't want to put my baby up for adoption, because I believed that one day I would be able to take care of her myself. After returning to Calgary, I began sending money every week with little gift packages. I hadn't taken her back to Calgary with me because I refused to go on welfare and live in a public housing project somewhere, so I tried to make sure she had a real family to care for her, which would allow me to be with her whenever I could. I felt I was doing the right thing under the circumstances.

Windsor Again

I returned from Alberta hoping for a normal life: a nine-to-five job with a quiet home and friends who were not from the fringes of society. I hoped I could become a true mother to my little girl. I was twenty-two, and it was 1981. For weeks I looked for a job as a waitress, a cleaner, or a secretary, without success. The money ran out, and I ended up back in a massage parlor in downtown Windsor. It had a reputation with the police as a clean establishment and was the only one allowed to operate in the city, at least up to that time.

This parlor employed only the most beautiful girls. Its atmosphere was the ultimate in classic sleaze, with tufted gold velvet furniture and soft lights. A large aquarium displayed exotic fish while gentle jazz played in the background. A private lounge upstairs resembled a cave, with real stone walls from San Francisco. The lounge featured an enormous heart-shaped, Roman-tiled sunken Jacuzzi, and the ceiling had special effects installed to resemble shooting stars. In this room, customers could view pornographic movies while they were bathed by beauties or massaged on a waterbed table. The salon offered topless or nude rubs as well as doubles.

I only worked there for the last few weeks of 1982. My boss did not have a problem with me refusing sex acts with the patrons, but when I refused *his* advances, I knew my days there were numbered.

One day a client offered to let me live with him and his wife if I would become his wife's "slave girl." My job was to pamper her (usually while he watched) or to punish him on her instructions. At first his wife was very much into this and loved my massages, which he was forced to watch with his hands tied behind his back. My prior experience as a dominatrix came in very handy, and she was delighted with the suggestions I made for her husband's humiliation and punishment. She gloried in the power of having a slave girl, and at my suggestion, she would also restrain and torture me when her husband was at work. She particularly enjoyed tying me up spread-eagled and tickling me. She became quite intoxicated by the feeling of power she got from this act. Sometimes she would tickle me for hours when she found a sensitive spot, and the more I struggled and begged, the crueler she became. These were intense hours for both of us. She would climax many times during a single session, and sometimes it seemed she couldn't get enough. If I wasn't ticklish in a given spot, she would pinch me, which was very painful. In order to avoid being pinched, I learned to fake being ticklish in places where I really wasn't.

For several months, I lived with this couple. They were comfortable in terms of having a house, a car, and money, but other than providing a roof over my head and food to eat, they did not pay me, telling me they could not afford to. Nevertheless they objected when I tried to get a job. When the husband became jealous and resentful of how much the wife enjoyed playing with me, I left. For her part, the wife seemed jealous of the fact that her husband often seemed more interested in me, the slave girl, and in the games that we played, than in his wife. They were also well into their thirties, and she told me she had to start thinking about whether they were going to have children.

Once again I was at loose ends. So, when a friend of mine told me she was moving out west in a few weeks, I arranged to go along. She did the driving, the weather was warm, and it was a good chance to enjoy a vacation and a fresh start back in Calgary, a city that I knew.

Chapter 3

Jail and Bail

Back to 1994 and the raid: in the police van on the way to the police station, Mistress Morgan and I were with the woman officer, so there was little we could do but speak in generalities. Morgan expressed a mixture of fury and sadness. My main concern was calming her and reassuring her that we had done nothing wrong, and that it was very rare for people to go to jail on the charges they had mentioned. It was now about four in the afternoon. At the police station, we were taken to holding cells with television cameras and microphones pointed at them. Morgan and I were in adjoining cells. We could speak to one another but could not see one another. The bed did not have a mattress. There was a washbasin and toilet.

Edward and Princess were told they would have to appear in court. Edward lived on the premises, and since he was able to produce a key, he could return to the premises in a few hours. Princess went home as soon as she could. Edward had been trained in security; he knew how to follow instructions, and I had prepared him for a situation like this. I knew how important it was to have someone on the outside arrange a lawyer and bail. I told him he was to be as quiet as possible but not to cooperate, other than to tell the police that he was in charge of security for the bungalow, that he had been working there for only a few months, and that he was just following my orders and didn't want to say any more.

I knew that Edward wouldn't be taken into custody—or if he were, he would not be held long. I was right. As soon as he left the premises, he walked over to the home of a trusted friend of his living in an apartment nearby. Edward followed my instructions, calling my lawyer, Ken Danson, to ensure I had a lawyer at the bail hearing next day at the York Region Courthouse. Ken was away, but his staff said they would send another lawyer who would represent both Morgan and me. Edward did not know that Morgan had been released. He called Princess and told her to lay low and that he would be in touch. He then called Judy and told her what had happened and not to come to work until further notice. Then he called Art and Scott, two of my most trusted clients I will discuss later in more detail.

Then Edward called Jerry, the owner of the property, and asked him to come over. Jerry came that evening. I had told Jerry when I moved in that in addition to Edward rehabilitating the property with my help, I was planning to run a small beauty salon, and also to make and sell some clothes. Edward told me later that when he brought Jerry up to speed on what was actually happening, Jerry was not angry—at least, not with us, for which I am grateful. He *was* angry with the police for dismantling so much of the house and for taking away some of his furniture. In addition, his property, the largest residential lot in the very upscale community of Thornhill, had probably lost hundreds of thousands of dollars in value because of the publicity. As he learned more about the case, he was very sympathetic to me and the others, but he really didn't seem to understand my world, saying that if I had broken the law, I would have to pay the price. He didn't seem to know that places like mine existed elsewhere. His business ventures, real-estate developments, and investments seemed to be what occupied him.

Meanwhile, back in the holding cells, the officers suddenly told Morgan she could leave, and that she would have to appear in court in the near future to face charges. Also that evening, two officers, one of them the main investigating officer, a young officer wearing a ponytail, came into the cell area. He told me that they had just come back from my house and said, "We cleaned everything out of your house and had a long talk with Princess."

"I want to call my lawyer!" I replied.

He shot back "Who did the female clients?"

The officers were smiling. I again asked to make the call. Finally, they let me call my lawyer. I suspect that they delayed the call until after business hours, when my lawyer would likely be harder to contact. Sure enough, he was not in his office, and all I could do was leave a message with the essentials with his answering service. As I said, I didn't know at the time that Edward had taken care of all this.

Then two officers, one female and one male, came and told me that I would be kept in that cell overnight and would appear in court for a bail hearing in the morning. I told them they were making a big mistake and that I would fight this all the way. They gave me a cold hamburger and a cup of coffee. I used the cup to drink water from the sink later in the evening as well.

The cell was cold, and after a while, I started to shiver. When they peeked in, I repeatedly told them I was cold, but it was well into the middle of the night before one of them finally showed up with a paper blanket. I lay on the hard bed, shivering most of the night, watched by the cameras and listened to by the microphone. I must have fallen asleep midway through the night. There was nothing to do or read. Mostly I just lay there, angry and depressed. Occasionally I wept a bit. But above all, I was mad. I made up my mind then and there that no matter what or how long it took, I would not let them get away with this.

Bail Hearing

The next morning, I was awakened and handed a packet of instant breakfast. Later a female and male officer came into the cell area. They opened the cell door and handcuffed me. They told me they were taking me to court and led me outside to a van. I was driven to the regional courthouse, where I was led into another holding cell. My handcuffs were removed, and I was kept there until the afternoon. Two legal-aid people visited, but I told them I wanted my own lawyer. Finally I was visited by a lawyer—not my own, but one whom Edward knew and had called. This lawyer said he did not understand the charges and that he expected no difficulty arranging bail. When he left, a female officer handcuffed me and took me for photos and fingerprinting. Then another female officer came in, rehandcuffed me, and took me to the bail hearing. I felt disheveled and grungy after spending the night in the holding cell. During the night, I had had to remove my blouse and skirt so that they would be fresh for the hearing, and I had been denied a blanket until the wee hours. So I was very tired from lack of sleep due to the cold and how angry and worried I was.

The lawyer called by Edward the day before spoke to me prior to my court appearance. He asked me where I would live if bail were granted, and we discussed what would likely be the conditions and financial requirements of bail. He then asked about my background, seeking information on previous convictions and outstanding warrants. He said he did not understand the charges, and he thought the police were behaving in an extraordinary and unacceptable manner. The entire meeting lasted about five minutes.

He also informed me that the Crown attorney, which in Canada is the term used for District Attorney, was seeking my incarceration until a trial date was set, without bail. The Crown also asked for an outrageously high payment, should bail be granted. Upon hearing this, I felt a myriad of emotions: anger, shock, frustration, outrage, humiliation. I couldn't understand why the Crown was so anxious to incarcerate me, as I hadn't committed any crime.

Finally I was removed from the cell in handcuffs by the court officer and taken up to the courtroom, where I was led to the prisoner's box and placed before a microphone. The Crown attorney, James McKeachie, was the first to speak. While he addressed the judge, all I could think was that if this man was a good example of a lawyer, the legal system as we knew it was in trouble. Here was a man who was perhaps too impassioned in what he was saying; his rhetoric amounted to a moral, rather than a legal, attack.

Red-faced, he almost screamed his remarks to the bench. According to him, my job was not a "real" job; I had never had a real job. I was a "menace to society," and the things I did in the bungalow were so bad that I should be kept in jail to protect society. He recited my previous record in related activities to show how "bad" I was. He said I had no ties to any community, nor did I have any of what he termed "community support." This angered me. I had interacted with more of the community than he could imagine, including the lawyers who were my clients. The jobs I had had and the volunteer work I had done were either unknown or unimportant to him.

Then my lawyer rose and stated that detention was unwarranted and that I should have no problem paying my bail. He pointed out the ways in which the Crown attorney's arguments were ridiculous. He requested that bail be set at $5,000.

The judge requested the names of three people that I knew living in

Toronto, as well as their professions and home phone numbers. I gave these. I then had to speak on my own behalf, but found it difficult. I was nervous and unsure of what to say, but I suspected that my response might have a bearing on whether I received bail. I told the judge that I did not deserve to be detained until my trial date, and that although I may not have had much formal education, I had been well schooled in life. I expressed my feeling that I was self-taught in many areas and my belief that not all education is learned from books.

The Crown attorney agreed to $5,000 for bail, but with conditions: I could not return to the house. I had to give the police any new address, at least until the charges had been dealt with. I was not permitted to communicate with most of the other defendants until the charges had been dealt with, unless we were in a lawyer's office. Finally, I had to sign in at the police station once a week until my trial date. He did not insist on his argument that I be held until trial. He obviously did not believe that I would be able to get the bail money or adhere to the conditions of bail. He was wrong. Not only was I able to post bail, but I signed in every week without fail for the year or so until the first trial date. If I missed a sign-in, I could be jailed.

Detention Center

I was taken to the Metro West Detention Centre in Toronto to be held until I made bail—or until trial, if nobody bailed me out. If you've seen cattle herded into a pen and processed for branding, you will have some idea of what it is like to be processed into a detention center. By the time this degrading (but, I suppose, necessary) process was finished, I had lost any sense of dignity, and the hopelessness began. They processed us one at a time, and the waiting seemed endless. When it was my turn, I was told to remove all clothing and put it in a bag. I disrobed, and a strip search was performed. I was told to stick out my tongue, run my fingers through my hair, and show the backs of my ears while the officer looked into my ears and mouth and up my nose. I was told to lift up my arms and my breasts so that the officer could perform a complete visual search of my body. I was told to bend over, squat, and cough to see if I were holding any drugs in any orifice.

I showered in the presence of the officer, and I received my assigned prison garb of a T-shirt and jeans. I was put back into a holding cell with several other girls. Throughout all of this, I was terrified. I didn't know how long I was going to be inside. I had no control over what was happening to me. I was not allowed to make phone calls.

At nine or ten that night, I was moved to the women's section of the center and placed in a dormitory cell with two other girls. The lights were out, except for the main light in the corridor. I wasn't able to sleep, so I tried to read some magazines by the pale light shining through the cell bars. It helped to calm me, and I managed to sleep.

I woke up at dawn, not sure of where I was at first. I listened to the sounds all around me and longed for coffee. I could have joined the other girls for breakfast in the eating area, but because I was so scared to leave my cell and was unsure of the routine, I didn't move as fast as the officer wanted and found myself in trouble right off the bat, missing both coffee and breakfast. In this and other matters, I had to rely on the other inmates to tell me the routine.

I spent the first of my four days in jail orienting myself to my surroundings. In this particular area of the center, we were allowed to use a pay phone, so I called collect to the house at about ten in the morning; Edward filled me in on his efforts to arrange bail and told me that our case was on the front pages of some national newspapers. It had also appeared in other dailies, on television, and on the radio.

Overnight I had become a bit of a celebrity, not only in the media but also in the jail. I was very surprised by this. I had thought that if I ever got raided, it would be a minor news item, if that. One of the guards showed me an article about me in the newspaper. The other inmates were curious and asked questions. Several of the girls asked me to spank them. I found that funny and decided to accommodate them. They were lined up. I have no idea why they wanted to be spanked. I spent the day answering questions about S&M. I also noticed an increased interest in me whenever I showered. Several of the girls were incarcerated for violent crimes, and I had been afraid for my safety prior to my notoriety, but after my identity was well-known, my new status seemed to offer some sort of protection.

Later that afternoon, I was spanking a fellow inmate in the common room. A guard watched us, laughing as she walked away, saying that she wasn't about to interfere, as the inmate was obviously in need of correction. After lockup that night, I was asked to spank one of my cellmates, who was curious about what I did as a dominatrix. I put her over my lap and spanked her, which amused several of the other inmates. She had begged me ceaselessly for this spanking, so I felt I had to oblige her. The next day, Sunday, I began teaching an unofficial class in domination. Several of the girls wanted to know the rules, and some asked me to speak to their boyfriends on the phone. I tried several methods to relax: reading, stretching, deep breathing, and, mostly, talking about my profession. If I hadn't been behind bars, I might have actually enjoyed this experience.

That evening, Ken Danson came to see me, and I told him all I knew and what had happened. Ken had represented me when I was charged in Toronto years before. He agreed to be retained as my legal counsel. He said he needed to view the documents of disclosure and meet with the police before discussing my case with me, and that would not happen for a few months. Edward had told him that my bail was being arranged and that Ken's help was not needed for that. Ken did tell me that he had heard the unofficial details on the radio and that I was the subject of a large headline in Toronto's tabloid, *The Toronto Sun*.

After Ken left, I returned to my cell in time for lockup. That night was uneventful, but I remained worried about my bail being posted. Two unsuccessful attempts had been made to post my bail. I was told that there were "paperwork problems." Monday afternoon, I was told that my bail was finally being posted, and I was taken to a small room where I signed paperwork in the presence of a justice of the peace. I was about to enjoy my first taste of freedom in four days. I gathered up my bedding and clothes and put them in the pillowcase for return to Admissions and Discharge, where I was processed for release.

Freedom

Just putting on my own clothes made me feel human again. Outside, in the sunshine, I was picked up in the parking lot by a friend of Edward's, who whisked me off to my new residence, where I was met by Edward himself. Naturally I had many questions. He told me what had happened—about how the police had taken almost everything out of the house, and about the press conference where Sergeant Norman Miles of York Regional Police had posed with the whips, spanking benches, and some other equipment. Edward had heard reports that the police had seized a copy of our client book and would be contacting the clients, and that the police had videotapes of clients entering and leaving the premises.

My name had been made public by the media, but thankfully not the names of the others charged. The news conference had been the leading story on the local evening news and a headliner the next day, as I noted earlier. (They did not let us read *The Toronto Sun* in jail because of its extensive focus on crime and criminals.) By the time of my release, everything had gone silent in the media.

Edward added that Jerry had generously offered to let us live in another property, only about a mile away and also in Thornhill, which also needed rehabilitation. However, to no one's surprise, Jerry had imposed the condition that I not restart my business.

So I moved in there and took stock of my situation. It was a nice, old home, and my needs were few. Edward was kept busy by the renovations and landscaping work. I helped where I could. But shortly after moving in, I got busy on the phone.

Before I continue, I want to introduce a couple of my clients who loom large in my story. The first is Art, who lived near the house. One of my first clients, Art was in his midfifties when the raid occurred. A wealthy and educated man, he was used to dealing with lawyers. He said he would be loyal to me and would share his good fortune in life with me. It galled him to see how the authorities were treating me and the property owner, whom he did not know. He was all too aware that if he had been at the bungalow that day, like the elderly client, then he, too, might have been charged, and might not have been able to hide it from his family. All through my ordeal, he was as good as his word, and I will always be grateful to him for helping us win the first round of our legal battle and the other support he provided. Art supported me by paying some of my legal fees, giving me money to live on, and arranging a conventional part-time job for me. I would value all this help at close to $100,000—and that amount bought more at that time than now, fifteen years later. The worth of that figure doesn't include his very valuable advice and leadership in the early days of the battle—for example, in dealing with the lawyers.

The other client, who will shortly be joining me at the center of my story, is Scott. Essentially Art's assistant in the early days of my legal battles, Scott took over from Art after a couple of years. When I was drafting this book, I asked him for a biographical sketch and his version of his early involvement in my case. I liked it so much that I offer it to you here in full. This is Scott in his own words:

> I came from a comfortable home and was well established in a professional career. I never married or had children, although I did have two very serious relationships, spaced many years apart. For years I lived almost like a playboy. My time was my own, I had money to spend, and I knew how to get along with women. When my last serious relationship ended, I traveled, took courses, and pursued some of my hobbies. I concentrated on my career and involvement in my professional organization. And of course I dated, but not with a willingness to make any sort of commitment.
>
> I was affluent enough to also consider living out my fantasies. I noticed the advertisements in some of the local entertainment papers for dominatrices. Eventually I responded and, for almost a year, tried out several of these establishments until I finally visited Madame deSade. Her house was out of the way for me, but it was the best one I visited, and after a while she offered to reduce my payments in return for doing chores and errands. I became a regular there. It was almost too good to be true. I would often stay for entire weekends. I was sometimes there during the working week as well. I was careful not to ask too many questions about the operation of the business or about her or her staff's private lives, but over time they would gradually confide in me, and often I could assist them in various ways. In return, I got to live out my fantasies. When there were paying clients in the house, I would usually make myself scarce in a remote part of the house or out back.
>
> It was like that for about a year. I knew that the house could not continue as it was indefinitely. It was awkward to run a business that has many visitors in a residential area. Plus, Bedford did not own the house, and said her landlord did not know the full

nature of her business. If he found out he might put a stop to it, and might also sell the property in any event. It also occurred to me that the police might even raid such a business, even if they found there was no sex for sale, because they did not want that type of service in that part of town. So I had this foreboding that this facility would not be there long, and I was glad to have such an opportunity while it lasted.

I was not at the house on the day of the raid. After Bedford got out on bail, I offered her my assistance, and she referred me to Art. I told him my experience and qualifications and offered to assist financially. Of course, the lawyers would be in charge of the legal battle, and I would do what Art or the lawyers asked. Before this legal battle, I was doing some volunteer work and giving money to charities and was helping friends in need. Now this would be the cause.

This cause was dear to my heart for several reasons. Bedford and her circle had taken me into their lives. They made my dreams, if you will, come true. I was intimate with them in a most profound sense. They gave me memories for a lifetime. I got to know them, their talents and basic decency. I cared about them, at that time, more than almost anyone in my life. They did not deserve what was happening to them.

There was also the morality—or rather, the immorality—of the raid. If I had been there that day, I would have been arrested or ticketed and, as events have borne out, never given a clear reason why. In my view, there was no crime. I spoke to a couple of lawyers about what was right and normal in these circumstances, and was told that Bedford was innocent but that the police routinely use intimidation and attrition to force guilty pleas. Here, for perhaps the only time in my life, was an opportunity to do the right thing when doing so was important. Also, I was simply furious, and I am not someone who meekly accepts this sort of treatment of me or my friends.

And finally, and frankly, I enjoyed the thought of being an important behind-the-scenes participant in a landmark and highly publicized event. Aside from what I cared about and who

I liked and what was right and wrong, this promised to be more interesting than anything else I had ever been involved in.

If he wanted to be part of a groundbreaking case, Scott would not be disappointed. Over the next few months, it was Scott, using his surprisingly extensive connections, along with Mistress Morgan, who pieced together how the raid had come about. Here's what eventually emerged.

The Story Behind the Story

We had a client who was the Reverend of a well-known Toronto church. He became obsessed with Mistress Morgan, and especially with a particular role-playing scenario with her. He even asked her to leave town with him if he left his wife. He very foolishly used his cell phone to call the house and make appointments. His wife saw the number on the bills, phoned the number, and of course figured it all out—except the part about Morgan. Some members of the church were police officers. His wife also hired a detective to follow him. So I imagine that the Reverend's wife must have blabbed to the police at their church. Anyway, that's what the Reverend said. These police officers reported the alleged activity in the house to their superiors, and the vice squad swung into action with a stakeout of the house. They had probably wanted to shut down my operation even before the Reverend was exposed.

However, the case took a different, and more political, turn during the stakeout. The vice squad got a big surprise: they discovered that a local official was a client of mine. A member of the squad told the mayor, who was a bitter rival of this client; meanwhile, the municipal elections were only weeks away. The media were told that the police had videos of the house and a client book and would be contacting my clients. The mayor was sending a message to her rival.

What happened in the next twenty-four hours or so was never made clear to us. But Sergeant Norman Miles, who gave the press conference the day after the raid that resulted in the headlines, was taken off the case, and a new spokesman appeared before the media who said plans to track down the clients had been dropped. We found out that a gag order for the remainder of the case had been placed on the entire police force—meaning they were not permitted to speak about the case to anyone except their superior officers. Miles was demoted from sergeant to lance corporal. Apparently his press conference had not been approved via the normal process. Apparently the senior police officials put a stop to political interference with their work. My case was now in the hands of the Crown attorney (the Canadian equivalent of the district attorney in the United States). To this day, the identities of the local official and the Reverend have not been revealed to the media. I will never do so.

This information reached me bit by bit over many months, and I could hardly focus on it. I was preoccupied with overcoming the rage and fear that came from having my livelihood, home, and possessions taken away and being powerless to do anything about it at the time. Jerry, Art, and Scott stepped up and enabled me to survive. Judy had another job, so she just carried on with that. She lived a long way from the house, so it was not such a blow to her when it closed. Princess simply found another part-time job in her effort to work her way through school. Morgan also found other work. Edward we know about; nothing much changed for him, except that he spent more time renovating and none at all on security. He also got some casual work in construction.

Another client, whom I called "Worm," had a cottage in Northern Ontario. He offered, and I gladly accepted, an invitation to stay there alone for a couple of weeks before I started looking for work. While I was up there, alone, I had plenty of time to calm down and think. I had some important decisions to make.

Chapter 4

BAD BIG GIRL

I moved back to Calgary in 1983, hoping to survive without drugs or prostitution. I found new friends who helped me get back on my feet. I looked for legitimate work, but my skills were minimal: I could type, and I had good telephone manners. That was about all I had going for me.

I answered an ad for an "assistant to teach Chinese children in daycare the English language." The job required me to attend night school to learn Chinese. I was hired for my enthusiasm and willingness to learn. The employer was an elderly Chinese gentleman, small and frail, with a wonderful sense of humor. As his assistant, I followed him everywhere. He was a very enterprising man, and my job description grew as time passed. At the same time, I was working at a charity bingo and going to Sunday schools to help children with their Christian development. During the week, I taught English to Chinese children in the daycare center. I handled the bookkeeping and other secretarial assignments at the daycare center, and at night I studied Chinese under my employer. I was given a room in his house as part of my compensation. However, after several weeks, he found that the school was not financially viable, and he had to let me go, but allowed me to keep my accommodation until I found another place. As 1983 drew to a close, I was surviving, but my earnings that year were so low I didn't even qualify to pay taxes.

I found a job in a clothing store in a mall, earning a commission on the clothes I sold. After about a month, however, I was laid off. I was unemployed and running out of money again in the cold Alberta winter. Proudly or stupidly, I still refused to go on welfare. After searching for a job in vain for a week, I gave up and called the escort agency for which I had once worked. I was welcomed back and put to work right away. It was a relief to have a couple of hundred dollars in my jeans that night.

My new crowd was snorting cocaine, and I soon fell back to my old ways, looking for new experiences as well as some kind of relief from my troubles. I loved to experiment with my friends, especially the kinky females. My erotic experiences mounted as I acted out my fantasies. My work, once only done out of need, now became a vehicle to satisfy my wants and desires. I felt a compulsion to be in erotic environments. I sometimes even paid girls to make love to me. At this stage in my life, I was very submissive to women and loved it when they were severe with me. I enjoyed being tied up and tortured by a beautiful woman. My sexuality was reaching all-time highs.

The drugs and the wild lifestyle began to take their toll. I realized I could not continue this way indefinitely, keeping these irregular hours and constantly getting stoned and drunk. One day late in 1985, I packed my things, told this new crowd I was going back east for a visit, and left for Windsor once again.

Back in Windsor Again

I went back to school on a government grant and tried to live on eighty dollars a week. The school was a community college. I took basic business administration. It was a co-op program, meaning it combined on-the-job training with classroom instruction. The school assigned me to a job at a recording studio. I liked the job and the classes, but I couldn't afford to stay in school. To put a roof over my head, I went back to being a prostitute and lived with one of my clients.

After a few months, I had saved enough money to start a singing-telegram service and talent agency, incorporated under the name T. J. Bedford Enterprises Inc. Of course the agency was also an escort agency. A friend who owned a small pub and needed weeknight entertainment allowed me to hold talent contests in his club. The arrangement worked well; I filled the place with talent without cost to my friend. He was raking in the dough.

I now had a stable of talent, so I went to work in earnest on the singing telegrams. I became acquainted with a woman who owned a costume store and proposed a plan: she would receive a commission and recognition on my business cards if she provided costumes at discount rates and promoted my business in her shop. The arrangement was profitable for both of us. My service was requested for parties, showers, stag nights, and various other events.

I got a gig once at an Italian Christmas party at a convention center. They requested Miss Piggy and Kermit the Frog. But in the washroom, I discovered the Miss Piggy costume was the wrong size, so I picked a woman from the audience to play Miss Piggy and gave her a quick lesson in the washroom on how to perform. Kermit the Frog did not show up, so I donned the Kermit costume and went onstage, but the children taunted me, pointing to my large breasts under the spandex costume.

Keeping in mind the old maxim that the show must go on, I expanded my repertoire to include a French maid, biker chick, party doll, Playboy bunny, Marilyn Monroe, and Mae West.

When I wasn't busy with the singing telegrams or the talent shows, I was working as an escort in my own service. (The singing telegrams and talent agency did not provide me enough to live on after expenses.) I operated out of my house until I leased a warehouse in the heart of downtown Windsor. I wanted to renovate it to suit my purposes, and I envisioned a medieval-type setting with a feminine touch. Also included in my plan was a dungeon.

Since no other dungeons could be found in town, success came faster than I had expected. My warehouse location had a hidden door to the basement, reminding me of an escape hatch used by fugitives. I kept a mat over the hatch, and nobody found it unless I showed it to them. I had a carpenter build a few furnishings to give the dungeon more atmosphere. I shopped for costumes for me and the clients. I even used kitchen aids and things from the hardware store.

My warehouse space had a large sitting room where clients watched television or listened to music. Black wrought-iron room dividers separated the space into sections; in one section was a king-size waterbed surrounded by black velvet drapes. I lived and worked in the studio.

My talent agency sponsored one of our acts in a contest at a local college. This was a young man who strongly resembled and impersonated the entertainer then known as Prince. We won and traveled to Toronto for the finals, where we won a second prize of $500; we had a wonderful time as tourists.

A year after I started the singing-telegram and talent-show business, I sold it to a friend and turned my attention to running the escort service and dungeon, which were much more lucrative. It was now 1986.

This steady progress ended one afternoon when I was raided by the police, just as my service had built up a respectable number of clients. I was arrested, charged with operating a common bawdy house, and released on my own recognizance. I returned to my studio and found that the police had not taken very much—mostly some sex toys and a few costumes. The furniture was intact. They had not discovered the secret entrance to the dungeon: a trapdoor under a rug.

I hired a lawyer to represent me on the bawdy-house charges. I continued to work the escort agency. The phone was still hooked up, and the ads had been running, but we stuck strictly to outcalls. I was lonely and discouraged. I stayed home alone for days on end, living in fear of being arrested again. I had the presence of mind to know that the police were keeping an eye on my studio and could arrest me again whenever they chose. I knew I had to get out.

A former employee of mine offered to take me to Toronto, where she was moving to make a new start. When we got there, we stayed in a cheap motel while we looked for work. That lasted about a week. One evening I came home to find she had stolen most of my money and disappeared. We had been doing drugs and drinking, and I was in rough shape. I had enough money left for a bus back to Windsor, and I took it.

When I got there, I was suffering from malnutrition and the effects of drug and alcohol abuse, so I went straight to a hospital. The doctors admitted me right away. I didn't tell anyone I was back in town, except for one police officer who had always been sympathetic. He and his wife had even offered to help me on a personal level, so I called them, and they visited me frequently.

It seemed to me that my whole life comprised a string of setbacks and failures.

I also called an old friend, hoping she would help me get back on my feet when I was discharged. She told me that my boyfriend was trying to locate me, so I told her to let him know where I was. I also asked her to tell him to check into detox as well.

One month later, I left the hospital and entered a drug-rehab program in a comfortable house setting. The occupants were all females recovering from drug and alcohol addictions. Occupants were expected to adhere to a strict regimen, with most of the day spent cleaning and cooking. I became weak with even light housework. After a few weeks, we were allowed to have visitors, so a friend brought me a birthday card with a marijuana joint in it. The joint was discovered, and I had to leave the house. I was too embarrassed to call my police-officer friend, because I felt that I had betrayed his trust.

I contacted an old boyfriend, Omar, who had checked himself into the hospital to kick his cocaine addiction. He had been abusive to me, but we had had great sex, and I had no one else I felt I could call. He checked out to rejoin me. I borrowed money from a friend and called another in Calgary to arrange a place for us. We headed there by bus.

Spending the next two days together on a bus, Omar and I seemed to become closer than before. In Calgary, we moved into the rooms my friend had found for us. We both found conventional work very quickly: he on a construction site, me waiting tables. For a while, we lived a quiet and compatible life, without any substance abuse. When we were both off work for the day, we went for walks, watched television, and saw the occasional movie. It was one of the islands of peace in the stormy ocean that had been my life.

Alas, after a few weeks, things fell apart: Omar began hitting me again, and he was fired for showing up drunk. A few days later, he drove up in a battered, old foreign car. When I asked him where he had gotten it, he told me to shut up, pack my things, and leave with him that night for Vancouver. We ended up in a cheap hotel located on one of the Vancouver's worst, most drug-infested streets. The room cost twenty-five dollars a night.

The next day, we were pulled over by the police, who seized the car and charged my boyfriend with theft. The car was valued at less than $500, so his bail was set at $1,000. Fortunately (or otherwise), I had enough money to bail him out after a few days.

We found a converted bus to live in on a camping ground, and soon we were receiving welfare. We didn't have to pay much rent at the campground, which made life a bit easier, but after several months, the authorities found out that we had not insured the bus, so we were forced to move to a rooming house in a run-down Vancouver neighborhood. We were only just surviving. Our social life consisted of buying and using drugs when we had some money. Omar sold drugs to get money to buy drugs.

The court date for my bawdy-house charges rolled around while I was still in Vancouver. In the habit of long cocaine binges, I woke up one morning in an alley not knowing where I was. I called some friends from a public phone and read them the nearest street signs. I had no money, and I was exhausted and hungry, so when my friends picked me up, they agreed to buy me a bus ticket back to Windsor and provide money for food during the trip. In that alley, I decided I wanted to get away from Omar and to deal with the charges against me in Windsor. I found out some years later that shortly after I left him, Omar was murdered by another drug dealer. I did not miss him after I left him, nor was I sorry to hear of his subsequent death. Whatever attachment I had to him also ended in that alley.

It was now late 1989. Leaving Vancouver, I hoped, would give me another chance to get clean and sober. I wanted three meals a day and a decent place to live, and I wanted to see my daughter again. I wanted to be loved and cared for. I knew that once I returned to Windsor, I faced a long jail sentence, so I prepared myself mentally for the worst. Jail at that time began to look like a refuge.

When I got back to Windsor, I called my police-officer friend to let him know I was back and that I was going to turn myself in at the courthouse the next morning. I called my lawyer and made the arrangements. I visited my daughter one last time before handing myself over to the authorities. I kissed her good-bye and explained to her that I was going on a trip for maybe a year or more and that I would write often. Even though she hardly knew me and was not sad at our parting, saying good-bye to her almost broke my heart. She looked like Shirley Temple and to me was every bit as sweet.

The next morning, I was off to the courthouse, where I was placed in a holding cell until I was called into the courtroom. The Crown and my lawyer had previously agreed on my sentence if I pled guilty to all the charges facing me: failure to appear in court, along with all the bawdy-house and prostitution charges connected to being a madam. I was given a fifteen-month jail term, followed by fifteen months of probation. I was relieved to finally deal with this problem and to put my past ordeals behind me. I was determined to be a model prisoner and put my best foot forward.

Vanier Prison for Women

The Vanier Prison for Women was a four-hour drive from Windsor, in Brampton, just outside of Toronto. As I approached the compound, dread filled me. The guards took me out of the van in a cold and hostile manner. I was stripped, searched, and given my supplies. Then I was taken to a "cottage" and given my cell. The place reminded me of Maryvale. I worked in the laundry and became friends with the man who ran the shop. I also went to school and upgraded my literacy and my computer skills. In the evenings, I took advantage of activities in the gym. I helped organize the Christmas show and became very involved with everything I could, including attending Narcotics Anonymous.

I became attracted to some female inmates, especially one beautiful young heroin addict from Toronto. She was now clean and remained that way for the year that I knew her at Vanier. I wrote love letters to her. Sometimes my letters were intercepted by guards who told me lesbian behavior would not be tolerated, but we became inseparable and made plans to live together after our release. Since she was scheduled to get out first, the plan was that she would set everything up for us. I lived for the day when we would have a life together on our own.

Fate quashed my plans again, however, when another inmate, a convicted drug pusher, managed to smuggle some heroin into the jail. She tempted my friend, who became addicted again after just a few fixes. Then my friend's supply was cut off. Since she had not been caught with the drug or related paraphernalia, her withdrawal symptoms were treated as if she had food poisoning or the flu. It was horrible to watch. A few weeks later, she was released. She did not come to the jail on my release date, as we had planned. I never heard from her again.

Toronto Halfway House

As my release date approached, in late 1990, I was scheduled to move to a halfway house in Toronto. A halfway house is usually located in a quiet residential neighborhood where women just released from prison can live and get support as they reestablish themselves in the community. I was looking forward to doing just that, as I was tired of living on the fringes of society.

The halfway house was run by the Elizabeth Fry Society, an organization dedicated to the rehabilitation and reintegration into the community of women who have been in trouble with the law.

I found work as a waitress, but the job didn't last long. After only a few weeks on the job, I slipped on an ice patch and twisted my foot severely, breaking my ankle. The break required an operation, and I still have metal screws in my ankle. The timing was awful, because the job had been going well; I was making friends and gaining confidence that I could live a calm and respectable life, and perhaps soon get back together with my daughter.

While my ankle healed, I stayed at the halfway house all day and night, reading, watching television, and talking with the other girls. My time spent in the Elizabeth Fry Society was very valuable to me, because the staff were great listeners and very understanding of the plight of the women coming and going through its doors. I was given some clothes with which to find a proper job and encouraged to attend meetings to help in my transition.

My ankle finally healed, and I looked for work again. Among the magazine articles I had read were some about dominatrices in Toronto and elsewhere, quoting police and lawyers as saying that what these women did was not illegal, provided there was no sex or communicating for that purpose. However, at this juncture, I was not anxious to start an independent business of any type, because as much as I missed the kinky lifestyle, for now I just wanted some breathing space to live normally.

On the job board at the house, I came across an ad from Frontier College for an assistant administrator to help with an ongoing project to help newly released inmates. I was hired right away and started work every morning at 7:00 a.m. I was an enthusiastic worker, and after three months, I was given a raise. I left the halfway house and moved into a rooming house, but soon after found out that in several weeks, the project was to lose its funding, and I would no longer be needed. I was unable to find a new job by the time the termination date arrived. Not only was I unemployed, but I was also ineligible for unemployment insurance because I had not worked the requisite number of weeks. I had few marketable job skills and very little money saved, so I needed to find a job quickly.

During my time at the halfway house, I had become a volunteer for the AIDS Committee of Toronto (ACT). I got to know four gay men who had been diagnosed with AIDS and could not live at home without someone doing their cleaning, shopping, and cooking, and helping them bathe. My involvement with the cause began when one male friend who was dying of the disease suggested I attend a seminar. I did, and it was heartbreaking, but it did tell me how I could help. I had the time, and helping these people gave me a nice break from the halfway house and an opportunity to phone for jobs. When I began working again, I still did the volunteer work, because I had become attached to the guys I helped. They in turn helped me prepare my resume and advised me in my job search. What a horror AIDS was and is. One of the guys was a top chef; one was a classical pianist and one of Toronto's leading accompanists for classical singers; and the other two held responsible positions in offices. They all died in the late 1990s.

Meanwhile my daughter was moved to another foster home, because the husband of the couple she had been living with died. The wife was ill, and the Children's Aid Society did not deem her capable of looking after my daughter, who was ten at this time. Another couple with two kids slightly older than my daughter took her in and were now eligible to receive the welfare allowance. All this happened without me knowing anything about it. They probably couldn't have reached me if they had tried. I was in Toronto, always moving, and this was before cell phones were commonly available.

I applied for a job as a masseuse and was hired to start the next day. Two days later, the place was raided by police. They did not believe that none of the employees had engaged in any sex acts, so I was charged with being an inmate of a bawdy house. Of course, I knew that the police were wrong, but I could not afford a lawyer, so when my case was heard some months later, I pled guilty. Fortunately for me, the judge was sympathetic to the fact that I'd only been working there a few days and that I had conducted myself well since coming out of jail. I was given a fine, probation, and a warning to keep my nose clean. I was in no mood to fight these results.

Less than a week after the raid on the massage parlor, I found work again in the massage business. I found a suitable apartment and moved in. I was barely making a living but had a roof over my head. By Christmas I was visiting my daughter almost monthly and living a relatively normal life. I wasn't breaking any laws at work. My new employer was more respectable than the last and also had a tanning salon on the premises. She tolerated no hanky-panky in her well-run operation, and I felt safe working there. I stayed for over a year and a half without incident.

Then this place was raided, too. The owner, the two other masseuses, and I were charged with being inmates of a bawdy house. I was innocent, and so was the owner, but since there were others who were not so innocent, we were all guilty in the eyes of the police. Everyone pled guilty to the charges; we were fined $500 each. My employer paid my fine as compensation for my troubles. I had asked a lawyer how much it would cost to fight the charges, but when I was told the amount, the fine sounded like a good bargain. It also saved the hassle of further court appearances, preparing the case, and possible jail time if we lost. The salon remained open, and I was told that I was welcome to stay, but I had been arrested three times on bawdy-house charges in the past five years, and I feared my criminal record couldn't take another hit. I decided to look for a different kind of job. It was now 1992.

I Become Madame deSade

For the next few months, I collected unemployment insurance, a respite that gave me a chance to gather my inner resources and prepare for the future. I researched what I thought would be a safer line of work: professional domination. I read extensively about the profession. I frequented such establishments to get an understanding of how doms ran their houses in Toronto. Sometimes I booked myself as a client; when I arrived, I said I would pay them just to tell me how to set up such an operation. Some of the places I visited were filthy, and others were inadequately equipped. I found that some of the girls were working from their apartments.

I decided that this pursuit would only be worthwhile if my business were in a first-rate facility with state-of-the-art equipment and costumes. I reconciled myself with the fact that it could take years to realize this dream, but I felt that after all I had been through, such a sacrifice of time and effort was justified. I wanted to wake up every morning with maids and servants at my feet, indulging all my whims, orders, and cruelties. I ask you: who wouldn't want a life like that?

After some time on unemployment insurance, I got a job in telemarketing for an investment firm in downtown Toronto. Through work-related social events, I met a woman and a young man with whom I shared my dream of becoming a full-time dominatrix. The woman had a friend with a house in need of extensive repairs, so we decided that the young man would live on the premises while he renovated the house and landscaped the grounds.

I moved into the house in early 1993. It was on one of the largest residential lots in Thornhill, a suburb just north of Toronto. The lot had the feel of a small forest, with a huge backyard and a creek running through it. It was expected that the property would be available for a couple of years. The renovations would take a long time, and the owner said it would be a couple of years at least before property values rose, so I thought that here, I would realize my dream. I calculated that by seeing a couple of clients per day, I could make enough money to pay a share of the rent and otherwise support myself. Edward, the young man doing the rehabilitation of the property, agreed to help me with my little business.

During 1993 my practice as a dominatrix grew. When I had no clients, I would work on setting up one theme room after another. I began to see that I could grow my business by advertising more and hiring some staff. The range and variety of my clientele were growing as well. My dream was quickly coming true: Madame deSade's Bondage Bungalow, as it came to be known, had arrived. It was such a wonderful change in my life. I no longer scrambled to provide for the day passing over me. I had the run of a large house. I was safe. I had money to spend. I was earning a living doing what I loved to do and making the dreams of others come true. I was able to send money back for my daughter and sometimes visit her. I was actually happy, and I wanted to make the most of it while I could.

Chapter 5

My Trials Begin

Our day in court would feel somewhat like a relief and an aftermath. As you will soon see, many things happen, or should happen, before you get your day in court (the trial). In fact, most people charged who are not guilty don't even see this day. So before I tell you about the issues surrounding my day in court, let me tell you what it took to get there, about more allies who rallied around me, and about some of the other events that occurred during that year, from October 1994 to October 1995. Five of us had been charged during and after the raid: me, Edward, Princess, Morgan, and Judy. We were the defendants, and our first decision was whether to fight or to plea bargain.

There are a number of reasons why so many people charged with crimes resort to plea bargaining—particularly those who face, as we were, the prospect of considerable media attention. A guilty plea means no trial. No trial means very little time in court, so the media have little to tell the public in addition to what it already knew. In our case, five people would thus be spared having their friends, families, and employers—past, present, and future—know about their intimate private lives.

A guilty plea has the added advantage of saving time and money. If the group fights the charges against them, each defendant is normally required to have his or her own lawyer; this is to avoid conflict of interest among counsel. Finding a lawyer requires time and missed work. Each defendant would also have to work with his or her lawyer to mount a defense, and then all the lawyers would have to confer. The preliminary hearings and trial also mean workdays missed. On average, the costs can amount to tens of thousands of dollars in fees and disbursements per client.

In our case, for example, three pretrial hearings were required for each defendant, and sometimes for their lawyers. For the five defendants, that meant traveling to Newmarket, some ten miles north of Toronto, for each hearing. That caused, generally, fifteen days of missed work or school for each pretrial hearing, along with a lot of time spent traveling and waiting at the court and a lot of money spent on legal fees. When Mistress Morgan was doing some babysitting, she simply forgot about one of the court dates, and the judge issued a warrant for her arrest. That meant that if she failed to appear at the pretrial hearing, she could be arrested and possibly held without bail. She therefore had to come from out of town, at her own expense, and miss two days of work just to ensure she made the next pretrial hearing.

And what happened at these pretrial hearings? Almost nothing! The two sides and the judge usually just exchanged a few documents and set the date of the next pretrial.

I think you can see that the prosecutors have at their disposal the tactic of attrition; at some point, they expect a defendant to screw up. When the prosecutors come to pretrial unprepared or unwilling to negotiate, they pay no penalty. But if one of us was not there, they took every opportunity to apply pressure. To our credit, however, we all made it to all the pretrial hearings, except in the one instance described above.

Also, the province's Legal Aid program for low-income people was only available to one of the defendants. Even then, the hours the lawyer would be funded would be inadequate for the huge legal battle that this case warranted. Also, expert witnesses would have a role in a trial of such complexity and significance, and they could be expensive. Legal Aid, in one of my applications to them for funding, recognized the potential broader implications of my matter, but refused me funding because the sentence or fine likely to be served or paid, if there were a conviction, would be too low.

Perhaps most important, plea bargaining before our trial began would probably have meant very minor fines or suspended sentences for the others charged, and only a fine or short jail term for me. If we fought and lost, criminal convictions could possibly be registered against all of us. We all would also have faced fines and possible jail time. It appeared that the "normal" thing for us to do would be to pay our fines or do a bit of time, and then reopen or go back to work for someone else.

But we did not do the normal thing. Shortly, I will tell you why not.

Not long after the raid, I went to see my lawyer, Ken Danson. The other defendants had not yet looked into getting lawyers, and Ken said he would arrange for their legal representation if it were required. First he had to see the disclosure—the package of documents, pictures, or whatever else the police showed the defense in advance of a trial to enable the defense to properly prepare. We had to wait about ten weeks for that, and then Ken would see the police before I finally met with him to go over my options.

I liked Ken Danson. He was a very handsome and fit man in the late prime of life, and he was also very friendly and charming. Scott went to see him to offer help, and Ken gave him a couple of things to do. Scott found him approachable and personable. Ken was a well-known criminal lawyer in Toronto and had handled some high-profile cases. His father had been the defense minister in the federal government and a veteran of the Second World War. His brother was also a high-profile lawyer who had risen to national fame representing the families of victims in one of Canada's most notorious murder cases. So Ken had a pretty good pedigree. He was also an activist lawyer.

Believe it or not, just a couple of weeks after I was raided, the National Leather Association held its annual convention in a hotel in downtown Toronto. They displayed equipment much like the whips and other things that Sergeant Miles had shown at his police press conference. Journalists interviewed doms who said they did the same sort of things that I did. When asked why they thought I had been raided, they said I should not have opened in a residential neighborhood. Ken went to the convention and gave a speech in which he attacked the actions of the authorities and maintained my innocence, but no one offered him much sympathy, as the participants at the convention feared that publicity from my case might cause a sort of overall crackdown. Ken was there because he wanted to gather information for my defense. He wanted to know whether other dominatrices were being raided and what services they did and did not offer; he wanted to see if laws were enforced differently in York Region than in Toronto. The media covered the convention extensively, complete with photos.

Also, coincidentally enough, just days after the raid, the movie star Dana Delaney came to town to promote her movie *Exit to Eden*, which also starred

Rosie O'Donnell. The movie was about thieves hiding out at an S&M resort island. When asked about the raid on my house, Ms. Delaney said, "I found that so funny."

The Dozen Begins to Form

At this point I should introduce the informal group to whom this book is dedicated: The Dozen. I described them as a group in my dedication, and I have told you about Art, number one of The Dozen, and Scott, number two of The Dozen. Now others are about to appear in my story, and their placement in the group is given in the order in which they appeared on the scene.

During these ten weeks, I acquired four important allies, three of them from the Community. I use this term here to refer to those who participate in running houses or services such as mine, to gay or lesbian activists or sympathizers, and to journalists who cover the S&M scene.

One ally from the Community was the prominent journalist Robert Dante. He published a glossy magazine out of Toronto called *Boudoir Noir*, which catered to the Canadian, American, and British S&M scenes. He was a leading activist in cases such as mine, and he served as a media spokesperson for the Community. He publicized the raid and reaction to it and set up a dedicated defense fund to receive contributions for my legal fees. He also helped Scott and me with the early drafting of this book. Of course the writing was subsequently put on hold numerous times throughout the next thirteen years, and Robert closed his magazine and left Toronto in 1999, but his early encouragement and assistance got me started on what grew into the book you are now reading. Robert was also famous as a performer with a whip and had appeared in movies. He had also written screenplays, directed plays, and published poetry. His wife, Mary Dante, was one of Toronto's most famous doms in her own right, but she was also well-known as a submissive to Robert. The Dantes had been the subjects of a few documentary films in which they were seen as aesthetes of S&M. Robert is the number three of The Dozen.

My second new ally from the Community was Patricia Aldridge. Paddy ran and runs Toronto's longest-running and most extensive facility for cross-dressers, called Take a Walk on the Wildside (a trademarked name) and located on Gerrard Street in Toronto. I had bought much of my cross-dressers' wardrobe from her store, so I knew her during the time I operated my bungalow in Thornhill. We are friends to this day. Walk on the Wildside offers cross-dressers a mini department store with an extensive selection of "women's" clothing and shoes big enough for men of all sizes. But that is not all. Paddy offers transformations in which her staff will help customers learn to apply make-up and select clothing. Customers can book sessions during which they can be dressed by Paddy or her staff. For example, this might involve lacing the customers into corsets or attaching garters to stockings. And to top it off, Paddy has overnight suites, so out-of-town customers can take a vacation as a woman. It is so important that men who like to wear women's clothing can do so with assistance, yet in a private, nonjudgmental environment. Prominent businessmen, politicians, and even blue-collar workers and farmers are among Paddy's clientele. So it should be no surprise that I now tell you that I am proud to say that Paddy is number four of The Dozen.

The third ally from the Community, Paddy's friend Roxy, was a male cross-dresser who worked for her. He was a business graduate who chose to retire comfortably from the U.S. business world at an early age. In normal clothes and situations he appeared as a tall, distinguished, middle-aged man. Like Paddy, he would play a critical role in my future life and legal struggles. Roxy worked with Paddy to help my matters move along and helped me a number of times in a number of ways. He is Number Five of The Dozen. However, it is with great sadness and regret that I must tell you that Roxy died just as I was completing my book. Paddy and I are devastated. She and I were with him when he died. So many others are grief-stricken. He was not only a wonderful companion for Paddy and a pillar of support for me, but a great presence as well. He was part of Toronto's landscape for many years. We have lost an original. In his last week he asked to see my manuscript. He read some of it and some of it had to be read to him. He told me to make sure my story is told. He did so much to make that possible. As I write these words I am crying.

The last of these four new allies did not participate in my legal matters, but provided financial support and personal support and gave some of us jobs. This was a woman I will call Phyllis. Phyllis, a friend of Scott, ran a rather technical business in a very conservative industry, and she was a ball of fire.

Phyllis hired Edward for some work and even rehired him from time to time, along with helping him in other ways. She also gave Morgan some work and even hired me at times, despite the publicity risk in doing so. I could go on at great length about what a great supporter Phyllis was on the personal front for me, too, but I am committed to ensuring her privacy. Let me just say, with great gratitude, that she is number six of The Dozen.

Phyllis introduced Scott to George Callahan, a lawyer who she thought would be very interested in my case. George was a lawyer in the middle of his career, with a background in entertainment law. Scott talked to him about doing a book about my house, and George advised and assisted Scott and me as we considered such a project while we waited for Ken to obtain the disclosure and meet with the police. George also had some experience in criminal law, so he gave me the benefit of his private insights on my case and provided me with legal help on a number of occasions that you will read about. As time went by and I observed George in action, I gave him the handle George "Bulldog" Callahan, because when he sank his teeth into something, he wouldn't let it go easily. George, when his time came, wanted to shake the flesh off the Crown attorney and run away with the neck bone. He was incensed with the way we, the defendants, were being treated. He also represented me to the tax authorities after the raid. That is a book in itself, but the upshot of it was that George negotiated an agreement after a few years that enabled me to declare bankruptcy afterward. He ensured that my rights and interests were protected and watched my back in matters not related to the case—although, as you will see, he did briefly appear in court on behalf of the defendants as well.

Finally, at this point, I want to thank a wonderful assistant David, who was there for me so much as well. His support is not to be minimized.

Lawyers and Hearings

Art said he would see Ken after the disclosure arrived and Ken had met with the police. The disclosure was about seven hundred pages long. Most of it consisted of an inventory of items seized, the logbooks of the police officers involved, and various statements. The document included photographs and diagrams. It looked very intimidating to me, but Ken said that to someone who did this all the time, it was nothing special.

The police visited Danson at his office a couple of weeks later and told him there would be a two-week trial, and that they would call the property owner to give evidence and the names of all defendants would become public record. They suggested, however, that if the defendants all plea bargained, the sentences or fines would be minimal. Some would even get suspended sentences. This option would entail none of the costs I mentioned earlier. The case would go away, and we could put it behind us. Ken told me there was no need to make a decision. The five of us even went to the first court date ourselves and obtained a routine adjournment simply by Ken handing a letter about our next court date to the court clerk and Crown attorney attending, who seemed to me to be unimpressed by the fact that Ken was my lawyer.

Meanwhile Art met Ken and got his permission and mine to take the disclosure to another lawyer for a second opinion. Art then met with another lawyer, met with Ken, and finally came to see me. Art also asked to meet Scott. When I introduced Art to Scott, they got along well. Art was about fifteen years older and had more social status than Scott, who paid full respect to Art's seniority as team captain. Scott agreed to pay about one-fifth the cost of the fight, to help out using his experience at research and analysis, and to coordinate things like making sure everyone got to court.

Art recommended that I replace Ken Danson with Morris Manning, saying that Morris was the best choice for this case. Looking at his credentials at the time, it was hard to argue. He had been the lawyer for Dr. Henry Morgantaler, the famous abortion doctor who was eventually honored formally by the Canadian government as a pioneer for women's rights. Dr. Morgantaler's trials were some of the most famous in Canadian legal history, and Morris's representation had won many accolades. But Morris's qualifications did not stop there. He was a Queen's Counsel (QC). When a lawyer puts QC beside his or her name, it is a mark of distinction conferred by the profession and the government on the recommendation of the legal profession and the laymen who advise the profession. Then, in perhaps the most convincing qualification of all, he had worked as a Crown attorney.

Art said that when he told Ken about the change, Ken had not been angry; Ken had said he was a pro, and that every pro knows that there is always someone better equipped for a certain matter than him, and he should never begrudge a client an opportunity for the best possible representation.

Morris told us that he could win the case, possibly without even going to trial. He pointed out that the Crown's case had many weaknesses, and that the Crown attorneys would know Morris would spot those weaknesses. He was very encouraging and said he was very pleased to get the case. I got no indication that he was even considering pleading out.

Morris's younger legal partner was Theresa Simone. This very attractive and urbane woman gave me some very helpful emotional support. She explained the process, as Morris had, and warned me that she and Morris would often be hard to reach if they were busy with other trials, explaining that lawyers in public practice always had hectic and often unpredictable schedules. Morris would represent me, and Theresa was to represent Edward.

Morris and Theresa were joined by Graham Pinos who would represent Morgan and Princess. Graham was an average-sized man with dark hair. He was quiet in his demeanor, but enthusiastic about the case and very protective of the girls.

Meanwhile, Judy was able to get a Legal Aid certificate and retain her own lawyer. So no risk of conflict existed among defendants then, as each basically had his or her own lawyer. We had formidable legal representation, ready to do battle, with the defendants all standing firmly against the charges. Scott asked some lawyer friends about what was typical in such situations, and was told that such a strong team of lawyers and defiant defendants is rare in cases such as ours.

We defendants went to the second court date without any lawyer. Morris said we did not need one, because he had given us a letter to give to the judge and Crown attorney identifying our new lawyers. This would automatically adjourn the matter to a later date, which could be worked out later, since the new lawyers needed time to review the matter. In the hearing, several Crown attorneys sat at the opposition table, and when they looked at the letter, their body language indicated panic. There was nothing for them to do or say at that time, but the look of shock was clear. Suddenly, instead of facing defendants with only one lawyer of moderate reputation, they were up against a most formidable defense.

Our work was done for a couple of months as far as our lawyers and preparation were concerned.

But the police were not through yet. Princess had not told her husband about what she was doing at the house. She had only been dating him at the time of the raid and had married him shortly after. He knew nothing, but, as Princess told me when we met at Morris's office to work on the case, she worried that if she did not plead out, or if she spoke to a lawyer, the police or Crown attorney would tell him. Not only that, but Princess had been on a student visa when she worked for me, and was not supposed to be working in Canada. (I didn't know this until after the raid.) So she was worried that the police would report that if she did not plead out or if she spoke to a lawyer. Princess asked Scott for advice. Scott said she might as well tell her husband, since even if she gave in to the charges, the police might have her deported anyway. It would also haunt her, he said, if her husband found she had continued to hide things from him. So she told all to her husband, and he spoke to Scott. Scott explained the legal representation and how her fees were being paid by him and Art. Thankfully, Princess's husband was not mad at her, but was mad at the police. When he met the rest of us and had all his questions answered, he was supportive in every way. At a preliminary hearing, when the police tried to approach Princess to testify in exchange for their dropping of the charges against her, her husband was firm in telling them to leave her alone.

Morris spoke to Art and me at his office in March 1995, six months after the raid and three months after becoming my lawyer. They told me that the Crown might bring the property owner to court to testify. The Crown did not seem to care whether the owner had even known what I was doing in the house. It seemed to me they were using the threat of his public embarrassment as leverage to push me to plea bargain. It seemed to me they were angry with him for giving me a place to stay when I was prevented from going home by my bail conditions. I say again that he had not known what we were doing. I had told him we were running a beauty and hairdressing business, and he said he understood we had to make a living. He never went beyond the kitchen, where he even had tea every couple of months. He was a kindly gentleman, very grateful to us for restoring the property. He was also a prominent businessman in conservative lines of business, with employees as well as customers. The exposure would cause embarrassment and loss to him, his business, and his family. The value of his property had probably lost hundreds of thousands of dollars already.

Morris and Art brought all this to my attention, as well as the fact that in a full trial, our legal fees would mount. It was also possible that the Crown would threaten to expose as clients those whose vehicles they had noted visiting the bungalow. Morris said he thought he could get me a three-month sentence, and the others fines or suspended sentences. He also pointed out that most of his retainer would be returned to Art if there were no trial. Art also said he would make use of the money and set me up in another house so I could resume my business once this had all blown over.

Plea bargaining was also attractive to the Crown. They would get a conviction that largely justified their actions legally and in the court of public opinion. By implication, then, other houses doing what I did would get the message that the authorities had a ticket to act against them, too, because those houses were offering S&M and the other services that I provided. Plea bargaining also saved the Crown time and money; they didn't have to answer for their actions as they would in open court.

This was not what I had expected. I told Morris and Art I needed time to think. I had to make up my mind within a few weeks. I did not know what to do. I had to get advice.

I got advice, and made my decision.

I decided to fight. So did the others.

Why We Fought

I told you at length the reasons for not fighting, for pleading out. But, as you know, we did fight. And here's why.

First, we happened to be innocent, and we happened to have been wronged. Anyone who has been so treated wants to clear his or her name and be rightly done by. Among us circulated a bit of the old-fashioned belief that you should only plead guilty if you are guilty.

Second is the matter of criminal records. None of the other defendants wanted criminal records. The simple fact was that a guilty plea would be irreversible for life, becoming a public fact. Also, as you will see later, my codefendants' mere threat to fight led to the dropping of the charges against them.

Third, it was a chance to make history by making law—even if I were convicted. A good judge would be a clear judge and would tell me that what about my actions was legal as well as what was illegal, and under what circumstances. Then I could reopen my business under the protection of the law. Previous houses or doms charged had not fought simply because of the temptation to plead guilty for the reasons I discussed earlier. As it happened, judges have cited the decisions in my cases when acquitting others subsequently charged under these laws. It was the ambiguity and internal contradictions that were at issue.

Fourth, I was advised that at trial the Crown's case might be proved a sham and their behavior excessive and wrong. This might open the door for me and the others to sue the government for compensation for lost income and legal fees.

Fifth, fame sometimes means fortune. A number of reporters said my story (even at that early date) would make a great book or movie. A long trial full of juicy evidence and testimony would get a lot of coverage and make me a celebrity, if I handled things the right way. One does not get such an opportunity very often. It was something to consider.

Despite the threats if we fought, and despite the temptations of pleading out, all five of us, not just me, were resolute in choosing to fight. It is a rare moment in Canadian justice when all the defendants are so united. It showed we all believed we were innocent. It showed that our lawyers wanted to fight and believed we were innocent, but had advised us on the logistical advantages of pleading out. We refused to let them treat the property owner or us as hostages. We met once, with Scott there, and we had numerous discussions over the phone, and we were in agreement: we were going to go all the way.

I was not adverse to publicity, but the other four had something to lose with the publicity accompanying such a trial. Yet still they wanted to fight.

I was at the opera with Scott one evening, and we ran into Ken Danson just after my meeting with Art and Morris. Ken said, "Terri, you can't plead guilty. Please don't plead out."

So I told Morris our decision and our reasons. Art said he would honor his pledge to pay the fees. Morris thought he could win the case on pretrial motions (that is, before I could even enter a plea). However, he insisted that I not speak to the media. I agreed. I knew that the property owner had already been embarrassed. I also knew that leading up to a trial, the authorities would have time to pressure any clients they had identified (using license-plate numbers) if I got those authorities angry. There would be plenty of time after the trial to go public, as it were. But it would be best to win first.

Also, Scott was looking ahead. He had me start drafting this book while events were still fresh in my mind, and I worked on it a few minutes each day or a couple of hours per week. Meanwhile, I was working as a phone psychic and telephone tarot-card reader, and Scott was discreetly gathering information and planning for the future. Our strategy was simple: as long as Art was paying most of Morris's fees, and as long as Morris was on the case, we were to lay low.

Days in Court

Finally the day of the trial arrived. The five of us gathered at our Thornhill home and left in two cars for Newmarket, the regional capital, on the blustery morning of October 24, 1995. Over a year had passed since the raid.

Our four lawyers met us at the courthouse. A couple of reporters from the Toronto newspapers were also waiting for us. Morris had instructed us not to talk to reporters, so we indicated our reluctant silence with smiling shrugs and pantomimes of lip zipping.

During the inevitable waiting period before the trial got started, a news radio station in Toronto called the public telephone in the lobby, hoping to catch a few words from me. I was right beside it and picked it up. I passed the phone to Mary Dante, who was there with Robert to observe the trial and report on it. Mary spoke on the phone for twenty minutes, during which the phone-in show accepted some calls from listeners. Each caller expressed surprise that the proceedings had progressed to this level, with the Crown showing so much enthusiasm and energy in prosecuting us.

We waited and waited. The judge and lawyers were in chambers for more than a day. They narrowed the issues, and a great deal of the Crown's so-called evidence was thrown out. When the courtroom sessions began, Morris had plenty to say about the behavior of the police during the raid. At one point, he loudly criticized them for seizing "truckloads of evidence" but not bringing any of it to court.

The trial itself was to begin the next day. Reporters entered the courtroom and began taking notes. Crown attorney James McKeachie sat on the right side, and Morris and the others on the left side, of the judge Justice Terrance O'Hara. The judge first offered to entertain motions. Morris rose and presented his first argument: that the charges were too vague to defend against. In charging us with keeping "a common bawdy house for purposes of prostitution or performing indecent acts," he argued, the prosecution had not informed the accused of whether we would have to defend against prostitution charges, or against charges that we had performed indecent acts—two separate and unique situations effectively lumped together under the original charge's wording. Morris said he could not be expected to create a proper defense because of this lack of specificity. The entire argument took three minutes, with judge O'Hara clarifying and nodding as Morris progressed.

McKeachie smiled and stood up. McKeachie said there was no substance to the motion. He cited many cases and explained them carefully. Judge O'Hara looked pained. The judge called a recess while he went to his study for another reading of the materials related to the motion. When he returned, he advised McKeachie that he saw merit in the motion and asked if McKeachie wanted a recess to examine the matter further and make further representations before a ruling.

McKeachie said a recess was unnecessary and that the Crown was ready to proceed.

Judge O'Hara sighed. He ruled that the trial would not proceed, and the charges were quashed.

McKeachie looked stunned. As I began a quiet celebration with my codefendants, a red-faced McKeachie quickly huddled with the police and other Crown attorneys while we planned the retrieval of our personal possessions from the police warehouse.

McKeachie turned to the judge and announced his intention to appeal the dismissal. Morris furrowed his brow. The case was already going to the Ontario Court of Appeal without a single word having been uttered in trial. As a consequence, our possessions remained in custody. I was too overwhelmed by media surrounding me and too pleased at the victory to have any reaction to their immediate decision to appeal.

Afterward people asked me if I had just "got off on a technicality." I did not win on a technicality. When the police enforce a vague law, such as the so-called bawdy-house law, they are obliged to be highly specific concerning the alleged offenses. In order to accomplish such specificity, they must specify in the charges as well as the evidence, using recognized wording and citing recognized laws, the logic of their case and its charges. Perhaps most important, in this context, is that they failed to say exactly what it was that I was doing that was supposedly illegal and what was not.

Papers were stamped and documents were signed. We tried to leave the courthouse, but outside I was stopped by reporters, with whom I chatted briefly. One major journalist, Rosie DiManno (about whom you will hear much more later), in her column the next day criticized the Crown for pursuing this small case as though it were a matter of national security. The embarrassment to the police and the Crown continued to grow in the press and elsewhere in the coming days and weeks.

But while we celebrated our victory, we realized that we had perhaps provoked the police and Crown by defending ourselves so vigorously. They went to some great lengths to close down the Bondage Bungalow and put me out of business.

Now would be a good time to tell you about the Bondage Bungalow.

Chapter 6

The Bondage Bungalow

At the end of a long, winding street, a small bungalow sat facing a large church. A lot of kneeling was done on both sides of the street. The bungalow had ten rooms: six upstairs, and four in the basement. I created a theme for most of them.

The Headmistress's Office

On a client's first visit to Madame deSade's, he would be led through the parlor to my office, which served as both consultation room and the headmistress's office. Ten large panels of drapes surrounded the erotically Victorian room, isolating parts of the room when privacy was required. Gilded flowers and golden thread were woven into the chintz fabric of the drapes. Books and magazines were available, and clients could read about cross-dressing, fetishes, or S&M. Many small, ornate decorations and theatrical props added to the mood. I would sit regally behind my desk and interview the client about his desires, after which we would take him on a tour of the house, or we would begin his first session.

For some scenarios, the office of the headmistress was like a principal's office at a very private school. The wait outside this office can be a test on any bad boy's nerves, especially if he is waiting on his knees—waiting to hear those high heels coming down the hall with lightning and thunder incarnated into each step, coming closer and closer to the intended victim. She grabs the offending pupil by the ears and ushers him into her office, where he is made to kneel on a spanking box. She twists his ear in order to force him to confess his sins and receive the proper punishment. For example, if the client was caught masturbating in class, the punishment was commonly twenty-five swats with the paddle or a hand across the buttocks. If the student failed examinations or did not complete his homework, he was likely to receive a verbal reprimand as well as being made to stand in the corner, write on the blackboard, or clean the washrooms. Some clients misbehaved deliberately in order to be sent to the office.

If the little culprit fidgeted too much while being spanked, his hands and feet were tied to the box, and punishment continued. The naughty student had to thank the headmistress after each and every stroke and then ask for another. If he didn't, he would be left alone, possibly with nipple clamps on. On the other hand, he might be spanked even more severely or caned.

The headmistress's office was also used as a waiting room for clients who arrived early, or for whom we were not yet ready, or those we wished to keep waiting. Many clients experienced a thrill of anticipation and a chill of excitement when one of the doms came for them and told them to rise and follow her. This office was in many respects the nerve center of Madame deSade's Bondage Bungalow.

The Parlor

Upon arriving, the client, almost always male, who had had a consultation on his first visit, was ushered into the French parlor to await the mistress. The visual setting for a scene is vitally important, so I attempted to capture the Victorian era by selecting prints that depicted lords and ladies at play in fine costumes. A large, gilded mirror reflected light from a candelabra on the piano, highlighting the room's elegant mystery. The scent of fresh flowers filled the air. The lighting was always provided by candles. A white lace room divider provided a screen for the mistress's costume changes. The parlor could also be transformed into a small conservatory where the "boys" or "girls" took music lessons and had their little knuckles rapped for poor performances on the piano.

In the French parlor, I held private audiences, during which the clients entertained me with intelligent conversation and displays of their talents. Since the parlor was such a large room, it contained many pieces of furniture and doubled as an elegant dressing chamber for ladies of the aristocracy. An extensive wardrobe hung in the parlor, composed of fancy hair clips; costume jewelry; masks; wigs of all colors and lengths; capes; riding boots; umbrellas; tutus; leather jackets; petticoats; gowns for all occasions; skirts; blouses; riding outfits; high-heeled shoes; thigh-high boots; pinafores; a large collection of lingerie in a variety of sizes; and a small collection of bridal veils with darling tiaras made of pearls and rhinestones. Little hats and gloves and decorative scarves were all there, enabling cross-dressers to indulge in hours of fantasy. A charming antique-glass display case held little treasures, such as garters, stockings, bras, fancy panties, bustiers, bunny outfits, harem-girl costumes, French-maid ensembles, and little leather odds and ends. More items were scattered across a small vanity, and rhinestones glittered everywhere, from the costumes down to the accessories. It was all collected in one room to reinforce the anticipation of clients waiting for the mistress. I was told by many that they had imagined that the salon belonged to an eccentric old actress from Paris. Some clients imagined that they were back in the time when ladies in waiting tended to their mistresses.

The Classroom/Nursery

On the main floor of the Bondage Bungalow was a junior bedroom. Painted pink, the space measured about fifteen by ten feet. In it were a couple of school desks. There was a large blackboard at the front, a notice board on the side wall, bookcases against the other wall, and a large number of toys and reading materials for young "children"—those seventy-five years of age and under. Drawings and photos on the wall showed adult babies being diapered and cross-dressers being laced into corsets by a dominant woman.

This room was incredibly popular with my clients, given the modest requirements of setting it up and the limited amount of space it occupied. Here they could act out fantasies in which they imagined that they were children at the mercy of a strict or cruel woman.

I often had clients who, at their initial consultation, were unsure as to which of the house's activities they wanted to try first. I usually suggested they start in the classroom and learn the ten lessons of servitude.

- Lesson One was Orientation. This was an extension of their initial consultation, where they learned what a dominatrix was and what the house offered, along with how these services and facilities fit their personal proclivities.

- Lesson Two was Basic Etiquette, as defined by me. Clients were required to take dictation on the blackboard. They had to write out and memorize the Ten Commandments, which, in my house, were the ten rules of servitude.

    - Rule One: the slave must always address me as Mistress.
    - Rule Two: the slave must always remain with eyes downcast.
    - Rule Three: the slave must never touch the mistress.
    - Rule Four: the slave must remain on knees or belly until told otherwise.
    - Rule Five: the slave must ask for permission to speak.
    - Rule Six: the slave must be dressed for his humiliation (in diapers or panties, or cross-dressed).
    - Rule Seven: the slave must always submit to the cruelties and extravagances of the mistress.
    - Rule Eight: the slave must anticipate the wishes of the mistress.
    - Rule Nine: the slave must obey any delegate or representative of the mistress.
    - Rule Ten: the slave must accept any punishment decreed by the mistress.

    Slaves were disciplined for inattentiveness or lack of deference to the mistress. They were also tested on the commandments and disciplined for incorrect spelling or lack of insufficient knowledge. If a client did not take the rules seriously, he would be punished even more severely.

    Most times, one of my assistants would act as either an assistant teacher or a fellow student. She would either intimidate the client or get him into trouble with me. She was my official tattletale. She would tell the client that he had to leave the classroom and go to the headmistress's office (my consultation office) for punishment, or I would make him stand in the corner, and the tattletale would giggle when I left.

Basic Etiquette also involved the demonstrating of special skills with which to please the mistress, such as performing arts, knowledge, or physical prowess.

- Lesson Three was Basic Training, which involved light spankings, reviews of Lesson Two, tests of obedience, and other slave training.

- Lesson Four called for the client to leave the classroom and go downstairs or into the boudoir. He would then be spanked or otherwise punished lightly to see how he reacted; this often involved some sort of bondage. The client would know the code words for safety and would have preapproved bondage and discipline in their consultation.

- Lesson Five involved transformations and role-playing. The slave had to submit to transformations as part of basic etiquette. He might have to be something like a baby, a bad girl in a convent, a singing student, or a promiscuous girl who was found out.

- Lesson Six was Domestic Servitude, where the slave was transformed into a maid, dressed appropriately, and taught how to clean a house properly.

- Lesson Seven was Physical Training, such as running on the spot, pushing pennies with one's nose, and walking in high heels, or pony training, in which the slave was ridden by the mistress. He would also visit the examination room for a physical checkup and pain-tolerance test.

- Lesson Eight was Behavior Modification. The slave was taught female superiority, how to serve his wife, and how to how to treat women generally. As in all the lessons, if he failed to observe the commandments, he was promptly punished. I often had to stop a lesson and use the client's time strictly for punishment. Sometimes when he returned for another session, I would continue the punishment for the first part of the appointment and allow him to resume his training only when I felt he had been sufficiently punished.

- Lesson Nine was Loyalty and Obedience, in which the client extended his lessons outside the house by writing reports at home, sending me letters, and calling me for permission to perform certain everyday actions, including sex. He might also have to call me to tell me how he was complying with his diet, his exercise program, or his effort to stop smoking or drinking.

- Lesson Ten was Graduation. For a cross-dresser, this was an outing to a lingerie store with the mistress. He, of course, would pay. Or I might accompany a client to a tack shop for riding or harness equipment. Or I might go with him to a fetish night or gay bar. Of course, the client had to pay for my time and expenses, but most clients were more than willing to do so by this time.

To use the room as a nursery, we had to rearrange the furniture, setting aside the desks and replacing them with a small wrought-iron daybed/playpen to which infantiles might be chained. On the floor would lay toys, games, coloring books, and a blanket to sit on. The client might be dressed in bonnets and frilly pink play dresses, and usually would have to wear a diaper and plastic pants. Rattles were offered as well, along with bottles filled with juice or milk. We would lay out stuffed animals and dolls for some as well. One of my assistants acted as nanny or babysitter if I were with another client or not in the house. The client would be played with, tickled, or pinched. The client was given a nap time, and sometimes the client could also have a bubble bath with bath toys. The client would be handled just like a real baby: he was not allowed to talk, only to make noises and scream or cry. If he did talk like an adult, he would be ignored or punished. Sometimes we would leave the client alone until he cried. And, of course, if he wet or soiled his diaper, he would be spanked.

This room was, for many of my clients, an escape from their daily adult male roles. None of my female or gay clients were interested in this room or these routines. Interestingly, however, couples were often interested in being brothers and sisters, or rivals, in such a scenario. I can't say I'm surprised, since many men remain fascinated by the things they did as children.

The Stage

The little stage was located in the room adjacent the throne room. It was constructed of wood, and the carpeting, valances, and curtains were all in red. Full wall mirrors encompassed the stage. The use of these mirrors on the stage enhanced the scenarios acted out in this area. We strove for a burlesque ambience in the theater, reminiscent of the gold-rush days of the Klondike.

A brass pole at center stage enabled participants to swing to music. The stage was used primarily by the cross-dressers and exhibitionists, who would perform stripteases and express themselves artistically. The stage was also equipped with a sound system that allowed the performers to choose their own music.

The mistresses were forbidden to strip at any time but were allowed to perform bondage and spanking scenarios on the stage (such as schoolgirl/teacher) and were appropriately and often elaborately costumed. Costumes always add to any scenario, but when worn on a stage, they lend a professional air to a production.

All the mistresses had to be able to act to a certain degree. Whenever the scenario required, a mistress had to be able to portray fear, joy, elation, anger, pain, and so on for a scene to be realistic. Facial expressions; makeup; wigs; boots or shoes; and the smell of leather, perfume, or incense all added to the realism of a scenario. The success of a scenario enactment depended on its realism for the client: he had to believe that whatever he was feeling or experiencing was real to the extent that he forgot his actual surroundings and became totally immersed in the moment.

The stage was also used for teaching. A television and VCR allowed clients to view their own sessions; the sessions would only be taped at the client's request. Client confidentiality was always respected, and if a session was taped, the client's identity was protected, usually by the wearing of a hood. The request for taping was not a common occurrence, but when it did happen, the client usually took the video with him.

Most of the videos shown as teaching aids were films purchased at the local adult video store. Two of the films were made by Toronto mistresses and sold through magazines that catered to the S&M community. These videos were used to demonstrate different types of bondage and discipline. If a client was unsure as to what he wanted or what a certain type of bondage involved, this was a painless and easy way for him to view what was available.

Clients were not encouraged to visit my house to just watch videos; my house was for active participation in the lifestyle. The S&M videos did not portray any sex acts, being limited strictly to bondage and discipline.

Exhibitionist clients liked to perform before an audience and often fantasized about it. Voyeurs were stimulated by observing S&M activity or by watching videos on the subject. Exhibitionism and voyeurism were often interchangeable and manifested themselves in the same situations. For example, some voyeurs who liked to cross-dress and prance and preen in front of the mirrors, performing for an audience of one. Some clients brought cameras and asked to be photographed as they posed on the stage. A house like mine provided the perfect outlet for both voyeurs and exhibitionists, and I provided a healthy setting for them to indulge in their desires without judgment or public censure.

In the role of instructress, I would help them discover their true inner selves and develop this potential. This was a process of discovery and exploration for the participants. It helped them connect with their feelings and emotions.

The Throne, Dungeon, and Examination Rooms

After a new or repeat client had finished his consultation phase, he would be led downstairs, often after being put into restraints, and shown to a shower room that was kept impeccably clean; the smell of disinfectant mingled with the ever-present scent of leather. Two doors accessed the shower room: one led into the examination (and punishment) room, and the other into the throne room. One of the exits from the throne room led into the dungeon, which contained a large open area and a large jail cell. A smaller cell was built into the wall of the throne room as well.

The throne room was dominated by an oversized chair atop a pedestal. After the raid, Sergeant Miles showed a photo of the throne at his press conference, saying that this was where the women would sit as men kissed their feet. He was correct. Many clients lived out their fantasies of having a leather-clad mistress tower over them as they groveled at her feet. Rings had been built into the throne; slaves could be fastened to the rings while being punished or displayed for the amusement of my assistants and me. I often sat on the throne and ordered my assistants to dominate their submissives. I loved shouting orders down and laughing cruelly as I sat there. As I related in an earlier chapter, during the raid, one of my girls sat on the throne while an officer kissed her foot.

The throne was used in interrogation scenes, in which the client might be strapped to it. I sometimes wore a large satin cape with a monk's hood, so during their entire session, the client would be unable to see my face or even my body. The cape was reversible: black or red.

Near the throne was a large cross attached to the wall; some clients enjoyed a biblical overtone during their sessions. Slaves were placed on the cross for punishment, repentance, or retribution, and it was also employed as a tool for humiliation, since on the cross the submissive client would be highly vulnerable and visible. They could be tickled, flogged, spanked, or just left there while blindfolded. I never actually suspended submissives ("subs") from the cross or put them upside down. Their feet always rested on the floor, but were restrained. One scenario required the sub to stand immobilized for a prolonged period, blindfolded, while listening to the sounds of other clients being punished or to sounds from other parts of the house.

The floor was covered by a large, blood-red Oriental carpet. The walls were painted glossy black, with a subtle pattern stippled lightly in silver. The lighting was very low—usually only candlelight. There were no windows, and very little light came in from the other rooms. The fact that we were usually dressed in black as well lent an atmosphere that many clients found enjoyably intimidating. Some told me later that they had nightmares about this room and the adjoining ones.

Next to the throne room was the dungeon, a large, open area about eighteen feet by fifteen feet. The room was renovated to look like a stable, except that its walls were painted the same glossy black as the throne room. A farmhouse door served as the entrance to the jail cell, which had thick wooden bars on one side. The dungeon was basically soundproof. Large beams across the ceiling enhanced the atmosphere and ensured safety for suspended clients.

Hanging from the ceiling beams were two devices: the swing and the stocks. The swing was suspended by chains and was made of high-quality leather, looking something like a large net. Clients experienced bondage by having each limb bound to a corner of the swing. It was one of our favorite devices, because it gave the dominatrix access to the sub from all sides, and she could be seen easily by him in this position, as he was partially upright. In the swing, he could be tickled, pinched, or punished by being rubbed with ice, having candle wax dripped on him, or having clamps applied. He could squirm more easily and safely than he could on a whipping bench, cross, or restraint table.

One scenario some clients found exciting was to be "discovered" in the swing by one of the doms. They enjoyed it when the assistant mistress would take advantage of their helplessness by teasing or punishing them, ostensibly without the headmistress being aware. Often, when I returned, the client would accuse the assistant of doing this. I would summon her, and when she denied it, I would punish him for lying while she looked on, giggling.

The other device suspended from the ceiling to about four feet from the floor was the stocks, a pair of wooden connecting planks with holes for head and hands. The holes were lined with fur. Sometimes the client was padlocked into the stocks as punishment for misbehavior in the classroom upstairs. He would often be fastened there fully dressed, and I would then pull down his pants and underpants; he would have to stand bent in the stocks like that. I was careful not to restrain the client's feet too close together, so he would not fall over or wrench his back when he tried to stand a bit. We could elevate the stocks for short periods if the client had back problems. I insisted on some foot restraints, so the client could not kick. Usually a short caning completed the client's time in the stocks.

I sometimes kept overnight clients in the jail cell. On some occasions, with the clients' permission, we kept one in the jail cell in hand and foot restraints while, just outside the cell, the swing was occupied by a second client. They were blindfolded and hooded so that they could talk without recognizing each other later if they happened to meet on the street. An interesting addition for these two was when, without warning, one of my assistants would come in and tickle the client in the swing but ignore the one in the cell. Or she might enter the cell and punish the inmate, while the client in the swing waited in terror that she might come for him, too.

Also in the dungeon was a large restraint table with metal rings at the corners. Many clients liked to be fastened with wrist and ankle cuffs, spread-eagled, and left for prolonged periods, or punished in that position. This table was important for obese clients or those with high blood pressure or other physical infirmities. Some clients enjoyed posing on this table during tours by other potential clients, wearing hoods to avoid recognition. You should have seen the faces on new clients touring the place when they walked in and saw a sub in a black leather hood with no eye openings spread out on the table in restraints. They were usually taken aback, even when I had warned them ahead of entering the dungeon and reassured them that the slave would not be able to see them. Sometimes the new client would see a slave on the table or in the cell wearing the hood as well as a big, black leather straitjacket, sometimes with feet also in restraint.

The examination room adjoined the shower room. It was painted in pink, so as to be infantile-friendly, and was intricately detailed to look like a cross between a doctor's office and a torture facility. Stethoscopes and other medical paraphernalia hung from the walls and rested on the shelves. Just as in a real doctor's office, disposable paper would often cover the seven-foot-long table in the middle of the room. Chains and restraint devices hung from the ceiling and adorned the walls. The room was mirrored at one end and could be either dimly or brightly lit. There was, as everywhere in the house, an on-off switch and volume control for the music tapes we played. Various canisters on the shelves contained feather dusters, wooden spoons, flyswatters, and kitchen implements, along with rubber, latex, and leather gloves. The walls were hung with whips, canes, straps, paddles, restraint cuffs, harnesses, spreader bars, and masks.

The examination room was used for doctor/nurse/patient scenarios. We'd wear leather or rubber with medical coats and latex gloves. Women seemed to be partial to this room. In its powerful and suggestive atmosphere, we could move from an empathetic stance to a cruel one with the client. The room was virtually soundproof when the doors were closed.

In this room, a common theme was the impassive woman doctor/nurse/inquisitor. The sub might first be examined, with some preliminary punishment. I had a large repertoire of routines for the examination. Next, I might declare that additional treatment was required, followed by the application of restraints and the continuation of punishment. In a very special scenario, the doctor would instruct the nurse as she punished or examined. Often, before starting a session, I would cover a client with clean sheets and leave him alone for a short while, during which he could think about what was ahead, and his sense of anticipation could build.

Another common situation called for the use of complicated restraints for prolonged periods. I would visit restrained clients with an assistant, and when they asked to be let go, I would instruct the assistant to continue punishment or maintain restraint. (Of course, this was the script they had asked for. I never actually held anyone against his will or disobeyed the code words indicating that he might really be in trouble, or that the scenario was not going according to his wishes.)

Many a client enjoyed a full or partial body shave in this room. Some wanted all body hair removed; some desired removal just in one area, such as the chest, or in a few areas, such as the legs only or the chest and armpits only. Some asked for their buttocks to be shaved before being whipped there. This was often done while they were in full restraint and blindfolded, which intensified the experience for them. Clients said that they enjoyed the tickling sensation, or that it was erotic or relaxing, and they seemed to look forward to feeling the stubble on their skin and against their clothing in the following days and weeks.

Rooms like these, in houses like mine, are often combined into one room and referred to as a dungeon. Some of the more elaborate houses operating today have separate rooms, as I did, that went beyond the definition of a dungeon. This is why I referred to my establishment as a house of erotica. Some clients spent some or part of their sessions in the dungeon, throne, and examination rooms. The looks on the faces of the police officers as they went through the house during the raid were familiar to me. Many of them, despite their outward show of nervous laughter, looked saddened to be dismantling the house. Here was a place where other men had enjoyed role-playing. Some of these officers probably had fantasies that they either repressed or acted out, and they may have felt disappointed to treat me as a criminal for facilitating the latter.

Costumes and Masks

The costumes of the dominatrix find their origins in Victorian undergarments and attire. A woman's garments were then very restricting. Corsets; bustiers; bustles; lacy and frilly panties and petticoats; layers of clothing; garters; stockings; hats; gloves; and riding attire, such as boots and riding crops: these are all accoutrements of the past, present, and future dominatrix.

However, the look has been altered to suit the times. Over the past twenty years, it seems to have been affected by the punk or biker-chick looks. Mistresses wearing leather jackets, Muir caps, sunglasses, piercings, spiked hair, shaved heads, and chrome jewelry have made their appearances. My clients preferred the whole range, usually in a blend of modern and Victorian. Rarely did they ask for the mistress to be totally Victorian or totally modern.

What does leather symbolize? Images of leather-clad German interrogators carrying whips or policewomen in leather carrying handcuffs are stimulating to many. Leather represents power, authority, and cruelty. Is it possible to see a woman in leather, with hard high-heeled boots that make her seem taller, as anything but dominant? Uniforms connote similar things to others. Many clients asked for the mistress to wear a nurse's uniform or a lab coat and latex gloves. This evoked an image similar to those that leather did for others: a harsh, cold, cruel woman who enjoyed their suffering. The look on their faces when such a woman appears is truly moving.

Some asked the mistress to wear a mask or sunglasses. At this sight, their mouths would turn dry, their eyes would open wide, and their jaws would drop. To them this was beauty incarnate. For others, fur, lace, satin, silk, and velvet, especially in black, red, or purple, were and still are the favored garments for the dominatrix to wear. For still others, the most stimulating sight was a woman dressed impeccably in a business suit. Yet others loved the look of a woman in rubber or vinyl. And, of course, some clients like the mistress in a miniskirt with high-heeled shoes and a low-cut top, perhaps also with a wig and lots of makeup. The common element here seems to have been that this was their own personal version of what makes a woman beautiful. Often the mistress's getup catered to a fetish, and merely being with woman attired in this way and being the object of her undivided attention was primary. The content of these clients' scenes often seemed to be secondary.

Most dominatrices love wearing a well-boned and tightly cinched corset, at least for a short time. In addition to enhancing her figure, it depicts her as refined and goddesslike. Corsets are ideal for playing a schoolteacher, governess, nurse, or nanny. We would have to be helped into these costumes. High boots would have to be laced up from behind, as would the corset. Stockings would be attached by means of garters, and this would require an assistant to attach the garters at the back of the legs.

Similarly, the submissive might be costumed. He might wear a leather mask, harness, restraints, or special clothing, such as a diaper and plastic pants. Needless to say, the cross-dressers had an endless repertoire of fetish clothing and makeup. Many men were thrilled to be dressed in exotic garments that they could neither put on nor take off by themselves. Many loved to be humiliated by being "forced" into such garments and undergarments. Many also liked to be paraded by or in front of the mistresses when dressed.

There is no end to the list of things that serve as fetish wear. Sometimes body parts themselves served as the fetish. Accessories were also fetish objects. Many men were stimulated when the mistress carried a whip or handcuffs or would enter with something the slave had to put on or be put into. Some clients enjoyed scenes in which, for example, they would be naked, and the mistress would enter with a diaper and plastic pants and argue with them about their need to put these on. Then he would be put into handcuffs, a straitjacket, or other restraints to prevent him from removing the diaper and plastic pants. These were, in effect, costumes for the client, and often the primary focus of interest.

One thing we never did for a client was to be naked or show our breasts beyond a bit of cleavage. When the client did not specify what the mistress should wear, the art of choosing the dom's costume was called into play. This art involved a combination of what looked most suitable for the client's scene with what the mistress most enjoyed wearing for such a scene, so that she would be as convincing as possible. The costume aspect of being a dominatrix was one of the most enjoyable parts of my trade. In some ways, it combines a woman's enjoyment in dressing up with the act of modeling. Knowing I was at my maximum attractiveness for the client was also deeply gratifying.

Perhaps one of the most effective costume pieces is a mask. A mask is a disguise, an identity you can change instantly. It is protection. It is power. Masks have long played a role in primitive rituals and theatrical presentations. They can frighten, alarm, shock, horrify, or offend. In medieval times, masked men maintained order and conducted executions. Masks were once used in the theater to impersonate a number of different characters. In sports, they are worn for protection, but they are also decorated to make the wearer intimidating.

Masks are usually conducive to good-natured fun and help to release inhibitions, encourage ribaldry, and permit anonymity. Masks also help express such emotions as anger, joy, and love. Masked clowns make people laugh, but they can also evoke fear, terror, and mystery. All of these factors were at play in the Bondage Bungalow.

It should come as no surprise that both dominatrices and submissives make extensive use of masks or hoods. Masks give a dominatrix a menacing authority. For the slave, a mask intensifies the experience or threat of punishment and humiliation. The cruel goddess actually

materializes under her mask, which is more elaborate and distinguished than that worn by the slave or submissive. Equally effective in endowing the dom with an air of authority is the Muir, or officer's cap, with mirrored sunglasses. This relates to some men's fascination with women in uniform, including policewomen with hats and sunglasses or nurses with surgical masks.

Many types of masks are available, from false faces held by a handle to complete head coverings. They can be made of anything from black leather to feathers, latex, rubber, fur, plastic, or even wood. Surfaces range from rugged simplicity to intricate design. Features can be distorted or exaggerated. The mask can be easy to put on or remove, or can have locks to act as a form or restraint. Black leather masks or hoods are traditional, as are cosmetics used to create a masklike image. The hangman and other executioners wear hoods. Wearing the mask of authority changes the internal and external expressions of the dom's character. She becomes brutal, manipulative, cruel, demanding, spiritual, crude, feared, worshipped, and adored. She becomes a real-life embodiment of a fantasy figure. She becomes the mask.

Submissive clients often liked to hide behind the mask to conceal guilt, shame, and pain. The mask can protect one's identity; for example, it may make a sub more willing to appear in a public humiliation. At the same time, his facial expressions thus remain private; this inability to communicate facially, or even see or hear, heightens his anticipation and fear. He loses his identity to the dom, and she cannot see his face. Many of my clients were stimulated knowing that their mistress never saw their faces.

The Bondage Bungalow boasted a wide assortment of masks and hoods. The police seized all of my masks as evidence of some sort of crime, and, in their press conference, they held one up as evidence, even though it had been purchased at a well-known store across from the Ontario Parliament buildings. The police never raided the store.

Chapter 7

My Trials Continue

The Crown's appeal of the court's decision to quash the charges against us was based on the argument that the charging document (the summons to court) did, in fact, disclose an offense known to law. This meant that the choice of words naming the offense should not be seized upon too narrowly by the judges. The Crown also pointed out that the disclosure given to the defense had described the alleged offenses using many different choices of words, and that the defense had many months to seek clarifications of what was in the disclosure.

In August of 1996, Theresa argued the appeal for our side; Morris was not there. She spoke for about forty minutes and cited case law. Then the Crown lawyer gave his rebuttal. Both lawyers were stopped periodically for questions or clarifications by the three judges. Cases heard at the Court of Appeal are normally heard by a panel of three judges. The judges called for a break before giving their decision.

The media were there, and Robert Dante called me when the case was over. He told me that newspaper reporters noted during the break that both Theresa and the Crown were using the same cases to argue their points as precedents for getting the decision they each desired. When the talking ended, the judges resumed their seats, and their decision was announced: in their opinion, the Ontario Court of Appeal felt judge O'Hara had erred in dismissing the charges. The original trial should have proceeded.

I was not at the hearing, simply because I was recovering from an operation and could barely walk. As I said Robert Dante told me the result and described what had happened during the hearing. I was very disappointed; I had not expected to lose, despite Scott's skepticism. Scott had spoken to his lawyer friends, and they had said the Court of Appeal was very conservative in matters like this and would be unlikely to sympathize with Judge O'Hara's decision.

I called Scott and told him what had happened and how I felt. Scott came by after work, and while he was there, I got the second installment of the day's double whammy: Art called and said he was "out." He did not say why. It might have been the threat of mounting costs or possible exposure, or both, or maybe he was actually being blackmailed. I never did find out. I felt betrayed, despite all Art had done. All his bravado was gone. It was very discouraging.

I passed the phone to Scott, who listened to Art for a moment. Scott said to him, "I understand. You have been very kind to these people. I would like to continue to fight with them, if it's okay with you." Art, of course, said that whoever is putting his money where his mouth is should have a big say. Scott thanked him again, winked at me, said good-bye to Art, and hung up the phone. He then turned to me and said that, other than the loss of Art's money, Art's departure from our cause would make things much, much easier. Scott added that he now had enough money on his own, and we could now openly seek help.

We had about a month to make some decisions. The first was whether to appeal the Ontario Court of Appeal's decision to the Supreme Court of Canada. If I decided not to pursue this course, the Crown would be free to either drop the charges or to continue with the original case. All observers believed the Crown would continue its pursuit of me and my colleagues.

The other defendants and I met in a restaurant, and we went over the options. We were unanimously in favor of a Supreme Court appeal by Morris. The actual hearing might not be for another year. Their legal bills would be very modest and would be paid for them. They would not be required to appear or do anything else, so they could travel and would not have to worry about missing appearances or work. Morris might win, ending their problems. If Morris lost, my codefendants would look at the matter then. It was explained to them that it would be about eighteen months until they had to make up their minds about how to plead, if Morris lost.

In fact, they had little to worry about in terms of a conviction. For some inexplicable reason the Crown dropped the inmate part of the charges against the five defendants. I'll explain. At first we had all been charged with being keepers and inmates of a common bawdy house. But in law, not everyone can be both at once. On the surface, I would be called the keeper, and the other four called inmates. But of course you cannot have five keepers of a place with no inmates. So there were no grounds to convict the other four defendants. However they would have to appear in court until the charges had been formally dropped.

Scott and I had talked very carefully about strategy. During the time leading up to the hearing at the Court of Appeal and in the months after, Scott had little to do on my behalf and was not very busy otherwise, so he offered to retain a firm to look at whether to sue the police, or perhaps even members of the media, for their actions. He explained that since I was broke, I was cost-proof and could not be made to post money in court in response to a motion to do so by the party I was suing. But first he wanted to set things up. He also said that if Morris lost, it may be better to engage another law firm—one Scott felt more comfortable with and one that would let him participate more. I had complete faith in Scott, and he had my blessing to proceed.

During this time, I had a partial hysterectomy and was incapacitated for about two months, but since I worked on my phone job as a psychic and did tarot-card readings from home, I only missed a couple of weeks of work. I had by this time moved out of the second vacant house that Jerry owned and moved in with a couple and their young daughter in their downtown Toronto apartment. I paid them a modest rent and I also did some babysitting for their daughter, who was in early primary school. They ran a gardening, landscaping, and renovation business that often occupied them both for extended periods several days in a row. It was a perfect arrangement for them to have me as a live-in nanny-type helper. It was a three-bedroom apartment in which I lived quietly in my own room for about three years. I worked on my memoirs—at a snail's pace, as always. But they were growing, as was the story. It was now late in 2006.

Klippenstein

Scott was greatly impressed by a lawyer who did some work for the party involved with the corporation where he worked. The lawyer was Murray Klippenstein, then of the firm Iler, Campbell, and Klippenstein. Scott asked him whether he and his firm would be interested in representing us in our likely upcoming trial and possibly countersuing on our behalf. They were promptly retained and had begun studying my case even before the Crown's appeal was heard. The focus at first was studying whether I could sue the police or the media for damages.

Murray was at that time in his midthirties, but he and his firm had already made a name for themselves on environmental, civil-liberties, and Native-affairs issues. He was a tall, slim, handsome man with a beautiful voice. He eschewed bluster in favor of demonstrating an understanding and appreciation of his adversary's position before opposing it. Judges seemed to love listening to him. Murray was the lawyer for the family of Dudley George in the famous Ontario case that resulted in a public inquiry (essentially a trial of governmental authorities). The public enquiry was called after a change in the provincial government came about, in no small measure because of the efforts of Murray and the George family. Dudley George was a native protester who was shot and killed by police. Allegations surfaced of police wrongdoing and political interference at the highest levels. Murray headed up the George family's legal team and was a key lawyer at the inquiry. He was therefore well-known when he took my case and became still better known, both because of my case and the public inquiry into the Dudley George matter that followed. Murray's involvement in the Dudley George case occurred before, during, and after his handling of my matter.

While Murray waited on standby to take over from Morris at any time, Scott also met and began a dialogue with Murray's partner, the highly regarded Charlie Campbell. Charlie was an expert in constitution and civil-liberty matters, and had in fact apprenticed under Morris. Charlie reviewed our case and sent Scott the opinion letter that Scott had requested. Scott and I reviewed it and drafted a reply. Charlie made a few changes. Scott finalized his position on whether we had cause to sue the police or the Crown for their excesses in raiding and publicizing the raid. This written and spoken dialogue, beginning with the opinion letter, cost thousands of dollars in legal fees. Charlie and Scott tried one another's patience as well, and they are both patient men. They concluded that we had limited cause for civil action, and such action would be prohibitively expensive. But Scott and I were very pleased with the exercise. He and I now understood many aspects of the law and police practices we had not previously understood, or even considered. Murray, who followed the discussion closely, was now much more thoroughly acquainted with the case. The exercise enabled all of us to be realistic and to all be on the same page.

Another good thing was that Wendy Snelgrove became involved in the case. She was a junior lawyer with the firm at that time and assisted both Murray and Charlie throughout their involvement in my matters. My case was of great interest to her, and she was very kind, attentive, and patient in working with all the defendants and Scott.

Charlie's analysis clarified a number of issues. The police had plenty of latitude in the raid, and the laws in this matter were quite vague, to the point of being unfair. It was also unclear whether they could be held accountable in a lawsuit for compensation for closing down my entire business because of some occasional, allegedly illegal activities. For example, let's say you are running a gas station, and you are charged with selling stolen cigarettes. Do the police then have the right to tear out your gas pumps and dismantle the diner on the premises as part of their seizure? Probably not. But in the case of my raid, winning a lawsuit would be an uphill battle, because I would have to (a) fund the lawyers and (b) establish what income had been lost and what I had done to mitigate damages. I was beginning to get the picture. Charlie never said so explicitly in his very responsible analysis, but it appeared to Scott and me that the so-called justice system had an unwritten rule: you don't fight back. Rather, in my case, it might be better if I spent my time and resources reopening my business elsewhere. It would be cheaper to "reoffend" a few times than to fight just once.

Scott and I then looked at the situation again. We decided there would be no civil action, but I would continue to fight the criminal charges. The only way the Crown could avoid a trial was to drop the charges against all of us. As I said, we knew the others would not be convicted, so there was no point in pleading out. And I was very much in a fighting mood. All my life, I had been held down and set back, and I had had to struggle just to survive. Scott and the other members of The Dozen then on board were squarely behind the strategy that emerged. They were organized, well funded, and well prepared.

This strategy determined my next decade. It was the right strategy. We were going to change the law, or at least the way it was enforced. We were not going to be blackmailed. We were going to fight and win a battle of attrition, and we would not blink. We would seek maximum publicity and be savvy in its use. We would keep a diary with which to eventually produce a book about this. And let me say again that the other four defendants were totally on board.

There was no going back. It was not going to be easy. But even if we had to eat the elephant one bite at a time, over many years, it would be worth it. We were going to make history and be the better for it.

Supreme Court

But first Morris, who knew nothing about these preparations, had to appear at the Supreme Court in Ottawa. He did so almost ten months after the Court of Appeal overturned judge O'Hara's decision. Paddy Aldridge drove me up to Ottawa and back to Toronto and was at my side the entire time, supportive as always. The appeal hearing was in June 1997. It took the court just a few minutes to rule that they had no jurisdiction to even hear Morris's argument. The Crown attorney never even had to get up. The reason was simply that the Court of Appeal's decision had been on a motion, not a verdict. So, almost three years after being raided, with my possessions still withheld from me, my business still shut down, me barred from the Bondage Bungalow, my legal fees paid, and my name and face a matter of public record, nothing had been resolved.

We Change Lawyers

Now we had to go through yet another round of pretrial hearings and then a trial. Theresa asked me to come to her office the following week with Scott to discuss matters. Scott said that we should ask Theresa a lot of questions, as if our minds were not made up about anything, and at the end we should say that first we had to speak to the other defendants and would get back to her. He wanted to use the occasion to gather information, and then Murray would write to Morris and Theresa, asking for the file and informing the Crown about a change in lawyers.

When we got to her office, however, Theresa told us that Morris was unavailable to continue on the matter and that she was willing to represent me. The others, as we noted earlier, only had to get to trial and would almost surely have their charges dropped or win acquittal.

The next day, Murray sent letters to Morris and McKeachie indicating that his firm was representing four of the defendants. Judy's lawyer would continue to represent her. At my request Murray was joined by George Callahan, who was very eager to help out.

But Murray, being the solid lawyer he is, went a step further. He enlisted Paula Roachman to advise him. Paula was a young, high-profile criminal lawyer and one of Toronto's rising legal stars. She had been mentored by one of the most famous lawyers in Toronto and worked at a well-known firm. As a law-school friend of Murray's, Paula advised him on the process ahead and suggested some tactics. She also gave Scott a standing offer to represent me if I were ever charged again.

It was time for the next trial, and we were nearly ready to go—but this time, it would be done our way. To add to the pressure, I found out that I needed another partial hysterectomy, to be done in the summer.

Once again, the pretrial hearings had to be attended to. At the first one, a new date for a pretrial hearing had to be set because the Crown did not have the right files. The next time, he claimed we were in conflict because not every defendant had his or her own lawyer, and that he would make a motion at trial to disqualify the defense team if that were still the case. Murray responded that that was only an issue if the Crown were going to drop the charges against my codefendants and call one of them as a witness. He added that no conflict existed in any event because the defense of each employee was identical. That defense consisted of the assertion that no sex or sexual acts had been for sale at the house. Furthermore, Murray asked McKeachie whether I had been charged with keeping a bawdy house for the purpose of prostitution, indecency, or both. Under Canadian criminal law, the prosecution must specify which. He did not receive an answer.

At one of the pretrial hearings, Murray was approached by another lawyer who was there on another case. This was Professor Alan Young, who taught criminal law at Osgoode Hall at York University in Toronto. Young offered his assistance without requiring a fee, as he would have time in the approaching summer. Murray mentioned the encounter to Scott and gave him Alan's phone number. Scott and Alan met subsequently. The upshot was that Young joined Murray's team, but as an advisor only.

On the other side, McKeachie was replaced by Peter Westgate. Westgate had attended law school in New Zealand and had been a criminal lawyer, as had Alan. According to some of the veteran reporters, Westgate was a "formidable adversary." He did indeed live up to his billing, but what he didn't realize was that the longer the trial continued and the harder he fought, the more it served our purposes.

Murray briefed us in his office. All five defendants were there. He was going to use the tactic of calling Morgan to refute anything Princess might say that might seem damaging, even though Murray or George could cross-examine her. Alan was not even going to sit at the defense table, but would be at court and would advise during breaks if called upon. Murray was going to call two experts to explain how S&M and other types of role-playing in my bungalow were a part of contemporary life and to establish that people did pay for this activity without expecting to have orgasms or even be allowed to masturbate. He was going to argue and demonstrate from the evidence disclosed that the bungalow was not a bawdy house because it was not frequently and habitually used for sexual activity, if at all. We loved working with Murray. He was so approachable and understanding. He stood for so many good causes, like civil rights and environmental protection, and this greatly impressed us.

Murray was also going to file motions: one would challenge the bawdy-house laws as impermissibly vague; and another that pointed out that by its nature and extent, search and seizure was such a violation of rights that the charges should be stayed, meaning frozen permanently.

However, the Crown was the first to file a motion. Westgate argued that since he was going to call Princess as a witness, and since the defendants were sharing lawyers, none of those lawyers were in conflict and none could represent me after the charges against the others were dropped. So he dropped the charges and brought the motion.

Murray was ready for the motion and had prepared a lengthy and well-researched argument against it. He again pointed out that no conflict existed, because the defendants, aside from me, disagreed on nothing; had signed waivers of conflict; and had not been told until virtually the last minute that their charges would be dropped. There were also the issues of rights to choice of counsel and the duty of the Crown to notify us, sufficiently in advance, that charges would be dropped. Murray even maintained that the charges against me should be dropped as well.

Westgate said that by established practice, Murray, George, and even Judy's lawyer should be considered ineligible to represent me, the only one now facing charges, because they had also represented the former defendants, at least one of whom Westgate said he was calling as a witness. Scott told me in advance that Westgate was correct, according to the manner in which things were done currently, but that Murray (who of course had plenty of peer advice from Charlie, Paula and George) had an opportunity to set a precedent. He and the judge had a chance to put to rest the despicable practice of attrition that prosecutors were using when they required each defendant to have his or her own counsel through a long process. A judge should consider whether conflict exists as it relates to interests clashing or evidence being compromised without having lawyers duplicating preparations and appearances—and billing for it. This is wasteful—assuming you have the money!

Young Takes Charge

Murray and Westgate made their points calmly and methodically. The judge, Charles Purvis, was going to retire soon and wondered aloud why he had been given this matter to hear. If he made a decision then and there in our favor, the trial would proceed. If he decided otherwise, the trial would be adjourned, and I would have to find another lawyer. He reserved his decision.

When we came back a week later to hear the decision, we were handed a seventeen-page written decision in which he weighed all the arguments and sided with Westgate. Murray George and Judy's lawyer would be in conflict if any of them represented me. But Justice Purvis said Alan was not clearly in conflict, so he was eligible to represent me.

The media were there in full force, anticipating a trial in which the questions of greatest interest would arise, such as "What is sex?" and "Which of the activities that went on in the Bondage Bungalow were indecent, and which were not?" and "Which acts were acts of prostitution, and which were not?" More succinctly, the media wanted to know what I was guilty of. So did I.

With the disqualification of Murray's team, I did not have a lawyer, so the judge gave me three months to find another one. Three minutes later, Alan announced to the media that I had hired him. I was now the only defendant.

Alan portrayed my case as a rare opportunity for the judicial system to rectify inconsistencies and injustices regarding how such alleged crime is defined and enforced. And Alan had three months to prepare on a matter he was already involved in.

In some respects, I was relieved. Murray, George and Judy's lawyer had busy practices and were hardly being paid, if at all. Also, Alan now had the benefits of their preparations and an entire summer with a troop of eager students. Scott had said he was virtually certain the judge would decide as he had, and that when it happened, I should act happy in front of the media, telling them that we had been victorious, because the others had had their charges dropped and I was looking forward to the trial.

The fact that our lawyers had been disqualified caused even more media interest in the matter. Some of the reporters told me they had known that the charges against the four would be dropped. They said they found a number of things about the case interesting—and they expected their readers would as well. Beyond the juicy details of the alleged crimes, they thought the way the court battles were being fought was a good story.

The costs on both sides were noted by the media. In man-hours, the costs to the government side, including police and support staff, courthouse operating costs, the time of the Crown attorneys, and their support staff, must have amounted to hundreds of thousands of dollars. The media undertook expenditures to cover the case. As for us, we had our legal costs, the sacrifice of the unpaid legal time, and, lest we forget, the time and money spent by the volunteers on our side.

The media smelled a barnburner of a trial yielding an array of stories. Scott told me to speak off the record to a few reporters who seemed sympathetic. That day at the courthouse, I told them that things were going as expected, and that at trial, they would very likely get enough in the way of salacious stories to get them working overtime. I assured them of pictures, films, experts, lively cross-examinations, and whatever else they wanted. They told me they would be there in force.

Mistress Morgan was, of course, very pleased that the charges against her had been dropped. After the hearing, she made a point of going up to the Crown attorney and lead investigator. She told them she wanted to testify and would tell the court how the officers had played around in the dungeon, propositioned her, and told her not to call a lawyer. She added that if they called any other of the former defendants, those witnesses would say the same thing. She got a ride back into the city alone with Alan and told me that evening how amazed she was at Alan's enthusiasm for the case. I found all this very encouraging.

For me, it was back to work while I prepared for trial and got ready for yet another partial hysterectomy. I was operated on about a month after the adjournment. My surgery went so well that even before I was fully recovered, we were back on the warpath. Our strategy included an amazing fund-raising event.

Chapter 8

RUNNING THE BONDAGE BUNGALOW

Before discussing the preparations for the big trial, I would like to come back to talking about the place the trial was all about. The Bondage Bungalow was an interesting place, of course. But people have always asked me about how to create and run such a business.

Where to Locate

From experience, I knew that small quarters would make it difficult to provide a fulfilling level of service. In small quarters, you are too close to your neighbors and unable to remain discreet while making noise. You also lack sufficient physical space to act out many of the scenarios requested by the clients. Clients would consider an apartment or basement facility ordinary and shabby. An entire house would provide the logistical advantages of having different rooms for various scenes. This would attract a greater variety of customers, and I would be able to charge higher fees in this venue. Such a facility would attract more affluent clients, as well as more educated and sophisticated people who might desire more intricate and imaginative scenes.

    A mistress must have a domain to preside over. New clients touring my domain looked amazed at the sight of these chambers that suggested that their dreams could come true. Without these facilities, that could not happen. Adult babies, or infantiles, needed playrooms and cribs. Psychiatric and prison fantasies were enhanced by jail cells and restraint tables. Cross-dressers needed mirrors and wardrobes. Classroom fantasies needed classrooms. Parlor fantasies involving petticoat discipline needed equipped parlors. Outdoor fantasies needed secluded outdoor settings. Reception and consultation called for a proper setting: the office of the headmistress.

The house also allowed me to live on-site, a great advantage when clients requested visits on short notice or when overnight or weekend stays were requested. In addition, more than one client could be present without being seen or heard.

Clients also felt a sense of mystery at the presence of many unseen chambers and unknown sections of this entire house available for their play. Sometimes they arrived expecting something different from each session, hoping to try something they had never done before. Some enrolled in detailed programs of training and discipline, using the full range of facilities. Others asked to be surprised by the contents of the session. Most dominatrices could only dream of the range of possibilities this house allowed. In my house, dreams came true.

Most dominatrices in the Toronto area operated in old warehouses or residential homes. They were in all types of neighborhoods. My being in a residential neighborhood was not, therefore, unusual for operating any kind of business, let alone that of a dominatrix. In York Region and Toronto, there were—and still are—doms operating in apartments, condominiums, and houses.

I wanted my location to attract a certain type of clientele—upper class, if you will. I did not want to be just another of the downtown crowd or operate a second-class facility in the suburbs. When one thinks of a dominatrix, one thinks of a luxurious or elaborate setting. The neighborhood should smack of power and influence. Many clients told me how they loved the location as well as the house, the facilities, and my operation. It made them feel as if they were going to Grandma's or Auntie's, but with a twist. For many well-heeled clients, visiting the neighborhood, which was in a very posh suburb of Toronto, and driving down the street was a treat in itself. Some said that driving down the long, winding street of near-mansions resembled a fantasy. Some believed, they later told me, that I was a wealthy lady who operated this business out of a genuine love of the profession, and they found this very stimulating compared to the many other such establishments they had visited, which seemed to exist only to make money. They also said that they felt safe in this neighborhood compared to visiting places downtown.

For many clients, the house was in their immediate community. At the press conference where he publicized the raid, Sergeant Miles of the York Regional Police said that many of my clients held high positions in the community. He was right, and these highly placed people were probably more grateful to me for what I did in creating this facility than they were to Sergeant Miles and his colleagues for what they did.

I took immense pride in living and working where I did. I loved working in my gardens and walking in the forest on the grounds. It was like having a cottage on-site. A small stream ran through the back and had a pretty pink bridge over it. It was wonderful to be able to offer these facilities not only to clients, but to visiting friends and to junior mistresses when they had a chance to relax during the summer.

Looking back, the bungalow was, despite my long hours and hard work, the nicest place in which I have ever lived. That is why, when the opportunity to move there presented itself, I knew it would be a great place to set up my business.

Naming Myself

How does a dominatrix name herself? Sometimes the name focuses on humor, sometimes on cruelty, and sometimes on a maternal image. Generally the names are geared to the vernacular of the S&M scene: Mistress Cruel, Mistress Domina, and so on. I found the names used by other mistresses to be unimaginative or ordinary. Some were too exotic; others were pathetic attempts to be cute. I wanted a name that would convey my business but not typecast me too narrowly in a range of paraphilia. The Marquis deSade, after whom sadism is named, was the most prominent figure in the origin of my craft. His name would add an air of sophistication, and I was pleased to note that no other mistress in Canada had used it. I felt that the many competing considerations were best served by calling myself Madam deSade. Acting under this name helped me to feel cruel, if the occasion demanded, and appear menacing to the clients.

My choice of name was a bold attempt to proclaim myself a preeminent dominatrix. I operated a premier facility, and I felt confident calling it Madame deSade's.

My advertising stressed other areas of paraphilia in my practice. Madame deSade's was not only a place where sadism was practiced by the mistresses; it was an academy of fantasy and role-playing. Bondage Bungalow was a name imposed by the media after the raid and did not convey the full range of activities. Madame deSade's House of Erotica conveyed succinctly, as mentioned above, not only that a dominatrix was in charge, but also that a wide range of activities were available. All advertising would detail these features after the name had caught the reader's eye.

I knew Madame deSade should be the ultimate focus of power, the sorceress who destroys the will of men. Her persona should conjure up brave new erotic worlds, so I became a real-life fantasy figure. I became, when the client wished it, a merciless vixen who enjoyed making them suffer. I became, when the client wished it, a reincarnation of his early teacher. I became, when the client wished it, a mother forcing him into clothing or scolding him as his mother had. I was the unattainable superior woman he secretly wished to worship. In my domain, he was now free to surrender to his secret desire to behave as he wished to but could not in everyday life.

Maintenance and Hygiene

Maintaining the Bondage Bungalow was a major part of my practice. By maintenance, I mean both the house's physical preparation and care of the grounds and premises. The driveway was swept daily in warmer months and shoveled and salted frequently in winter. Lawns and hedges were cut weekly. The exterior of the house was painted once each year and washed monthly. This was the routine after Edward and I renovated and landscaped the property, which occupied us for six months after we moved in.

A few select clients, as "slaves," would work under Edward's direction in maintaining the grounds and the outside of the house. Some of them, who had never done physical work in their lives, told me they took great pride in performing their duties. Others did so as barter for their sessions. Some actually had backgrounds in relevant professions, such as gardening or farming. Some were greatly stimulated by the mistress or mistresses waiting inside, where they would come in after hours of labor in the cold or hot sun, only to be laughed at or punished for their efforts by such a great lady of luxury. For many, it was their actual fantasy.

The interior of the house was meticulously prepared each morning. Before the first client arrived, a detailed cleaning regimen began. Unlike the outdoors, the indoors could only be maintained when no clients were present. Sometimes clients could arrange to provide their cleaning services in the mornings, but usually they could only do so on weekends. We (my staff and I) usually had to do the cleaning ourselves. Floors had to swept and polished; carpets vacuumed; furniture dusted and polished; chrome polished a couple of times per week; bathrooms and kitchen scrubbed; equipment washed and disinfected; laundry washed, dried, and folded; supplies replaced; room furnishings arranged; and repairs and replacements attended to as needed.

I cannot emphasize how important it was to me and to the clients that the house was spotless and well decorated. For health and safety, such cleanliness was important as well. Clients would often be on the floor or affixed to equipment or tables. A spotless house also reinforced the luxury component of the fantasy. Many clients complimented me on how clean my facility was compared to others. Cross-dressers appreciated a clean environment that made them feel more feminine. It also seems appropriate that a dominant woman would have an impeccably maintained home and dungeon, yet not have a single broken fingernail from performing domestic duties.

Security

The most important thing for me and my clients was a comfortable setting. In a first-rate facility, the client could park his or her car in a driveway in full view of the street, where no vandal would be unseen. The entrance to the house should seem secured. The affluent neighborhood was also a safe area at night. The size of the property helped to ensure discretion if a client were worried about being recognized.

To prevent break-ins, we had screwed plywood and insulation over basement windows. This also facilitated soundproofing. The house had a ventilation system. Doors to the outside were upgraded with the best-quality locks and bolts. All windows were blinded and curtained. The exterior of the house was lit at night, and six sets of motion detectors connected to automatic floodlights. Edward was present almost all the time. He was trained to respond to the slightest raising of women's voices. He placed fire extinguishers and first-aid kits in several locations around the house. He was more than capable in dealing with unruly clients if the need arose. Luckily, during the entire time I was in practice, we never had a fire or injury. On a few occasions, we asked clients or those taking tours or consultations to leave, but we never had to rely on security.

If a client was suspected of being drunk or on drugs, he was asked to leave. Anyone who appeared to be mentally distressed or physically ill was not allowed to stay. Clients who refused to stop asking for sex or indecent acts were told to leave. Only scheduled appointments were allowed, so security could always be in place.

Thankfully, we rarely had any of the problems I've just mentioned. Not one client ever filed a complaint or needed medical attention as a result of visiting us. We never had to call the police, and none of our visitors had to be forcefully ejected from the premises. Most of our clients were well mannered and respectful. When told that security was present, they responded positively, as it reinforced their positive impressions of my establishment.

Advertising

Professional domination is a business, and like all businesses, it must advertise. There are many ways to do so: ads in newspapers, in trade magazines, in supermarkets, on the radio, or on television. These ads may include pictures and may be succinct and to the point or lewd and suggestive. You can also stand on a street corner and hawk your wares. Word of mouth was, of course, another way in which Madame deSade's got itself known.

I pondered other considerations. In order to sell a product or service, I needed to identify a potential market and demand for it. When should I advertise? Was any time better than any other? Should demographics be a consideration? Should I limit my advertising to trade magazines that specialized in my area of expertise, or advertise more broadly? In advertising my services, I wanted to get two ideas across to potential clients: the realization of their fantasies by a professional and, at the same time, the protection of their identities and the promise of confidentiality.

Several magazines regularly advertised professional dominatrices and their services, preferences, and specialties—mainly small, independent publications. (Remember, this was before the Internet was in common use.) An even better type of advertising, however, was through word of mouth from participants within the Community. Patrons would return with wives, girlfriends, or secretaries, and then the domino effect would begin: these companions would tell two friends, who would tell two friends, and so on. I also received referrals from other dominatrices who recommended my facilities through fetish nights, business cards, and so on. Attending fetish nights enabled me to demonstrate my prowess as a dominatrix and my professionalism in presenting scenarios that were realistic, safe, and entertaining.

I was lucky in that I was one of only two complete houses in the area devoted to this type of adult entertainment. I was able to provide an entire range of playrooms, from cross-dressing to the enactment of scenarios. Clients were encouraged to make an appointment for an initial consultation and take a tour of the house. This was also, in itself, great advertising. Of course, when making the initial appointment and upon their arrival for the tour, prospective clients were told that sex would not at any time be offered as part of any package.

I placed new ads every week in order to emphasize my weekly special, which might feature spanking, voyeurism, or some other nonroutine service. I wanted to reach a broad range of clients and often had clients who wished to experience something new and different. Often a client would not know what he wanted, but when he saw what was offered that week, it could trigger a response. I offered a wide range of services, and by changing the ad weekly, I gave the readers something to look forward to. These specials also advertised the extent of my craft.

Since interest in dominatrices and their establishments existed worldwide, there were always clients who were willing to pay any amount and go anywhere to realize their dreams. Clients have come to my house for a weekend from the United States, France, Greece, and Russia. In other words, advertising enabled me to have an international business without ever leaving home, and I credit advertising with the success of my business, along with the excellent service I provided in a nonjudgmental atmosphere.

Administration

Without proper administration, there would have been no Bondage Bungalow. The most important aspect of administration was paperwork … and more paperwork … and yet more paperwork. Each client had a file that had to be kept current in case substitute mistresses did their sessions. There was also the usual paperwork common to any business, such as financial records and staff scheduling. So it was important to keep the paperwork organized and accessible. Unfortunately, my slaves were not permitted to help with these responsibilities. All contacts with clients were recorded in their files. I would usually sit down at the end of each day and update all files for clients who visited during the day or called with some new requests or information. I had a part-time secretary trained to handle some of the filing and other paperwork, which included ads, financial matters, staffing, schedules, appointments, supplies, correspondence, and the writing out of scenarios.

Clients filled out forms during their initial visit, and these were kept in their files under code names. Reading the account of a client's previous visit was also a way for me to prepare for that client's upcoming appointment, especially if he didn't visit often. Cash exchanges were recorded in a journal, along with appointment times and client codes. Bookkeeping was done as fully as possible. New ideas and task lists were constantly updated. An inventory of all equipment was maintained. Supplies were regularly examined, and when they ran low, replacements went on the list for the next shopping trip. Advertising preparation and scheduling was crucial.

Finally, I had to pay close attention to the scheduling of the staff. Two or three times a day, the day's schedule for all staff would have to be updated to account for no-shows, cancellations, illness, or absences for other reasons. And since we were always very busy, free time was used wisely. Thus, if a client failed to appear as scheduled or cancelled at the last minute, we could catch up on training, paperwork, maintenance, or shopping. Running the Bondage Bungalow made me into an administrator as much as a dominatrix.

Recruiting and Training Staff

In the beginning, I had only two or three clients per day, so I spent most of the business day in the office, handling the phones, consultations, advertising, tours, record keeping, and cleaning. In time my personal clientele grew, and with reluctance I hired administrative help.

But it also became necessary to hire other dominatrices, or apprentices, not only because of the increasing clientele, but because some clients wanted more than one mistress for sessions or wanted to watch shows given by the staff. The first employee I had was only hired to handle the phones and administration. When I asked her to learn to assist me in sessions, she was unfamiliar with the role of a dominatrix, but intelligent enough to understand the basic concepts. Within a month, she was fully capable of answering almost all clients' questions. She always ensured I had a synopsis in front of me when I began my consultation with a client. This ensured a professional environment for the consultations, which impressed the clientele greatly. She would also greet clients at the door, take their coats, and usher them into the parlor or consultation room. She performed the duties of a regular secretary, such as updating appointment books and maintaining financial and inventory records.

But in addition to her, I also needed other dominatrices. I needed days off occasionally, and clients would request physical attributes other than those I had to offer. Also, as I have mentioned, occasionally more than one dom was required for a session. Additionally, with more staff, more clients could be in the house at the same time. I felt that the best place to advertise for new dominatrices was at the bottom of my ads in the trade magazines. Tradition dictates that an apprenticeship of about two years is needed to become a fully qualified mistress. I had no criteria for hiring except that the girls had to be honest, intelligent, and artistic or creative.

The best way to teach the arts of the dominatrix was to have the apprentice with me in session. I would also give her everything there was to read on the subject, including psychology books and articles. Magazines that catered to the S&M scene, such as *Boudoir Noir*, were invaluable for suggesting scenario-enhancing techniques. Books such as *On the Safe Edge* served as virtual manuals. There were and are, as well, innumerable publications catering to fetishists and cross-dressers. Most of these were easily available at mainstream bookstores and specialty shops in the Toronto area. It was important to give and get feedback from trainees after sessions. I would mother these apprentices like I did some of my clients. Sometimes, though, I had to fire an apprentice; others quit because they felt uncomfortable in the scene. Still others found the location of my facility too remote.

I always made it clear that S&M and working with cross-dressers was not for everyone and that trainees did not have to participate in any scene that made them uncomfortable. I always tried to hire people who were uninhibited about what we did. Strange as it may seem, the biggest inhibition seemed to be about accommodating the cross-dressers, not about inflicting punishment or humiliation.

The most important thing my apprentices had to learn was that slaves must teach their mistress to be effective. Allow me to explain: when some clients meet a mistress, they set about training her in the art of training them—that is, they explain what they like and don't like, and how different props should be used. She must be charming and gracious when the occasion requires, or cold and remote if that is what the client prefers. She must have a keen understanding of what the client's limits are in terms of being too soft or too hard with him.

Thus a good mistress learns to respond to client cues and directions while remaining in character. She knows when to reassure him and when to scold him. She must appear to enjoy what she is doing, even when she is being cruel. She must pay attention to the five elements present in a scenario: adoration, discipline, humiliation, commands, and threats. She must invoke all of these elements at various times in a session. She must at all times be a superior woman, so the client will adore her. She must be firm. She must constantly, with words or looks, humiliate her slave while commanding and threatening him. She must do all of this while being beautiful, desirable, feminine, and unattainable.

I taught the apprentices how to speak in a commanding fashion, how to express themselves facially, and how to appear physically dominant and menacing. I would often have them stand before a mirror in full leather with stiletto heels so they could experiment with their expressions and appearance as they spoke. It is amazing how a hand on the hip, combined with nose in the air and one foot forward, can accentuate the forcefulness of even someone as naturally intimidating as a leather-clad, spike-heeled dominatrix.

The importance of ritual also had to be taught. The masochistic contract usually leads straight into ritual, which in this case normally took the form of organized worship in order to direct the client's energies into a spiritual channel. Rituals may also be used to invoke supposed magical powers. And, since fetishism is a form of worship or idolatry, some of the more common rituals involved the kissing of feet, groveling before the mistress, or verbally expressing adoration—all under the threat of punishment and often done while the slave is helpless in restraints.

If anyone wonders why dominatrices usually charge large fees for their time, they need only consider how much goes into making the sessions of the clients effective. Not only are equipment and decoration required, but also the skills of an actress who must play several roles in a day. In truth there is a shortage of truly dominant women: there is only about one dominant woman for every ten submissive men. So when you consider the skills and abilities I have just mentioned as essential to a good dominatrix, you get some sense of why so many men consider truly professional doms so special.

Chapter 9

THE BIG TRIAL: GETTING READY

Before I tell you about the fund-raiser, I want to tell what happened behind the scenes to prepare for the big trial.

Crown Attorney Westgate had at his disposal vast resources. He could call upon the lead investigating officer, who would also be a key witness, as would the officers who visited the Bondage Bungalow as clients. He also had at his disposal the resources of the police and the Crown attorney's office. According to the media, he said he might call an expert witness of his own to establish that S&M was a sexual act. He did not have to raise funds to do so, and I doubt he had a tight budget for this case.

On our side was quite a team as well: Alan Young, Leah Daniels, Alan's students, Scott, Paddy, Roxy, the former defendants (all of them ready to help in any way they could), the other members of The Dozen, and our seven expert witnesses.

Alan Young should, and I think will, be made a member of the Order of Canada. That is the highest distinction the country can confer. Alan wrote his own book, *Justice Defiled*, in which he all too modestly says little about his qualifications and achievements. The book is an eye-opener in exposing the flaws in our system of law enforcement. Alan had clerked for the Chief Justice of Canada. He was for some years a criminal lawyer in private practice, mentored in part by Alan Gold, one of Canada's leading criminal lawyers. For many years, he has been a professor of law—including, of course, criminal law—at Osgoode Hall, one of Canada's most prestigious law schools (at York University in Toronto). Alan teaches at the University of Toronto as well.

Alan is justly one of Canada's most famous lawyers. My case was just part of that fame. Alan, as he told Scott, saw his mission as getting government out of the private, consensual behavior of responsible adults. He has fought to legalize the use of marijuana, and his speech to the Canadian Senate committee studying the matter some years ago should be heard or read by all Canadians. He has doggedly and courageously fought hypocrisy and corruption in the Canadian legal system and the legal profession.

Life in this country is, I believe, better than it would have been had Alan not been Alan. He took the path of fighting for what is right, rather than building a law practice and making millions, which I am sure he most certainly could have done. I hope that in reading these memoirs, you can gain an appreciation of the greatness of his achievements and what a fine man he is. I am also pleased to be able to tell you that Alan and his wife, Laura, have also become good friends. I babysat Alan's dog Salem on a regular basis several years ago. To this day, his son and my grandson are friends and have regular play dates together. They are both now seven years old.

Naturally the opportunity to work on an important and high-profile case would be an attraction to anyone, even though the job didn't pay. Alan recruited a very talented former student, Leah Daniels, as his main assistant on the case. Leah, in her early thirties, was a professor of paralegal studies at one of Toronto's community colleges (where people train for specific trades). Leah had much of the summer to dedicate to our battle, and she took workdays off from the college to do so as well. She was hardworking and supportive of me. It was good to have a woman with me in court to give me support. I am old-fashioned in that way.

Several Osgoode students who were available in the summer also signed on to our cause. They helped prepare the book of authorities (precedent cases), researched the leading experts relevant to the case, and offered the insights of those experts. Scott attended one of their meetings at Osgoode and was very impressed with how intelligent, hardworking, and passionate they were about this matter. One of the students also accompanied Alan and Leah throughout the trial to assist as required. I extend my gratitude to them all.

The prosecution's strategy, which they were required to disclose to us in advance, was to avoid the issue of whether S&M, cross-dressing, or various kinds of role-playing were sexual in nature. They would say that this issue was a red herring, adding that we had allowed the clients to masturbate themselves, if they wished, and provided a context to facilitate this. They were also going to point out that genital contact, such as brief grabbing of the penis or squeezing of the testicles, did occur from time to time. Also, they had a video that showed me inserting a dildo into the anus of someone who was in restraints. They were going to ask the court to conclude that we were selling sexual services, even though they had no evidence of intercourse for sale.

In his detailed defense strategy, Alan was going to argue that the law required that for my Bondage Bungalow to be deemed a bawdy house, the Crown had to prove that acts of prostitution had occurred in the bungalow frequently over a long period, and that they were the mainstay of the business. Clearly that could not have been the case at my establishment.

Alan was also going to argue that the tape the police had taken from the house was not part of my business. It was one tape on a shelf of about one hundred videos of conventional as well as commercially available S&M and cross-dressing. One tape was all they could find, demonstrating one incident of penetration, without proof it was a commercial act. I repeat: one tape.

Alan was going to move for dismissal of the charges because of the excessive manner in which the police carried out and publicized the raid. They had oversearched, overseized, and overpublicized. They had violated the constitutional rights that protect the citizen against unreasonable search and seizure.

Finally, Alan could cross-examine Princess, whose charges had been dropped. Some media wrongly reported that her charges had been dropped in return for testimony. Not true. She was an involuntary witness who had made no deal. Alan was going to use his cross-examination of her to show that she was not a prostitute. She was more our witness than theirs, if only the court would be fair.

Alan was also going to make extensive use of expert evidence. I quote from his book the reasons for the experts:

> The experts were there for three purposes. First, as part of an overall press strategy, to give the public a better understanding of the issue. Even if we were to lose in a court of law, the case would still be a small first step on the road to law reform, as

public demystification is a necessary first step in any law reform enterprise. Second, to indicate that the pleasures arising from commercial S/M activity were not entirely sexual in nature. ... Third, to create confusion. We really don't understand S/M fantasy role-playing. This lack of understanding would allow me to argue that the Crown had failed to prove beyond a reasonable doubt that S/M activity is sexual activity. Confusion is the polar opposite of proof beyond reasonable doubt.

The Experts for the Defense

Now let us meet the experts of the defense. In the order in which they appeared at trial, they were Trevor Jacques, Luc Granger, Roy Baumeister, Shannon Bell, Darryl Hill, Robert Dante, and John Allan Lee.

- Trevor Jacques, a tall, slim, handsome man, was a physics graduate from England who became well-known for his book *On the Safe Edge*, a primer and manual for safe and effective S&M play. He also wrote a widely sold guide to alternate-sexual-lifestyle contacts and facilities in North America. He spent over a decade studying these communities and researching these works. He was also a well-known speaker in the media on these topics.

- Dr. Luc Granger was a francophone from the province of Quebec. (Canada has two official languages, English and French.) Dr. Granger was fluently bilingual but had a pronounced accent. He was a little above average height, in his fifties, mostly bald, but very fit looking—due, I suppose, to his avid participation in martial arts training. He was a professor of psychology and head of the psychology department at the University of Montreal. He was also a regular consultant to the Correctional Service of Canada, the department that runs Canada's federal prisons and related facilities. His expertise was in sexual offenders. He had thirty years of professional experience to share with the court.

- Dr. Roy Baumeister was a professor of psychology at Case Western Reserve University in Cleveland. He had taught and studied social psychology around the world. At the time of the trial, he had published over 175 publications, some in book form. Many were on S&M. In particular, he was the author of *Masochism and the Self*, a full-length book explaining masochistic behavior. He looked quite professorial with his neatly trimmed, greying hair and beard and his large glasses. It seemed to me he needed an Austrian accent to complete the package.

- Dr. Shannon Bell was a professor in the political-science department at York University, the campus where Osgoode Hall was located. She was a longtime professor, but you would never know it looking at her. A blonde with a good figure, she looked like a combination movie star and socialite, but she was a bit small to be a convincing dominatrix—too bad, as she certainly had the performance skills. She had published extensively on cross-dressing and S&M in various cultures and had done extensive research and acquired much personal experience in Toronto's S&M scene. Some of her works had been translated into other languages and published around the world.

- Dr. Darryl Hill was a lecturer in psychology at the University of Windsor, my hometown. He was in his thirties, but had already published in a number of prominent journals and had taught for several years. His research expertise was in gender identification. Specifically, his professional research into the phenomenon of cross-dressing had brought him to the trial. (Remember that almost half of my clients were cross-dressers.) One of Dr. Hill's students, Julie Fraser, also attended some of the trial as part of her research on the role of the distribution of male-female power in relationships, a major theme in her thesis. The soon-to-be Professor Fraser at Windsor, and later Dr. Fraser, will figure in my story again later on.

- Robert Dante, who I mentioned to you before, was a Texan. He was not as tall as Dr. Baumeister, but otherwise looked very much like him. Robert had some impressive credentials as well. He was mainly an accredited journalist, with twenty years of experience and hundreds of articles in mainstream newspapers and magazines. He had directed plays professionally. He had written books of poetry, including poems about S&M. Over the years, he had become more active in the S&M community, and it began to occupy more of his time professionally. At the time of the trial, he was the publisher of the world-renowned glossy S&M monthly magazine *Boudoir Noir*, which kept its readers—those into the scene or just interested in it—up to date on all the S&M news. Robert's chief claim to fame, however, was his worldwide reputation as an expert wielder of the bullwhip—the long and thick whip. This implement requires skill to use at all, and certainly to use safely. Robert had been a longtime activist for the reform of Canada's bawdy-house laws since moving to Toronto, and led the coalition formed to have those laws amended. After I was raided, he got in touch with me and established a defense fund to assist my fight. Although he would obviously be a partisan witness, he could speak to the facts of the S&M scene in Toronto.

- Dr. John Alan Lee was a professor of sociology at the University of Toronto, a post he held for thirty years. He was approaching retirement, but looked younger than his years. He was an expert in the sociology of sexual relations, especially S&M activity. The sociology of S&M differs from its psychology in that instead of focusing on why, his main research area was about who and where. The list of accredited courses he taught and his publications over the years was as long as my arm. He was also an active participant in Toronto's S&M scene.

My View

Now that the experts have been introduced, and before they have their say, I want to digress and give my own personal so-called expert opinion on an important subtext of the trial and its aftermath: the explanation of why a dominatrix is not a prostitute.

The Winston Dictionary (College Edition) defines prostitution as an act wherein a woman offers herself for "indiscriminate sexual intercourse in return for pay." The typical description of a prostitute would encompass her heavy makeup, her very short skirt, her extremely tight sweater, her fishnet stockings, her high-heeled shoes, and the street corner or brothel where she can be found. (While referred to as "she" in this passage, the prostitute can also be a man.)

Under the current laws a prostitute cannot always be discriminate in her choice of clients. Basically, all prostitutes are at the mercy of their clientele. A prostitute's chief goal is financial satisfaction, often achieved in cheap motel rooms or the backseats of cars. The more clients she services, the more money she earns. Often, the money earned is used to support a drug habit or a drinking addiction. If the prostitute has a pimp, she has to turn over her money to him, receiving very little of it for herself. In other words, under the current laws, her life is not her own.

A dominatrix is different from a prostitute in many ways, the main one being that with a dominatrix, the act of sexual intercourse or other sexual penetration does not occur. Also, a dominatrix can be very selective in her clientele and in what occurs between them. She may or may not let the client masturbate himself. The dominatrix offers fantasy role-playing. The planning and execution of these fantasies often entails much scripting, costuming, and—most importantly—staging. The dominatrix is specific in the performance of the fantasies, and the client controls his participation to the degree of his own comfort level. The dominatrix provides domination, bondage, cross-dressing, and other forms of discipline. Her clients are very specific as to their choice of fantasy fulfillment, which often occurs in a house or rooms dedicated to these types of fantasies. In most cases, security is provided on the premises for both client and dominatrix safety.

While a prostitute deals almost exclusively with the achievement of genital sexual gratification of her clients, the dominatrix uses most of the client's senses to help him achieve satisfaction. She uses sight, with the costumes and the look of leather; smell, with incense, candles, or leather; sound, with music or recordings to set a mood; and touch, with props like coffins, fabrics, and restraint jackets. All in all, the presentation by the dominatrix is as important to the client's experience as the psychological or physical achievement of his gratification. Not only do most dominatrices find the thought of having sex with a slave repulsive, but the act is simply out of the question. The key point is that the dominatrix facilitates role-playing.

Other Preparations

While the lawyers were preparing our case, other matters had to be attended to, including amassing resources—mostly money to fight the battle and publicity for our cause.

But before I discuss the financial issue, let me discuss what was done without pay or reimbursement. For starters, Alan dedicated much of his summer break to preparing and conducting the trial. Just think of the money he could have been making in the open legal market, rather than representing me for free. But that is not his mission. In other summers he has taken on cases consistent with his mission of keeping government and others out of people's consensual behavior in their private lives. He has also written during his summers.

Leah Daniels also dedicated much of her summer to preparing for and attending the trial. She is a fully qualified lawyer, and she could have done paying work or taught that summer. Do that math as well. Paddy took time away from her business and personal life to organize the fund-raiser that you will soon be reading about. Roxy assisted her every step of the way. Both of them recruited volunteers. Scott was in charge of making travel and accommodation arrangements for expert witnesses from out of town and ensuring that when they arrived, they were looked after and transported to court. He took trial days off from work.

We also incurred expenses for the experts. Dr. Hill came in from Windsor to testify, and when the court day ended behind schedule, we had to fly him in for his testimony a second time. We brought Professor Baumeister from Cleveland. He had flight and accommodation costs as well. Expert fees and honorariums were paid. All told, we spent over $5,000 on expert testimony. I might also add the costs of traveling to Newmarket, some fifteen miles north of Toronto, for all concerned. Let's just say that amounted to another five hundred dollars of disbursements.

Nor would it be fair to exclude expenditures by the prosecution and police. Imagine the cost of eleven days of trial time, preparation, and disbursements on their side. Further, one should consider the costs of the court, which are paid by the taxpayer.

All of this was spent on convicting one woman of a bogus prostitution charge for which the penalty would be a fine or short jail sentence, if they won. And even then, they virtually guaranteed the costs of an appeal.

How does one justify this? Obviously the importance of the matter led to many individuals coming forward to volunteer and give money. Also remember, this was my third trial.

Obviously, this case was running into the millions when costs in full are considered.

The Fund-Raiser

The fund-raiser was held in July 1998, two weeks before the trial began. Alan and I thought we should have a fund-raiser to raise money and as a show of force. We wanted to show the other side we were anxious for publicity, that we could attract media attention and financial support, and that we had a broad base of support. We also wanted to give our lawyers a platform to speak about the case. The thinking was that all these reasons for the fund-raiser would continue to attract contributions and support in the coming months. Alan, as established earlier, recognized that this might be just one chapter in an ongoing legal battle. He was, of course, right.

I'd never run a fund-raiser before, so I sought help and advice from friendly professionals throughout Toronto's gay and S&M communities. I was recovering from my recent hysterectomy while strategizing for the fund-raiser, and I would have gladly promoted and exploited myself shamelessly for the cause had I not been in such great pain. You don't know who your friends are until you find yourself in a monetary crisis. I found on my campaign that the gay community embraced my cause as if it were their own. So many wonderful, colorful people came out to offer support and encouragement. They made me feel like a real celebrity.

Before I tell you about the event, I want to thank so many people for their time and generosity in helping make the event a success. Once again I give great credit and appreciation to—you guessed it—Paddy Aldridge. Yet again this magnificent and talented woman went all out, with Roxy by her side, giving so much of her time and using all her organizing skills and contacts to make many of the arrangements. It was Paddy who arranged the advertisement, used both as a poster and newspaper ad: a full-page picture of me smiling sweetly while spanking a slave's reddened bottom. It advertised various facets of the event: panel discussions, cocktails, a movie, a buffet dinner, a cabaret drag show, a drag fashion show, a masquerade ball, games, mistresses to serve, spanking booths, door prizes, and S&M demonstrations. The date was July 5, 1998, at Buddies in Bad Times Theatre, a Canadian theater company that caters to the subculture in the Toronto gay community. The event was titled "Bottoms Up!"

Some potential guests expressed apprehension about attending for fear that the event may be raided. We were asking for money in exchange for spankings and other titillations. Was that legal? We decided it would be great publicity if my fund-raiser were raided. For one thing, it would happen on live television, amid a slew of lawyers. So I decided to call a press conference and invite the media so as to attract as much attention as I could in that one day. I sent out a press release to all media outlets, inviting them to a panel discussion with my lawyers and other professionals. The topic: S&M and the law, and how it pertained to the Bedford case.

We needed to petition sponsors for the event, so I ventured out to speak in person to shop owners who catered to the fetish community. I invited them to attend the event and asked if they would sponsor me with hundreds of dollars in gift certificates, toys, equipment, clothing, and services to be auctioned off or given away as door prizes. Among the sponsors (besides, of course, Take a Walk on The Wildside, which was Paddy's store) were Northbound Leather, Doc's Leather, He and She Clothing, This Ain't The Rosedale Library, Orion Bookstore, Urban Primitive, and Aura Borealis. At the time, these were some of if not *the* premier retailers catering to alternative lifestyles in Toronto. And of course we had at our disposal the fabulous wardrobes from Paddy's store.

I called upon Toronto's premier professional dominatrices to respectfully volunteer their time and equipment to a mutual and worthy cause. Needless to say, they came out in full regalia with their staff and slaves in tow. For a ten-dollar donation, guests were spanked, caned, and paddled, or they were made to serve drinks and worship feet. The real masochists endured to the end of the night and were passed down the line from one mistress to the next, making a contribution every ten minutes or so.

Scott had access to a printer and volunteered his time and resources, producing copies of my draft manuscript (then obviously in its early stages), which sold for $25.00 each; the proceeds went toward the defense fund set up by Robert Dante. Some of the retailers sold copies of the manuscript and told buyers I would personally autograph copies at the fund-raiser.

The first panel featured activists such as Robert Dante and a well-known local gay activist whom I would consider to be a pretty boy. His long, flowing red hair hung down to his waist, and his tall, skinny body poured into a tight pair of jeans made you look twice. A signature macho-man handlebar mustache came down the sides of his mouth to his chin, and his mouth opened wide into a sheepish, toothy grin. He looked very much like an archangel on a good day. I'm not sure how many projects he had on the go at once. He was instrumental in bringing out lots of gay men to the fund-raiser fetish party later that evening.

A prominent local psychologist catering to the gay community was also on the panel. He reminded me of Arnold Schwarzenegger in *The Terminator*. I found him by looking in the phone book for psychologists and psychiatrists in the gay community who would volunteer their time to come out and speak to the media in favor of the S&M scene. After I placed a dozen or more calls and left detailed messages on voice mail, he was the first one to return my call with a "Yes, I would love to help." At the fund-raiser, he and the other panelists fielded some very difficult questions from the media and the moderator, as well as commenting on what the other panelists said. Later that evening, I spotted him partying the night away with his lover on the dance floor.

The second panel consisted of my lawyers: Alan Young, Murray Klippenstein and George Callahan. Each one gave his legal and personal opinion on the case and the law. They then commented on each other's remarks and answered questions from the media.

The panel discussions were a great success, due in no small part to the moderator, Don Cullen, a well-known Toronto actor, comic performer, radio writer, and television director. He is most famous for his regular appearances on the Wayne and Shuster comedy specials over a twenty-two-year span (Wayne and Shuster, one of Canada's most famous comedy teams, hold the record for the most appearances on *The Ed Sullivan Show*.) Don brought forth all his communication skills in making the panel discussions a tremendous success. I shall always be grateful to him.

Then there were demonstrations by some of Toronto's leading S&M specialists. Free tongue piercings were offered to brave volunteers, and Vlad the Impaler demonstrated his pain tolerance by putting ten-inch needles through his arm.

At seven that evening, the guests were served a catered buffet dinner: hot and spicy Cajun dishes, including stuffed crab cakes, jambalaya, bouillabaisse, and beans and rice; as well as tamer dishes for guests with a temperamental palate, including cabbage rolls, buns, green salad, corn bread, and baked beans. We provided plenty of food, with some left over at the end of the night. For the first hour during dinner, we were entertained by a violinist, followed by pianist Michael Beers, who played for an hour or so afterward. We hired a DJ to play during the evening between live acts. Disco music from the 1970s kept everyone dancing. At nine, a live cabaret drag and fashion show dazzled the guests with performances by the superb Jasmine Fox, Bitch Diva, Empress Rose XI, Fancy, Niki Le Blanc, Sugar Bouche, the Grand Duchess Michelle DuBarry, Savanna, Chas Parkway, Sophie De Lee, Dale Barnett, and George Hollyoke. The show included the hilarious comedic stylings of John and Hardy and the outstanding Carrie Chestnut on saxophone. Standing ovations were given to all. It was something to see.

The host(ess) for the evening entertainment was a flamboyant Lucille Ball look-alike, who in real life was our own Roxy Wildside. At midnight, Mistress Morgan and her band played until it was time to shut down. Throughout the evening, dominatrices offered sample S&M sessions for a fee to raise funds.

Among the people who bought tickets to the event were patrons of the multicultural and liberal arts; psychotherapists; authors; intellectuals; artists; musicians; actors; lawyers; doctors; civil servants; businesspeople; army veterans; and famous media personalities. Word sure got around. The evening went off with without a hitch, and great fun was had by all. The fund-raiser was a success.

I had invited the media to stay all afternoon and evening to film the fund-raiser and even get punished, for free. How could the media resist? They were excited about the invitation to the masquerade and fetish party because it gave them an opportunity to be voyeurs behind the camera. One of Toronto's local television stations, CITY TV, covered it all day and night. The event was aired live on the eleven o'clock news, including short interviews and shots of the party in full swing. Bulbs flashed everywhere. I was pleasantly surprised by the coverage. Guests were fully informed that they may be filmed and didn't seem to mind at all, even if they were identifiable. The masquerade party allowed the camera-shy to be masked but still participate fully in the event and even answer questions from the media.

Perhaps the most significant moment of the fund-raiser occurred when I met a man I will call Albert. This elderly, distinguished-looking gentleman came up to me and told me how wonderful I was. Then he handed me a big check, gave me his phone number, and told me to call him if I needed more money. He was as good as his word. When the money we got at the fund-raiser ran out, he gave us what was needed for the experts and disbursements. He was also financially supportive afterward. Scott made sure all uses of Albert's money were fully reported to him, complete with receipts and summaries. Albert was a player, meaning a participant in the S&M lifestyles, and was known to a number of dominatrices. At this time, he was in his midseventies.

Albert's story is so moving that I want to tell you a bit about him. He told me that he had lived an entirely conventional lifestyle until his wife died when he was sixty-one and he retired the following year. He then engaged in the lifestyle of which he had always secretly dreamed, along with pursuing other interests for which there had never been time. He said he had never really started living until he retired. Scott told me that Albert served as a mentor for him and advised him on many things. Urbane and sophisticated, Albert appreciated good causes.

Albert is gone now, but may his example be remembered. He was a gentleman in every sense of the word. I am proud to say he is member number seven of The Dozen.

The fund-raiser netted us several thousand dollars and many offers of volunteer time toward winning the case. We were bolstered by the show of support and the attention paid by the media. It meant that even before the big trial, I was an established public figure, and my case was seen to have merit. Now it was time to see if I could win.

Chapter 10

SESSIONS IN THE BONDAGE BUNGALOW

The government was going to put my private behavior and that of my clients on trial. Let's take a good, detailed look on what they were going to try to put me in jail for.

Fetish Role-Playing

A fetishist is someone who derives intense pleasure from certain smells, textures, and tastes. This person is sexually stimulated by contact with certain parts of the body, such as feet, hair, belly buttons, necks, fingers, fingernails, lips, breasts, and buttocks. Other fetishes may include garments, such as high heels, stockings, leather, panties, boots, silk, satin, lace, rubber, and latex. Some fetishists prefer that their mistress wear fetish garments, while others like to wear female garments under their own business suits. These fetishists will wear female lingerie, such as nylons, panties, bras, stockings, and garter belts.

The most common fetish is foot worship. There are many opinions about the origin of this fetish. What makes someone passionate about something as ugly as a foot? I have had men make passionate love to my feet, caressing them and licking every part of them, including between the toes. Some men like it when your feet are sweaty and stinky. I had a client request that, prior to his arrival, I wear running shoes without socks for a few hours. He wanted to sniff my runners throughout the entire session. Of course, he licked my feet clean—a harmless scenario, but some people may think he's a pervert or weirdo. There is nothing perverse about it at all—he was just kinky, not crazy. He paid a lot of money, held an executive position, and was quite polite.

Some women spend a lot of time on their feet to make them objects of desire; some also spend hundreds of dollars on expensive shoes and pedicures. Women in some cultures adorn their feet with jewelry. When the foot is manicured, toenails are polished, and shoes or sandals are of fine quality, the foot can become an object of worship. Hands, faces, or any other part of the anatomy can also become art objects, worthy of all the attention given them.

I was amazed at the multitude of men who engaged in foot worship, but had no one to attend to or understand their needs. This constant desire ate at their souls; they desired foot worship just as other men crave the satisfaction of sexual intercourse. It can become a full-time preoccupation to the fetishist, a harmless inclination so frowned upon by "normal" society that he has to find a secret outlet. Only someone who cares enough to understand this type of behavior will martyr themselves for its legitimacy.

In the bungalow, the foot-fetish scenario usually took place in the throne room. In one very common script, I sit on the throne, wearing stockings, a garter belt, stiletto heels, or thigh-high boots (it was the client's choice); I might even be barefoot. I also wear a corset and wrap myself in a reversible red/black satin cape. My face is not visible. I also might wear an officer's cap, my eyes concealed by sunglasses or a visor pulled down over them. The fetishist is not worthy of gazing upon the goddess, and to do so is an infraction. Men like to look; when denied, their sense of anticipation and excitement are increased, because only a few feet or inches away is a woman in the most exciting and enticing situation they can imagine, yet it is denied them. This element of humiliation reminds a man at a deep psychological level of early infantile rages only highlighted by being, now, an adult male being manipulated by an omnipotent maternal figure. My assistant would usher the slave to my feet, where he would kneel and wait for my commands.

The slave would then be chained by the wrists to my throne's armrests, leaving just enough slack to enable him to kneel, with his head bowed down at my feet. The discomfort of this position only heightened the slave's pleasure and pain: he derived pleasure from licking my feet but was unable to hold them or caress them, and the more he struggled to lick what I would not give him, the more excited he became.

As a prelude to worship, it was common practice to have the slave prepare a moisturized footbath for me, in which he would bathe my feet and massage the oily water into my feet. He would also have the honor of removing my stockings. This was very erotic for me, and I thoroughly enjoyed all the attention. The slave would next trim my toenails or file them with an emery board. He would dry them off and apply cream, massaging it deeply into my feet, calves, and ankles. Afterward, he would be allowed to paint my toenails—but first, he must protect my little toes with cotton balls between them; only then would he be allowed to apply the polish. If the slave did a very good job, I would reward him with the pair of stockings I had been wearing. When presented with my stockings, he would either smell them or wear them. He would continue to show his adoration until his departure time. He would often bring gifts for my feet, such as scented oils, expensive stockings, and shoes. Many times the client left with the shoes, because he wanted to smell them later at his leisure.

Infantile Role-Play

Infantiles are adults who want to dress, behave, and be treated like actual infants, physically and verbally. They want to be comforted, or "mothered," by a maternal figure, preferably a full-figured woman. They feel that only a large woman with big hips, breasts, and so on, and one who is strong in mind and body, can match their idea of the needed authority figure. Mothering involves both comforting and disciplining, so infantiles prefer a strict maternal figure to a lenient one, or at least my clients did.

Infantilism is the fantasy of having the attention of an eroticized authority figure totally devoting her all to one's inner infant. The best scenes of infantilism balance cruelty with tenderness.

My infantile clients would invite discipline by coyly misbehaving. Their scripts called for me to scold and punish them. The scolding would involve raising my voice, telling them they were bad boys, and mentioning some of the punishments they would incur if they were not sufficiently submissive. They would get very excited as I listed punishments like being spanked, restrained, or put in diapers. They might also be forced to suck on soothers (pacifiers), wear women's clothes, be put in a straitjacket, be wrapped in a sheet, or just to be ignored. Being ignored was, believe it or not, their worst fear. I did not hesitate to inflict these punishments and more. A particular spice was added when their punishment was witnessed by other clients or my assistants.

It was my impression that the infantiles were younger, less independent, and less affluent than my other clients. They often told me that they were still living with parents, or that they were single, if on their own. They tended to be moodier and more self-conscious than other types of clients, particularly about their physical attributes.

Bill was a typical infantile. His fantasy usually started with me ordering him into a bubble bath with his toys. I would keep him there until the water was cold and his skin shriveled. Then I would take him out of the bath, dry him off, and lay him on a bed. I would rub him with baby oil and powder and then put him into a fresh diaper and plastic pants. Then, wearing only the diaper and plastic pants, he would go into the nursery/classroom and be told to play on the floor with the toys there. One of my assistants would then come in to babysit him while I pretended to be off on errands. The "babysitter" would have written instructions for feeding, naps ... and, of course, discipline.

Sometimes, instead of acting out the nursery/classroom scenario, I would dress him up for an outing, which was basically a walk around the house, or a trip to the doctor's office. Or we might go for a mock visit to an aunt or uncle, played by one of my assistants. The infantile would be dressed in baby booties, a bonnet, frilly pink panties, and a baby dress.

At the doctor's office, which was a room with an examination table surrounded by walls covered with hanging bondage and restraint equipment, he would be examined by one of my assistants. She would wear latex gloves and a doctor's coat—often with long, black boots and a corset underneath. If he were uncooperative during the examination, he would be placed in restraint. This was the furthest that Bill would want to go in his allotted time.

Many clients used infantilism as a prelude to full masochistic activity. Usually the client understood that any physical resistance, unless in full restraint, was dangerous and would cause the session to be terminated. Such restraints marked the high point of the session, as the application of restraints made real the sense of childlike helplessness. This was further reinforced when punishment was added, along with verbal admonishment. Now the client felt a loss of power along with his pain and humiliation. Many clients requested these elements to be extended to the point where they would cry and beg for mercy. At the end, they would be consoled and allowed to get dressed and leave.

Others received gratification from being permitted to rest their heads on my lap, or by being rocked to sleep as they lay across me. Some enjoyed being in a cell overnight and then being allowed to watch cartoons in the morning.

Another interesting scenario was when clients who like to be diapered would be deliberately mischievous by taking a laxative before coming to the house. They would then mess their diapers intentionally to incur my wrath. I would have to bathe their bottoms and change their diapers. Of course, they would then be spanked.

I think the most common feature of the infantiles was their desire for attention. They loved to give me reasons to yell at them, change them, and check on them to make sure they were not drowning in the bathtub. They loved to get my attention by shaking rattles, yelling, and annoying me with baby talk. I in turn could provoke more of this behavior by ignoring them, and so began a great parent-child reenactment in which they could never be sure whether they were about to be soothed or disciplined.

It seems to me that these men enjoyed a great release by regressing to this behavior. No man completely outgrows being a boy. Some play contact sports to very advanced ages, or go mountain climbing, or even just play golf competitively. My infantiles relived childhood directly with me. As I mentioned, they were generally younger and less mature than most of my other clients. I think that reaching their inner boy would require my more mature clients to look too far backward to behave like infants or young children, so they may have just accessed elements of their youth by cross-dressing or being submissive.

Cross-Dressers

Most cross-dressers preferred scenarios that allowed them to express their feminine sides. Most would have a female pseudonym. The costumes, makeup, settings, and scenarios all played an important part in making the fantasy as authentic as possible. I did a lot of shopping for these clients. At a few bargain outlets, I was always on the lookout for large sizes, and from time to time, I would also visit more expensive stores and look for items. But I did most of my shopping at Paddy Aldridge's store, which I told you about earlier.

My shopping trips involved three goals. One was to buy clothes for use in the Bondage Bungalow. Another was to buy garments that clients would take home with them. Finally, the third was to take a client shopping. The latter trips were almost always to Paddy's store. Some clients loved this. They had a desire to act out the fantasy of being taken to try on women's clothing, such as corsets. They would be my clients, rather than Paddy's customers, because cross-dressing was only part of their fantasy.

Cross-dressers sometimes arrived at the house already in costume and often sought immediate approval for their efforts. They always tried for perfection in their deportment and attitude as women. Several of my cross-dressers wished to start dressing as schoolgirls and work their way up to dressing as mature women.

One day, I opened the front door and beheld a figure wearing a three-quarter-length black rubber skirt, hair shaved down to the scalp, large earrings, exotic makeup, and no shirt or blouse to cover his masculinity. I was genuinely (rather than professionally) revolted. I gave him a good scolding for not having an appointment and for his decidedly unladylike appearance; he looked instead like something that had crawled out of a laboratory test tube. I had nothing against his fetish and always welcomed the cross-dressers who wanted to arrive in full costume, but I strongly felt they should respect me and my neighbors by presenting themselves as if they were truly ladies.

Cross-dressing scenarios took place in all rooms of the house. The client may have wanted to dress up as a schoolgirl, prom queen, or prostitute. Or he may have wanted to be tied up and left helpless in the dungeon, or made to pose in front of mirrors on the stage. Once dressed up as a French maid, he might be taught to clean a house properly. Cross-dressers' scenarios became elaborate theatrical productions. Once cross-dressers were prepared for their scenarios, they were taught how to walk properly in high heels, how to sit properly wearing dresses, how to be coquettes, how to flirt, how to smile, or and how to smoke cigarettes.

In public the cross-dresser had to mind his manners and play according to the laws of etiquette. This included giving the mistress her due respect at all times, regarding her house and neighborhood as sacred ground, and avoiding calling on her without permission. This indiscretion might cause him to be banished from the house forever.

Most often, my perfect little ladies showed up in dazzling evening wear, usually on weekends, when they could afford to spend extended time and money losing themselves in a world of fantasies, escapist recreation, and chitchat. Most found pleasure attending my house to dress up, and they seemed to go out of their way to make a lasting impression on me. They were hungry for exceptional female company, sometimes spending most of a weekend locked in the dungeon, bound in their garters and stockings. They might be ordered to give body massages, head massages, or footbaths, make bubble baths, brush hair, make tea, or entertain the ladies of the house with staged performances in my private burlesque parlor, strictly used for transvestite entertainment. Decorated in red velvet and surrounded by walls of mirrors, this room became their own little world where they could dance and express themselves as if they were really sexy dancers being heckled by an unruly crowd. They dressed in the finest costumes, including long feather boas, high heels, opera gloves, wigs, bikinis, or whatever the mistress wanted to see them in that evening, even if it were pink diapers and bonnets.

No matter what their costumes, the cross-dressers were always surprised to see themselves in feminine clothing. Their male attitudes totally disappeared once their feminine counterparts were in place. The feminine beings now flirted with themselves in mirrors and became more submissive to their mistress. Femininity became the objective of their training programs. Their male sides were made to think of themselves as the weaker sex, so their strength would be useless. They now had to learn the arts of gracefulness and daintiness while acting female in all ways, even when sitting to use the toilet.

Some instances of transvestitism might have represented desires to identify with Mother by dressing in her clothes. After cross-dressing, a client might undress and continue to playact naked. Only some exhibited homosexual impulses. These men, unlike others, wanted to watch pornography that featured males.

In their female personae, they liked to be threatened and badmouthed by the mistress. They seemed to be gratified by being seen as sex objects; they relished the sensuousness of the clothing. I had to be prepared with elaborate compliments when they needed reassurance. A healthy psychological diet for cross-dressers included a mixture of reassurance, instruction, advice, and encouragement from me.

As their mistress, I listened patiently as cross-dressing clients told me their worries, asking questions of perhaps the one woman with whom they could be close and seeking her advice. Their eagerness to please me, their concern with winning my approval, and their readiness to report their feelings and to ask me to satisfy their appetites with physical affection: all this brought to mind the behavior of a daughter with her mother.

Nearly all cross-dressers enjoyed exhibitionist fantasies, including teacher and student; mother and daughter; nanny and ward; mistress and (female) slave; boss and secretary; Mother Superior and student; aunt and niece; and babysitter and teenager. Often, a male role was played by a client who was an actor by profession. He became schoolmaster, father, uncle, boss, boyfriend, or stranger. His importance was paramount to cross-dressers because he provided a male presence in their scenarios, which lent an air of authenticity.

I was constantly challenged to devise clever little plays or scenarios that would take hours or an entire weekend to act out. Fortunately, patrons with extended stays painstakingly crafted their own customized scenarios well in advance of their visits, sometimes calling to confirm every detail before their arrival. If I required any items to complete their fantasy, I ordered the clients to make the necessary purchases. Patrons often came bearing gifts for me and my assistants—usually flowers, but sometimes chocolates, lingerie, jewelry, money, or leather toys. They appreciated our theater and its players, spending many hours lost in escapist recreation. Their dreams came true.

Here are a few of the more common scenarios.

Strip Parlor

If a scenario involved something like a strip parlor, more participants were required. In this case, other mistresses or trainees became the audience or hecklers or whatever was required. If the scenario involved a babysitter and baby, an assistant was assigned to play the babysitter, the client was the baby, the mistress was the mother, and my actor client was the father. Typically, the baby would be punished for disobeying the babysitter, who tattled on the baby to the mother or father.

Beauty Parlor

The beauty parlor was another popular scenario. This psychodrama enabled patrons to feel special and pampered. They were given bubble baths, massages, pedicures, manicures, facials, makeup treatment, and skin care, and they were costumed in elaborate wigs, false eyelashes, and fingernails. The goal was to treat them as if they were really women. Being pampered at their favorite salon brought them back again and again to have their fantasies realized.

In most cases, the scenarios were enacted at the house, but once in a while, some of the "girls" liked to go to gay bars to strut their stuff on their mistress's arm as she kept them in line. They would be humiliated in front of the bar patrons and paraded on leashes. The opinions of bar patrons would be sought in order to heighten the experience for the participants and to allow them to openly and actively defy their mistress in public. Such public interaction gave them the exposure they sought and allowed them to parade in an accepted manner. The gay bar offered a nonjudgmental atmosphere where they felt safe and, to a degree, accepted. This would not have happened in a heterosexual bar, where they ran risks of being arrested or being heckled in a psychologically damaging manner.

In the scenario of the boss and secretary, the boss would sexually harass the secretary by suggesting what she should wear to work, how to sit, and what she had to do in order to collect her paycheck. She would be told how to "treat" clients and what would happen if she didn't treat them in the expected manner. The boss (aka mistress) would tie up the secretary at lunchtime, use her as a piece of furniture, and eat lunch off her. The secretary would be humiliated for both real and imagined errors, and punished for wearing panties to work. She might, in fact, be punished for almost anything the boss felt was not in keeping with her job specifications. This scenario worked as behavior modification for clients who were bosses in their professional lives and had secretaries: it taught them to respect women through role reversal by giving them firsthand experience of the emotional and debilitating effects of such abuse.

Teacher and Student

In a teacher-and-student scenario, cross-dressers usually portrayed students between the ages of thirteen and sixteen. The students sat at authentic school desks, which lowered their positions in the classroom. Lesson One would be written on the blackboard for each student to copy into her notebook. One assistant in the room acted as a student who antagonized the cross-dressing student into actions resulting in the cross-dresser being punished by the teacher. Usually the "bad" student would be made to stand in the corner, with the back hem of her skirt pinned up over her panties to the back of the dress. The other student(s) would laugh at her, tease her, and provoke her, especially when the teacher had left the room. When the teacher returned, the snitch would have a list detailing the infractions of the offending student, such as pulling down her panties, mooning the rest of the classroom, sticking her tongue out at the other students, and so on. This always ensured that the cross-dresser would be in serious trouble with the teacher.

When the lesson was over, the offending student would be brought to the office of the headmistress or schoolmaster, where she would be put over the spanking box for punishment. The list of infractions would be submitted, and the offender would receive five paddy whacks for each infraction, administered with a hand, cane, or paddle. The offender was made to count out loud the number of whacks. This scenario was usually best suited to a novice, helping to slowly build up the trust between mistress and slave.

Nurse's Office

If a participant were already experienced with the teacher-and-student scenario, further humiliation and discipline would be incorporated into the scenario. A trip to the nurse's office might be required because of an offense committed on school property, such as masturbating, playing with other students in the washrooms, carrying dirty books, and so on. Infractions could be either real or fantasy.

Once the client was in the nurse's office, an extensive examination began by having the cross-dresser fully disrobe down to bra, panties, and stockings. She would then lie on the examining table, where the nurse put her into restraint as prelude to the examination while making humiliating remarks about the offender's body, cleanliness, mental health, sexuality, or any other area the nurse felt would call forth a response. Once restrained, the student would be contorted into position, her derriere shaved and spanked, and her legs suspended by chains over her head. She would then be blindfolded and gagged (as prediscussed in the initial consultation, with code words and safety responses). Further punishment might be meted out with implements such as riding crops, wooden spoons, or ticklers. The scenario ended with the offender being allowed to shower, dress, and return to class, where the teacher would dispense homework for the next session.

French Maid

My own favorite scenario with cross-dressers involved the domestic discipline of the French maid. To effectively participate in this scenario, cross-dressers had to be dressed in full regalia, especially shoes with three- to five-inch heels. The cross-dressers had to be completely presentable because of their high visibility by visitors. The stereotypical French maid wore a very short skirt, white apron, white cap, fishnet stockings, low-cut bodice, and blonde wig. She also had to be heavily made up. She was not allowed to talk until permission was granted, and she would then be punished for disobedience, because she had asked for permission to speak.

The French maids were taught to anticipate and understand my every need and want, and to obey all whims, orders, and cruelties. They learned to serve, cook, clean, wash dishes, scrub floors, sanitize bathrooms, clean leather equipment, wash walls, wipe down windows, do laundry, fold, iron, and garden. When the mistress demanded a bubble bath or massage, they had to prepare these in an artistic fashion. They also had to take orders from anyone else in the house, including company, without question.

Some of the scenarios involving the maids were performed in exchange for cleaning. This service was mutually beneficial: the cross-dresser acted out her fantasy, had the satisfaction of a job well done, and was rewarded afterward with another session to look forward to, meaning more cleaning and discipline. Meanwhile, someone was doing the chore of cleaning for me, and I had the satisfaction of seeing my house always in an immaculate and presentable state. If the work was not done to my satisfaction, which included a white-glove test, the job had to be repeated until it was completed properly. The punishment may have resulted in rice being placed inside her high heels, or tying her ankles together, along with her wrists, making it very difficult for her to complete her tasks.

Mother and Daughter

In mother-and-daughter scenes, I dressed in a matronly outfit—skirt, blouse, and low-heeled shoes—with my hair pinned back in a bun. The cross-dresser usually wore a schoolgirl outfit with bobby socks; braids or a pageboy-look wig; a white blouse and tartan skirt; and a schoolbag. The scene would progress one of two ways, depending on the client's needs and requests. In one scenario, I played a loving mother who nurtured her daughter and brought her up to be a proper young lady, educating her in all areas of hygiene, culture, and refinement. In the other, I portrayed a strict, verbally abusive, overbearing, dominant mother who made her daughter feel like less of a person and like a second-class citizen, one who deserved whatever treatment she received at the hands of others. It is my experience that novices at the start of their experimentation usually chose the first scenario, while hardcore players who had a deep-seated need to be punished opted for the second scenario.

Cross-dressers were encouraged to talk openly, ask questions, verbalize fantasies, and abandon established gender roles. They were also encouraged to engage in activities that appealed to them and to explore all facets of cross-dressing. In short, they were given the courage to be themselves and express themselves in a nonjudgmental, safe atmosphere where they could only be limited by their imaginations.

Some of my most memorable professional moments were spent watching men fantasize about their femininity. Once out of their cocoons, they could spread their wings, and the glorious display of colorful animation could begin. They started out as men exuding an air of authority and prosperity—usually older, distinguished members of society, such as bankers, lawyers, doctors, and engineers. They would then transform into beautiful, desirable women, delinquent schoolgirls, loyal handmaidens, blushing brides, or godless whores.

Some clients wanted to portray girls in need of superior discipline. Heavy-handed spankings would control these vulgar little lovelies, who might also receive discipline while in bondage and be given the cane instead of the hand or paddle. If a sassy juvenile delinquent wore her black leather jacket to class, it would be recommended she be sent to a convent school for rehabilitation. If her antics in class were lewd and suggestive, or if she deliberately disrupted the class, she was punished before her peers.

The cross-dresser who fantasizes about acting out the role of bad girl is truly a masochist. She encourages the schoolmistress to smack her for her brazen attitude and wants to be harshly punished for committing the ultimate crimes in school. She wears very expensive perfumes, stockings, and garter belts under her school uniform. When she is spanked and humiliated in front of the class, she is excited by their responses when they see that under her skirt, she's not wearing any panties. She is put through humiliating scenarios: cleaning toilets, washing floors with a toothbrush, scrubbing pots, disinfecting washrooms and kitchens, or cleaning the schoolroom. Other chores that served as punishments were kneeling for long periods of time, praying, or begging for mercy, always followed by more punishments and stern scolding.

Fairy-Tale Scenarios

Fairy-tale scenarios incorporate many elements into the enactment of a fantasy: religion, rituals, customs, cultures, ceremonies, initiations, interrogations, behavior modifications, domestic discipline, and basic etiquette. For me, fairy tales acted as a building block to kinky and fun-filled playtime. These lascivious little games were enjoyed equally by novices, cross-dressers, infantiles, and students. Clients' needs and fetishes were always met, and limits could be gradually extended. In a nonjudgmental atmosphere, clients could learn the basics of role-playing to heighten their enjoyment and participation.

Exploration and trust were encouraged when clients revealed their fantasies and preoccupations and when they developed a certain image of me. Trust is the most important element in a successful fantasy, whether the mistress is an evil queen, sex goddess, or fairy godmother. The fantasy figure must be free from inhibitions, liberal, sensually wise (in her portrayal of a sexually attractive figure), and able to extract feelings and emotions.

The Evil Queen and Snow White

The evil queen had captured Snow White and forced him or her into servitude. The client, who had a foot fetish, would spend his days attending to the feet of the evil queen while she humiliated him. If he were a fetishist who liked to be spanked or humiliated, the scenario would go as follows: Snow White had caught one of the dwarfs sniffing her panties, so he was put over her lap and spanked. The panties would be put over his head, with the crotch covering his nose, in front of the other dwarfs, who were incorporated into the dialogue as invisible entities. Note that with costume changes, props, and a vivid imagination, the mistress could play as many as five roles in a single scenario. This scenario could be exhausting and taxing but was also rewarding for both mistress and client.

Cinderella

For a cross-dresser who wanted to be transformed from peasant girl to a beauty queen, I would call upon the Cinderella scenario. If my assistants were available, all the better. The mistress would play the stepmother and fairy godmother, as well as the prince, and the assistants would play the wicked stepsisters. The client would be Cinderella. The cross-dresser may like bondage and discipline incorporated into his scenario. Some of the lengthier scenarios required a kind of script, because the client had several requests that had to be satisfied in the course of his scenario. Sometimes a client was forced to memorize his lines as he was taken through his scenario. Since failure to do so would result in discipline, some clients would intentionally act up or flub lines in order to receive this discipline. To make a scenario as authentic as possible took years of collecting pieces, costumes, and props, just like a real theater.

In the scenario, Cinderella was forced into domestic servitude by her evil stepmother and teased and tortured by her stepsisters. She was forced to perform acts of humiliation in front of them. She had to pretend that she was a virgin and endure humiliation at the extreme vulgarity of her stepsisters. She was disciplined, humiliated, and put into bondage by everyone in the household (including the fairy godmother, when Cinderella missed her curfew). Prince Charming tricked Cinderella into marriage, where he became her master and she lived in a different kind of servitude, happily ever after. This was usually an all-night scenario.

Little Red Riding Crop

The Little Red Riding Crop scenario was actually two scenarios here. In one, Little Red Riding Crop would meet the big, bad wolf (the client) in the woods and tell him to lock up her grandmother and wait for Red Riding Crop in bed until she arrived at the grandmother's house. Once Little Red Riding Crop arrived, she tied up the wolf and spanked him with her riding crop. Upon the release of the grandmother by Little Red Riding Crop, both the grandmother and the wolf were tortured further by Little Red Riding Crop. This scenario worked well if the client enjoyed fetishes, erotic role-playing, bondage, light discipline, domination, and submission.

This scenario began in our private woods with me dressed in a red cape, tartan skirt, blouse, bobby socks, and flat shoes. The wolf was stripped naked in the woods; he could put his clothes back on for the walk back to the house, but upon his return there, he would again strip and had to be waiting in the bed, under the covers. He would be helped by an assistant who would let him into the house and then hide in the closet. While in the woods, he would be made to kiss my feet, and I would tease him with the riding crop, telling him what a good time we would have if he'd go to grandmother's house and lock her in the closet. We would then have the privacy to do what we wanted. Little did he know that he was being set up for bondage and discipline for his naughty wolf ways.

In the other scenario, Little Red Riding Hood was actually the cross-dressing client. He would be attired in the same costume I was wearing as Little Red Riding Crop. This time I would be the vixen. This story began in the woods as well. The traditional fairy tale was played out, and I was the one who greeted Red Riding Hood while dressed and waiting in bed as the grandmother. When Little Red Riding Hood returned to the house, she entered the room and pulled back the covers; I sprang to my feet dressed in mistress regalia. At that point, I resumed my persona as the wolf or vixen and let the grandmother out of the closet. We would apprehend Little Riding Hood and throw her in the dungeon for mild torture and humiliation. The end of the scenario came when the client became exhausted from physical and emotional play. The scenario was evaluated at its conclusion. If it was all he had hoped, then he was destined to return. If not, he would never return. (Most often, the clients returned because of the realism of their particular scenario and the emotional releases it provided.) The client would then be escorted to the shower, where he would resume his normal persona. It should be noted that most clients wished to retain the euphoric excitement brought on by stimulation, visual as well as verbal. I have read that endorphins were released by the physical pain and pleasures produced by the paddlings, spankings, tickling, bondage, and mild tortures inflicted upon them at their request.

Whipping

Five elements are involved in a masochistic scenario: command, discipline, adoration, humiliation, and threats. The mistress stimulates the client with fantasies. Sometimes the client himself will indicate which fantasies stimulate or excite him, usually during his initial consultation. I always respected the client's pain threshold and was careful to build his trust. What was right for one person was not right for another. My only requirement was that the client agreed not to touch me and not to try to exchange roles, unless invited. I explained that security was present on the premises at all times. In other words, before we began, I required a clear understanding of the rules of the game. Their main concern seemed to be their desire that I convincingly appear to enjoy the session.

I never whipped someone who didn't beg for it or deserve it (at least consensually). Usually, the begging came first. Even if whipping were in their script, I would make them ask for it.

Worm, as I will call him, was one of my favorite whipping boys. Worm would have a supervised shower after arriving. He would have to undress in front of me and hang his clothes neatly. I would stand in front of him, usually in thigh-high black boots and a corset and short skirt. Sometimes I would give him some variety and wear a latex body stocking. Often I would wear black gloves and hold an instrument of flagellation as I instructed him in each step of disrobing.

Before stepping into the shower, he would have to spread his legs and bend over for a detailed inspection. Through the glass shower stall, he could see me observing him closely. I would occasionally scream orders, such as "Scrub harder!" This screaming and supervision aroused him greatly. I would give him a fresh towel to dry himself while I shouted at him to hurry and pointed out wet spots he had missed.

When Worm was dry, I ordered him to his knees and then left the room for several minutes in order to increase his sense of anticipation. When I returned, I would order him to crawl into the dungeon, naked, on his knees, or squirm there on his belly. During his journey, I would encourage him with kicks and blows.

When we arrived in the intended room, I or my assistant would fasten a number of restraints on him: wrist and ankle cuffs; a collar; a gag; and a mask with a blindfold to start. Then the true process of restraint would begin. I might hang him from the ceiling, tie him to my whipping post, fasten him to my cross, or put him across my whipping box. I also enjoyed using a leg spreader when he was on the floor and in a body belt to fasten his hands to his sides.

Of course, a previous consultation had determined Worm's limits and capabilities. He might agree that we would try to expand these slightly during each subsequent session. He knew the universal code words if he felt he were in any real danger. And he also would be asked before he began to undress which whips should be used for this session.

Then his whipping could begin. I would start out lightly by warming up and desensitizing his buttocks by lightly spanking him with my gloved hand. One of my favorite gloves was my leather gauntlet glove, which went up the forearm to the elbow and fanned out at the top. This glove was very heavy and applied a nice stinging sensation to the buttocks. Sometimes I would spray water on his bottom and spank him with my bare hand to warm him up.

After the warm-up, I would hit him lightly on the buttocks with the tip of the whip, a bit harder than in the warm-up. I would do this about five times on each cheek and then make him beg for more. If he didn't beg, I would put the whip down and leave the room for a few minutes, during which time he would be helplessly suspended or pinioned, usually blindfolded. Often he would call out, "Mistress, are you there?" and when I felt that his anticipation had grown enough, I would ask him if he was ready to beg for more. If he said yes, I would make him tell me why he deserved it, what a disgusting creature he was, and why I should hit him harder this time. He had to be imaginative in describing his deficiencies, or his punishment would again be postponed, and I would leave the room.

Tormenting him made me absolutely tingle with delight. The power was absolute, because not only was he physically helpless, but I would make him suffer whether he did the right things or not. Toying with him made me feel like a spoiled little girl. I could giggle with delight when I wanted, and when I became angry with him, I could punish him when it pleased me, or make him suffer when I could not be bothered to punish him.

Worm enjoyed a prolonged flogging of the buttocks, with the position of the restraints changed during the session. I would continue whipping with greater intensity, sometimes screaming insults or obscenities at him. I would order him to beg for mercy and laugh in response. It was very important to this client that there be continuous interaction and communication. I would usually finish by changing from the whip to the cane, which is generally more painful. But I would also tease and tickle him with my fingernails to add to the variety of sensations.

Worm was married, so it was important that I avoided leaving any marks. This dual need for secrecy and severity called upon all my skill and judgment. Sometimes I had to apply an ointment to ensure that I produced no welts or swelling.

When I finished the whipping, I would remove him from suspension but would fasten his restraints so he could move, but was still basically helpless to defend himself. I would then order him to kiss my hand, boots, or even my bum through my skirt or leather pants. As a special treat, I would sometimes allow him to lick my boots.

When Worm had groveled enough, I would remove his restraints. I would then let him have a few minutes alone, locked in one of my jail cells, to recover and, if he wished, to masturbate. After a few minutes, I would return, unlock him, and tell him to go and shower if he wished, and get dressed and come upstairs. When I heard him coming upstairs, I or one of my assistants would greet him in the hall and escort him to the front door.

Worm would generally visit about twice per month. I asked him why he didn't visit more often, and he said he couldn't afford to. He said if he could afford it, he would have at least one session per week, and with this greater frequency, he could enjoy some variety in his script—most likely more elaborate role-playing. I told him that if he visited more often, we could reduce his fee somewhat, but I had my staff and other expenses to pay. But he said that even a twice-monthly, one-hour visit was a lifesaving outlet for him, and he looked forward to it so much.

The Straitjacket

The straitjacket was used by clients with bondage fantasies. It was constructed of leather, with full-length sleeves and buckles that wrapped around the torso. Straps also wrapped through the legs and up and around the crotch, fastening to the bottom of the jacket. The client was usually naked from the waist down, although diapers and plastic pants may have been worn if the bondage was scheduled for several hours or even days. The client's goal was to escape the straitjacket, often hurling insults at the mistresses to ensure further punishment while in the jacket. The client might also wear a full hood, ensuring even greater sensory deprivation.

Often the client was suspended in the swing while jacketed, with his legs in the air. The swing was like a hammock, with the client's derriere exposed to enhance the sensation of bondage. His feet could be tickled, or he could be rocked back and forth in the swing. This bondage usually occurred in the dungeon, and the client was usually left alone, often for hours at a time. Sometimes the client liked to be taunted by the mistresses, who would hold a discussion on whether to let him go, just leave him alone, or torture him. Some clients had even more elaborate straitjacket scenarios to act out.

The feeling of helplessness was the major goal of the time spent in the straitjacket. But strangely enough, some clients loved the challenge of escaping, or trying to. Amazingly, some did.

The Coffin

When most people think of a coffin, horror movies come to mind in which the mummy springs from an upright coffin and surprises his victims. Coffins are also associated with the ritual of funerals and grieving. They symbolize our final resting place. I think the general public would be surprised to know that at the bungalow, the coffin was used both as punishment and as a place for sensual experience.

Enclosure in the coffin provided full sensory deprivation, with the slave sometimes in chains, often naked, and enjoying the sensation of the fur-lined enclosure. It is hard for some people to imagine the coffin as a thing of both beauty and sensuality, but the coffin used in my house was full-sized and very realistic in its design (but with adequate ventilation to ensure that no one suffocated).

Sometimes the scenario would involve the death of the slave, which involved the rituals and associations of death. The scenario would end with the slave's rebirth and the cleansing of his soul and body. For the slave, this scenario symbolized leaving the past and starting anew.

Some clients were able to use the coffin as a completely isolated place to simply rest or sleep. Being bound, chained, and unable to move enabled the slave to surrender control, meditate, and experience sensory deprivation. In order to understand the emotions and feelings of my slaves, I also lay in the coffin in order to experience the sensation of being locked in and completely surrounded by the darkness. In some ways, being in the coffin felt safe, as if protected from all that was fearful. I was chained and locked into the coffin for about an hour. It was serene, quiet, and almost sensual to feel the fur around my body. It was cold outside the coffin, yet I felt warm and secure inside, almost like being in a cocoon. I had several clients who rested in the chained and padlocked coffin overnight. Some said it was the best night's sleep they had ever had!

One evening, as I was making the rounds of the house, I spotted a nice pair of leather Italian shoes still sitting by the door. I was sure that everyone had left for the day and that there were no clients in the house. As I proceeded on my inspection, I heard a faint knocking sound coming from the boudoir. As I approached, the noise increased in volume, and I noticed that the coffin was still chained and padlocked. I had forgotten that a client was still entombed there. He had been there for about two hours, and it was past his release time. He thought it was an intentional delay on my part, but I really had forgotten about him. He was actually grateful because I did not charge for the extra time.

Unusual Clients and Scenes

These scenes, and the clients who sought them, were rare. But I am telling them to you just as they happened.

The Fly

One of the most unusual scenarios I was asked to enact was "The Fly." In its simplicity and innocence, it was a very unusual scenario. It usually started with the client as a fly caught in my web. I played the part of the spider woman, and the actions continued with the fly escaping my web while I searched and hunted for him in every part of the house.

The client wanted to be the fly, acting as an annoying, pesky insect. He would buzz realistically, and I would verbalize how I was going to hunt down the fly. I would pretend I didn't see him as he "clung" to the wall, and I would talk about how I would find that fly and remove his wings, pull off his legs, and generally dismember him. In my opinion, this verbalization of the dismemberment was the main objective of this scenario. I also used a squirt gun, which was supposed to be a ray gun, to annihilate the fly. He would hear it and fall to the floor, or jump out of the way. My flyswatter was used to swat whatever part of the body I could reach as he ran by. I would often hide, waiting for the fly to appear, hoping to surprise him.

This playacting would continue for a couple of hours, until I caught that pesky fly. His exhaustion would generally end the scenario, and with my squirting him, he would verbalize being caught and playact dying at the hands of the spider woman. I would often tickle him until he was rendered helpless on the floor. This scenario was enjoyable for both of us.

The Floor Tile

In this scenario, at the client's request, he was naked, as floor tiles don't wear clothes. His hands and feet would be bound with leather restraints. The client would then be laid on the kitchen floor, where he had to act like a floor tile, not showing any emotion. As he was also chained to the kitchen table, he was not able to move in any way. He was instructed to act as a nonentity, as if no one indeed knew that he was there. He was literally to become an object. His head was completely covered in a hooded mask, with only slits for the mouth and eyes. In this fashion, he could see and hear what was going on around him, but the mistresses would ignore him as he lay there, often for eight hours at a time.

As a floor tile, he was swept, stepped on, kicked, washed, used as a footrest; he had to accept whatever happened to him. He was able to listen to the mistresses clicking their high heels on the floor, look up their skirts, and hear conversations around him. He didn't have to make any decisions or talk to anyone. He could literally retreat from his own life and participate vicariously in the lives of others around him.

The kitchen was the hub of the house. Here the mistresses applied makeup, enjoyed a cup of coffee, had meetings, and relaxed. Meals were prepared and eaten there so that the experience for the client involved many senses: smell, hearing, sight (although limited by the slits). Watching a mistress prepare a cup of coffee while wearing thigh-high leather boots was very stimulating to the client. Naturally, food was dropped and drinks were spilled on him, just like on a real floor.

At the end of the playacting, the client would be untied so that he could shower and dress before leaving. This type of scenario did not involve a lot of preparation on the part of the mistress. Normal activity was carried out, although I would purposely wear an outfit that was unusual for the kitchen:

short skirt, garter belt, and stockings. The main focal point for me as a mistress was the client's satisfaction, no matter how odd the request may have been. In this case, the client was satisfied with very little effort on my part.

The Food Fighter

In this fantasy, the action took place outside. Everyone wore bathing suits, and the client was the target. The "weapons" were spray cans of whipping cream, bottles of chocolate syrup, meringue pies, chocolate cakes, Ding Dongs, peanut butter, honey, jams, jellies, ice cream, and anything else gooey and sticky. The client brought the food for the food fight, which lasted for about an hour.

Outside on the patio, the mistresses pelted the client with food, and he would return the assault, until eventually everyone was covered in goo. This was one of the more fun-filled fantasies for us to enact; although it was very messy, it was also was very entertaining. Everyone has a secret desire at one time or another to fling food at someone, and this playacting allowed everyone to fling with abandon.

Touching the body of either client or mistress was not allowed. The whole fantasy was simply to throw food and be covered in return. At the end of the scenario, I would hose them all off with cold water, and then the client would help clean up the patio where the action had occurred. He would then shower, dress, and leave, with no one on the outside the wiser to his secret desire.

The Fart Man

This scenario may seem gross to most people, but the client wished to smell the sweet essence of the mistress. He would get down on his knees behind the mistress and beg and plead for the fart to waft out and assault his senses. He wished to literally savor the moment.

For the Fart Man, I would wear thigh-high latex rubber boots, corset, garter belt, stockings, and black silk panties. Although there wasn't much preparation required for this fantasy, it was unbelievably difficult to fart on request. It often took two or three hours to achieve the desired effect for the client, but he was usually willing to wait.

At the end of the scheduled time, if the desired effect had not been achieved, he would offer to pay more money and wait until the mistress was able to deliver. He would plead for even just one little fart, and if the one delivered was simply noisy and not aromatic, then the result was the same. When he left the premises, he was one contented and pleased client, and I felt that, once again, I had another satisfied customer who would return.

The Panty Stealer

Clients usually waited for their appointments in the parlor, which was decorated in the Victorian theme, with curio tables and spindly furniture. This particular client was left alone there for about twenty minutes, and when he was brought into my office for a consultation, he was wearing a trench coat.

As I questioned him, I noticed something frilly and pink sticking out of one of his pockets. When I asked him what it was, he hesitated and appeared flustered. Upon pressing him, I asked him to empty all of his pockets. I was astonished when he then proceeded to pull out lace panties, teddies, and other underwear. In all, he had hidden about ten items of intimate clothing. If he had done this in a department store, he would have been charged with shoplifting.

This was not always a preplanned scenario. In such instances, I told him that stealing was a crime and that I was within my rights to call the police and charge him with theft. I then told him that in order to escape prosecution, he could subject himself to a spanking and put himself at my mercy. He agreed to be spanked, and pulled down his pants so I could proceed. It is my opinion that he deliberately stole the items in order to be spanked—of course he wanted to be spanked! I would often continue spanking until he begged for mercy.

It should be noted that the above-mentioned underwear was in the possession of the York Regional Police for over six years. The garments were seized as evidence by those dashing police officers during the raid. Perhaps the officers enjoyed the sensuous feel and smell of my underwear, free of charge.

Things We Refused to Do

First and foremost, there was no sex. We told those who called on the phone, "No sex." When they came for a consultation, they were told, "No sex." If they asked for sex during the session, they were refused. If they insisted, the session was ended. If they wanted to watch sex, they were refused. If they asked to see lesbian lovemaking, they were refused.

I now know that when the police investigated my establishment undercover, they offered extraordinary amounts of money, above the usual fees, to watch a staff member have sex or engage in a sex act in a show. They were refused, and one of the detectives was even told that if he continued to persist, we would call the police.

What do I mean by sex? I mean sexual intercourse of any type. I mean masturbating a client in any manner. I mean oral sex of any type. I offered none of these. After I was raided, Toronto police were quoted in the media as saying that convictions were not obtainable against places such as mine unless overt sexual activity were demonstrated, and that police had not previously investigated places such as mine for this reason. Furthermore, we were as concerned about sexually transmitted infections as everyone else. Therefore we wanted to remain within the law and remain healthy. I was not about to lose the huge amount of money and effort I had invested in developing my practice and facility by knowingly breaking the law. I followed the prescription of "safe, sane, and consensual" at all times.

In addition to requests for sex, other clients made requests that we were unwilling to fulfill. Burning, cutting, and bleeding were all refused. We did not go into these extreme activities, which were and are offered elsewhere. My establishment was more psychological in its orientation than many other facilities. Other doms had more specialized facilities for intense punishment and torture. I never had to call an ambulance or help a client leave, nor was there ever any complaint by any client other than when I was not as severe as requested.

This did not mean that my whipping, strapping, spanking, or pinching techniques were never severe enough to cause them to scream or cry, but I never drew blood or left serious marks. I also never suspended anyone upside down because of the obvious risks. If one of my submissive assistants was being dominated by a client, they were chaperoned.

If clients arrived under the influence of alcohol or drugs, they were sent home. We supplied no illegal substances or alcohol to any client. In one rare exception, a client brought a bottle of champagne, which he drank by an outdoor bonfire while in chains.

Some requested scenarios were refused. One client asked us to pretend to kidnap him in public, take him to the house in the trunk of his car while handcuffed and blindfolded and gagged, and then interrogate him at the house, while seeming to hold him for ransom. This was refused for the obvious reason that if observed, it would appear real, and the scenario presented physical hazards to him as well. Another man wanted me to cut his fingers and make him wash dishes in hot water with bleach. Another wanted me to sew his arms to his sides, actually stitching skin to skin. Yet another wanted to be electrocuted with a cattle prod. All these were refused. I cannot begin to count the number of men who asked me to urinate or defecate on them. This was refused as well.

I refused to provide many extreme services despite some extraordinary financial offers. My activity was not nearly as extreme as that provided in other establishments, where body piercing, heavy S&M, scarification, and other extreme measures are offered. The police did not charge the operators of these numerous establishments, yet I was demonized, even though mine was one of the less extreme of the thirty-odd dungeons and similar facilities in the Toronto region.

Me at five

Shall we get started?

With Val and Alan

Smile for the camera

Shop window

Crossdressers' parlour

Tools of the trade

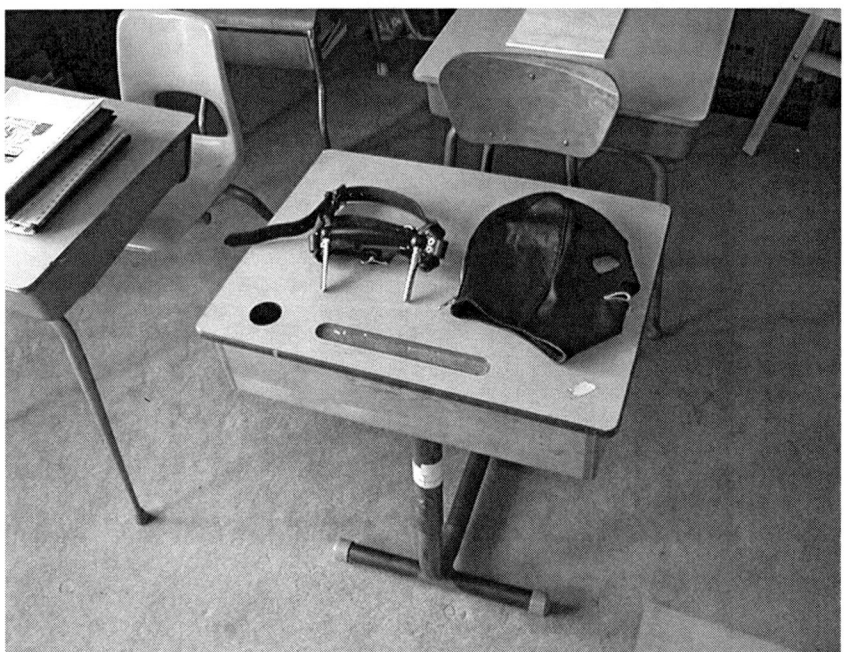

School Time

No place like home

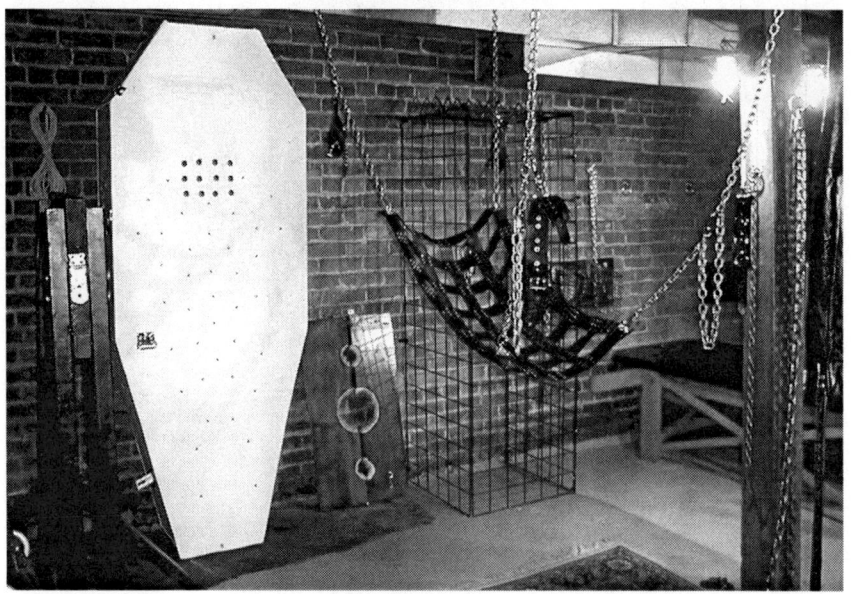

Rest and relaxation

A day at the office

Dinner is served

Law and order

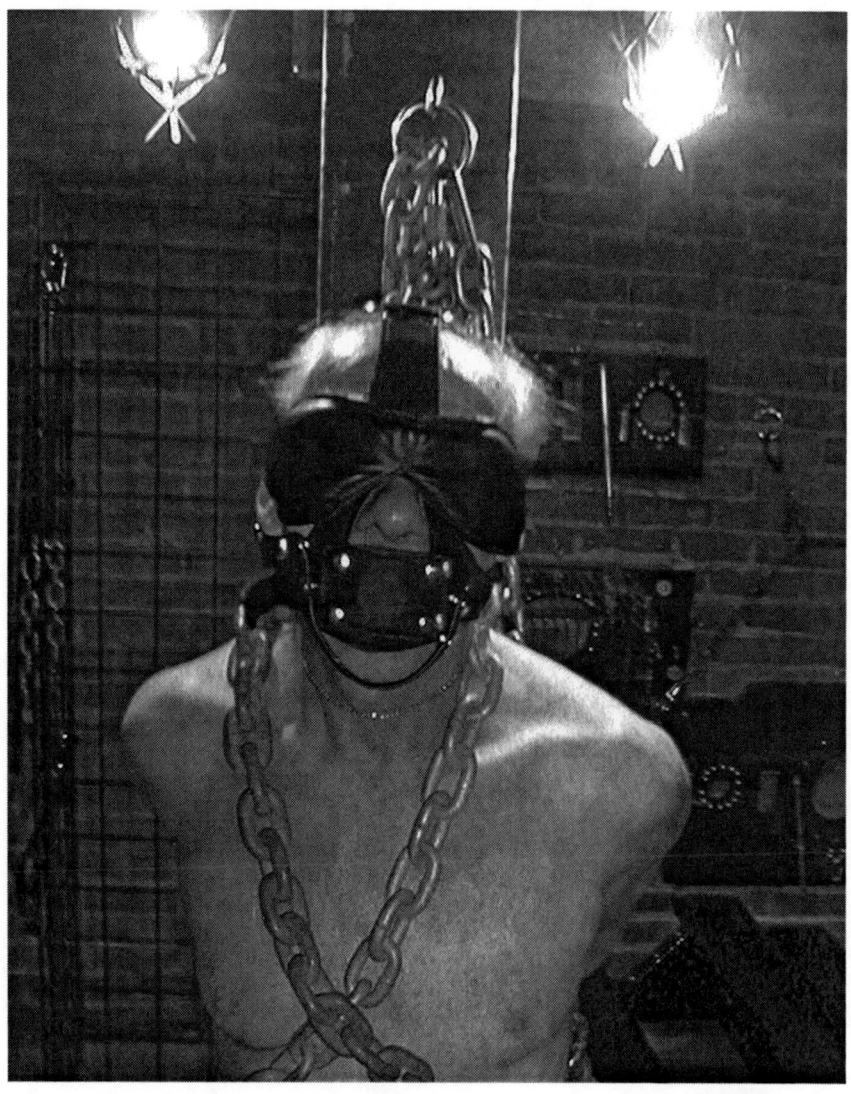

Hanging out

Paddy and Roxy

Getting my stuff back

Media scrum

Print what I say

Val and me at court

I'll be back

Chapter 11

THE BIG TRIAL: WHAT A SPECTACLE!

Alan picked me up early that July morning in 1998 for the ride to Newmarket and the beginning of the trial. We were accompanied by one of his students, who was to be Alan and Leah's assistant during the trial. Adam was a tall, good-looking young man who looked like a football player. He was very supportive of me in every way throughout the trial.

Alan told me that the judge would be His Honor judge Roy Bogusky. He was a gray-haired gentleman who had been on the bench for many years. Most of those years had been spent in the vast spaces of Northern Ontario. He would fly to sparsely populated areas to decide cases. Now, it appeared, he was in a position to make big-city history.

When we arrived at the courthouse, we had to walk through a media gauntlet to get inside. At the lunch break and after the day's proceedings had concluded, Alan and I gave interviews. The media had done setup pieces prior to the beginning of the trial. They couldn't wait to see what would happen next. Scott told me people in his office were openly talking about the case. On some days, when we were inside, along with the reporters, Scott would stop by the courthouse and chat with the camerapeople to find out what they were thinking and what had happened so far that day. Some days, Scott and I would have a word together before I addressed the media on the court steps, to ensure they got good copy that day. These interviews must have frustrated the police and Westgate, because they did not answer back directly. However, Westgate did get his picture in the paper.

Judy came to court for support on some days. Princess came, of course, because she received a summons ordering her to testify as a prosecution witness. It was odd for the prosecution and media to see a prosecution witness and I embracing (we hadn't seen each other for some time) and chatting. Fortunately the judge was about to impose a publication ban on her name appearing in the media. Amusingly, he also imposed a publication ban concerning not the name, but a description of the chief investigating officer, whom I will call Officer Smith. This officer, who apparently also did some undercover work, usually wore a ponytail, but he appeared in court the next day without one, after the media had reported his hairstyle. I guess he got a taste of his own medicine when it came to publicizing identities. His new look would probably impede his busting more cross-dressers.

I pleaded with some of the reporters not to reveal the names of the other defendants whose real names, and not just their stage names, might come up at the trial. However, it was obvious, at least to me, that Smith took every opportunity to repeat the real names of the defendants, as did Westgate. Game on. They were going to get a bit of their own, all right. Their publicity had hurt many people, and now we were going to repay the favor as we made our case.

I will have much to say about the media coverage later on. Aside from the coverage by the electronic media, a vast amount of written material has been clipped from the newspapers and magazines by me and my supporters (remember, the Internet was just getting going then). The clipped material is two feet high when stacked.

But for now, let's stick to what happened at the trial. I will first discuss the testimony. Later I will move on to the motions, rulings, and verdict. The eleven days of trial were spaced out over about eight weeks. The transcripts of the trial proceedings and testimony amount to almost 1,400 pages (averaging about 220 words per page). There are also lists of exhibits and submissions and motions. But the trial is only part of my story, and I want to keep my story somewhat brief when selecting which details to include. At the same time, when I think it is important to elaborate, I will.

For the first hour, Alan and Westgate made arrangements with the judge about how the trial would proceed, and motions were filed.

Then I was asked to plead, and I did: not guilty.

Testimony of the Witnesses

After my plea, the witnesses began to testify. Two bylaw officers and two investigating police officers testified. Among them was one expert who was leaving the country that evening, so he gave his testimony earlier than he otherwise would have. Then Princess testified, followed by Officer Smith. After some rulings on the admissibility of evidence, I testified. The closing arguments followed and, finally, the rulings, including the verdict. As I said earlier, I will for now keep to the testimony and discuss the motions, rulings, and verdict last.

Three officers had visited the Bondage Bungalow as clients, all men in their thirties or forties. As a group, the York Regional Police at that time had a terrible reputation, not just for my matter but for a whole bunch of acts of corruption, incompetence, and a bad attitude, from the top down. The force was mainly a gang of old boys drawn from an old, narrow, and fading part of society. Fortunately, as people from all over the world immigrated to York Region in the following years, some of them joined the York Regional Police, changing the face of the force.

The officers entered the premises posing as customers. They all gave the same testimony: they had been instructed that they could not buy sex and that the mistresses would not masturbate them. They had been informed of their fantasy role-playing options and told that they could masturbate themselves at the end of the sessions. They had been given a tour of the premises and asked to fill out questionnaires about what kind of sessions they wanted and their limitations, preferences, and dislikes. They had pressured us for sex acts and had been consistently refused. They had come back a number of times to see whether they could buy sex acts if we were convinced they were regulars. Same result. They had done this over a period of a few months. They had seen one of my regulars being punished and wrote about it extensively in their notes. Alan cross-examined them to establish that the bungalow was distinctly different from brothels and massage parlors they had raided as bawdy houses, and that these officers, at least, had never raided a place like mine. The officers confirmed this.

Princess was then called to the stand. Westgate seemed very nervous. She was clearly a hostile witness, and he had to assume that Alan had prepared her. Westgate was right, and he had reason to be nervous. Remember that Morgan had told Officer Smith that if she were called to the stand, she was going to tell them about how the police had kissed her feet and had engaged in mock swordfights with the whips, and so forth. So just before the trial, a sworn statement arrived from one of the police officers disclosing that had he kissed her feet and witnessed the horseplay. The Crown may have been afraid that if they suppressed evidence, that might cause the judge to dismiss the case.

As it turned out, Princess testified to the same things Morgan had threatened to tell, and more. She told the court that the house's bottom line was, no sex. She told the court about the officer slapping me and telling me to call him master, about the officers wearing wigs and dueling with the whips, about being paid fifty dollars out of petty cash by an officer, and about the police holding over her their promise not to tell her boyfriend what she did so long as she cooperated. All of this made the headlines in the media.

After Princess's arrest, the police had told her that a lawyer could not help her and that if she spoke to anyone other than the police, she would be jailed and then deported. Princess was in Canada on a student visa and was not supposed to be working. She knew nothing about civil liberties or rights. After she had a lawyer and we spoke to her, she told us how angry she was at how they had treated her. She said she would make no deal to get the charges dropped and, as you will see, she was solid. She did not believe we were guilty. She had to wait four years for the charges to be dropped, for her day in court.

Princess had previously visited the police, and they had recorded an interview with her. She had been too frightened to refuse. Alan, in fact, referred to the interview and her thirty-page account of her days at the bungalow to show how sketchy her memory was and how confused she was by Westgate's questioning. Westgate's questions for Princess were obviously intended to elicit an admission that sexual practices occurred in the bungalow. Repeatedly, Princess said that by "no sex," she meant no intercourse, oral sex, or masturbating the client. She said those were the rules of the house, and they were followed during the half year she spent there, working an average of three days per week. It was established that at times, a mistress would humiliate a client by slapping his penis with a stick if it became erect or tie up his genitals with a rope. Also, shaving of the anal area was offered as a service. Additionally, dildos were found on the premises. These were for decoration (really) and were not used for clients. However, they were used for friends and fellow S&M players who were not clients. Westgate questioned Princess about this from many different angles, and she went to great lengths to explain that clients were told that what was offered in a whorehouse was not offered in my house. She explained our procedures in great detail.

I have before me the transcripts. I counted Westgate's and Alan's questions to Princess, and the total is 178. All that to make the case I have just told you in a few hundred words above. Meaning, no sex. Meaning, some genital contact. Meaning, some clients got erections, but we never touched their genitals when they did. It came back to what Alan had established earlier with the officers: if a man wanted sex, ours was not the place.

Next on the stand was Officer Smith. Westgate went through the official version of the origins of the investigation. Westgate asked Smith about a complaint about the business that had come from the mayor's office and was eventually referred down to the police. Smith said he was ordered to investigate the possibility that a bawdy house was being run at that address. Most of Westgate's questions were of the damage-control nature and led Smith to admit that some police misbehavior had occurred during the raid. What was really interesting about Smith's testimony was how he had gotten the search warrant, how he justified using a SWAT team for the raid, how he justified seizing over seven hundred items of evidence (most of them commonplace), and what he considered to be prostitution.

Smith began by giving the official version of the origins of his investigation. He said a complaint had come to the mayor's office, and on it went from there—via, of course, officially sanctioned procedures. After his investigation, he consulted with the Crown attorney and got a search warrant from a justice of the peace, and the raid was on. Remember that the Crown attorney at that time was not Westgate. The Crown attorneys prior to Westgate had taken four years just to get even one of us to trial. That suggested to me that the advice Smith had gotten from the Crown Attorney Office was not credible. In time, I will tell you about how a lawyer who later became a judge wrote eloquently to the Supreme Court about the flaws in the search-warrant process, particularly as it applied in my matter. I don't think Smith knew about the Reverend and his wife, or that the mayor and others were out to embarrass a colleague who was taped going into my bungalow, until after the raid. But if and when he did know, he could have spoken up.

Smith's testimony then turned to why he thought prostitution was going on when his investigators, as we have seen, found no evidence of intercourse, oral sex, or genital manipulation. Let his own words speak for him:

> Well like I consulted with the Crown. I went over what the observations of the officers were. I felt that there was—the mere fact of the—the acts that were taking place there and the fact that the—the patrons were allowed to release themselves having watched these acts of violence and degradation that they could combine that with masturbating themselves that it was a form of sexual gratification and I felt that we had enough grounds to obtain a search warrant to search for that residence and to charge the individuals that were in charge of it.

Articulate? Note that Smith does not say that cross-dressing is violent or degrading. What about diapering? What about spanking? He was all over the map, and the media ridiculed him for it when Alan cross-examined him. It appeared that we did need experts, after all, to answer the questions that everyone was asking outside the court: What is sex? What is prostitution? And, of course, the all-important question: who decides?

So even though courts had ruled that the behaviors he mentioned were legal if conducted in private, Officer Smith had passed judgment, he says in consultation with a Crown attorney, and ordered his SWAT team into action. Is this beginning to sound like the Keystone Kops? The media certainly made it sound that way.

Now, let's examine why he used the York Region SWAT team. There were eleven team members, if you include the investigating officers accompanying the team plus other officers, for a total of fifteen. How did Smith justify so much force? In both his testimony and cross-examination, he didn't do so convincingly. Nor could he justify seizing women's clothes, a dictionary, a small chandelier, a common chair, and common kitchen implements. Alan had moved for a stay of proceedings because the citizens of Canada are protected from unreasonable search and seizure. The police had also ripped apart the jail-type cell I had had a carpenter build for me in the bungalow. They had also done other damage to the property in addition to seizing all those items.

Their motivation was clear: they were hoping to prevent me from reopening elsewhere. They ruined me economically, and they misused their power to pass judgment on what I could and could not do. They took my wardrobe, as well as that reserved for the cross-dressers. And remember, the trial began four years after the raid. Is this justice? Surely the judge would throw out the case based on overseizure alone. Most in the legal community seemed to think so.

There had to be limits on police power. We would see.

Testimony of the Experts

Next up to testify were the nonlegal experts I told you about before. Of the 1,400 pages of pure transcript, over 850 contain expert testimony and the cross-examination of the experts. Interestingly, Westgate did not call any experts. I think if he had done so, the very fact of his doing so would have supported Alan's argument that there was uncertainty as to what sex is and what prostitution is. Here are some of the highlights of the testimony of the experts Alan called to the stand.

Trevor Jacques was on the stand for almost three hours. He outlined how far-reaching S&M and other types of fantasy role-playing are in the world today. The range of fantasies that people pay to act out was incredible and surprised even me. No wonder Trevor had written so many books and articles about it. He also pointed out that bondage was a very common interest among Internet users. Westgate attacked his credentials and said that the fact his books and articles were widely published did not qualify him as an expert. Trevor and Westgate sparred about some of his findings. Westgate was trying to convince the judge that Trevor's lack of formal credentials showed in his work, and so his evidence should not be allowed.

Next up was Dr. Luc Granger, who testified for over two hours. He explained to the court that S&M practitioners came from a cross-section of society and are not deviant, that different things satisfy different people, and that many things could be sexual, or not. Dr. Hill, who was from out of town, was also due to testify that day. It had to be postponed. Westgate's lengthy questioning of Dr. Granger with some absurd questions put out the intended schedule. I say "absurd" because they were trying to prove that I was a prostitute, and they had already dropped the charges on the four other defendants, so what was the point? I think one sample of the exchange will suffice.

> Westgate: Okay. You used an interesting example of astronomy. You can't displace the moon. But you'd agree with me that astronomy or astrophysics is based on irrefutable, repeatable laws of physics, correct?
>
> Dr. Granger: More or less. It's correct in a way as long as you consider the laws of physics are absolute, which they're always not. If you read in physics, you'll see that there's a lot of controversy about—in cosmology, especially about the big bang or not big bang. ... So you cannot expect that science (psychology) to be as precise as natural science. It doesn't mean that nothing is and that we're just blabbing out mouth and speculating.

I wanted to displace Westgate to the moon. Dr. Hill's testimony had to be put over to another time because he had to be in another city the next day. I should mention that Dr. Granger is a Francophone Canadian, meaning French is his mother tongue, and the transcripts are a direct quote.

Next was Dr. Baumeister, whom we had flown in from the United States. He was on the stand for almost three hours. He established for the court that people who have sex after masochistic behavior might enjoy it more. His well-known book was accepted as an exhibit. Westgate had Dr. Baumeister read excerpts aloud and argued with him about everything but the kitchen sink, including the punctuation. The media reported on Baumeister's testimony, simply saying that he distinguished between buying role-playing and buying sex. Again, Westgate was attempting to attack the credentials of the witness as an expert, as well as attack his testimony. Westgate was doing his job. It wasn't pretty, but he did it. The press and public in the courtroom were almost put to sleep.

Dr. Shannon Bell was the next expert witness. Alan had her speak about the psychological drama of power games and how these related to the social context. Again, Alan was looking to put my work in a nonsexual context and show that nonprostitutes play power games. Westgate and Bell got into quite a sparring match during cross-examination. Bell was very combative, and he did not like it. She was actually questioning his understanding of the different meanings of "orgasm" and the different contexts in which ejaculations occur, for both men and women. Meanwhile, the legal billing meter was continuing to run for everyone, including the taxpayer. I couldn't wait to hear the judge's conclusions regarding the definitions of sex and prostitution. Stay with me; his turn to speak will arrive too.

Finally, Dr. Darryl Hill made it to the stand and was on for about ninety minutes. Previously, he had driven to Toronto, where he stayed in a downtown hotel, and then drove up to Newmarket the next morning—and never made it to the stand. He had driven back to Windsor that evening. This time, he flew in and was picked up at the airport by Scott, who drove him to the courthouse. At the end of the day, Scott drove him back to the airport.

Hill, you may recall, was a professor of psychology who had researched the phenomenon of cross-dressing. You may also recall that cross-dressers made up, by my estimate, 30 percent of my clientele. Cross-dressing was the single most popular activity in the bungalow. Maybe Dr. Hill would shed some light on whether sex meant men putting on dresses. As you've probably guessed, the answer was negative. As Dr. Hill's testimony suggested, the cross-dressing part of my business was hardly sexual, if at all, and certainly not sex.

Next witness: Robert Dante. He, too, was on the stand for about ninety minutes, testifying that what I did in my house was done regularly in public venues in Toronto. He was referring mainly to the S&M and fetish scene. Fetish nights were popular attractions in Toronto. For example, you could go to a fetish night and see dominatrices in full leather, whipping and disciplining slaves. You could also see fetish fashion shows. In his cross-examination, Westgate questioned Robert about his efforts to support me and his appearance on one of the panels at my fund-raiser, suggesting that Robert was a biased witness. Robert replied that he was head of the coalition to repeal the bawdy-house laws, and my case was a part of that initiative. Robert was also firm in his testimony that professional dominatrices do not provide sexual services. The media got some great footage of Robert outside the courthouse after he testified. He had his bullwhip, and from about ten feet away he snapped a banana in half as it was held by a woman reporter at the courthouse entrance. The clip was shown across the country that evening.

The last expert witness was John Allen Lee. He shared his learned insights and easily dealt with Westgate's questions. His evidence reinforced what we had heard previously. He and the other expert witnesses achieved at least one of Alan's goals: they helped get the word out that if a bawdy house sells sex and sex is understood to be the house's purpose, my establishment was not a bawdy house. If it were, getting an erection at the barbershop or a strip-joint might make those establishments bawdy houses as well. They also got the word out that S&M, cross-dressing, and other forms of role-playing are not normally associated with ejaculation. Again, those seeking sexual gratification could go to places other than mine if that was all they wanted. At my bungalow, if a client wanted to have an orgasm by touching his penis, he had to do it himself.

My Testimony

At last, I took the stand. The place was packed. We had been building up to this for a very long time. I was the last witness. My time on the stand took up about one full court day. It was divided in half by a break of ten days, due to courtroom availability. Alan prepared me for it by reviewing the answers I had given to his questions and suggesting ways to keep to the point. He told me never to lie. He gave me some sample questions and follow-up questions I could expect from Westgate.

For the first hour, Alan questioned me about my past, which you have been reading about in this book. Then he asked me in great detail about what we did in the house and what we did not do. No need to repeat here what you know already. But I also took this opportunity to tell the court how Princess was threatened by the police and to answer what she had said in her testimony. Furthermore, I demonstrated the theatrical nature of my business when I told the court about the fly and the fart man and some of the other unusual scenarios and scenes you have read about. Needless to say, the media ran with that. Finally, I spoke about the raid in detail and its huge economic impact on me and others.

Then Westgate cross-examined me. The press was really looking forward to this. He went through my criminal record and numerous prior convictions. Most were for shoplifting as a teenager. We had an argument when he wanted me to read into the record an ad that appeared beside my ad in one of the local papers that overtly advertised sex. When I refused because of the language and its implications, Alan interjected that Westgate could read it into the record himself rather than insist that I read it. So Westgate read the ad as part of a question, and of course I replied that my business was not like that other business, despite the decision of that newspaper to put it into the adult-entertainment section of its classifieds. He spent quite a lot of time on that. He also spent a lot of time reading scenarios written by clients, and I told him what we would and would not have done in those scenarios. Westgate harped a great deal on the terms "erotica" and "erotica room."

Alan used most of his re-examination to stress all the points made throughout the trial. There did not seem to be much to refute in what Westgate had done, despite how aggressive he had been.

The next day, the judge began making his decisions. It was expected that his judgments on admitting expert testimony and staying the charges because of the search-and-seizure excesses of the police, and, of course, his verdict, would make Canadian legal history and set precedents. What happened instead came as a big surprise.

Chapter 12

CLIENTS OF THE DOMINATRIX

Why They Do It

Paraphilia means "extra love." Paraphilia is not sex. Sex involves direct stimulation of the genitals and intercourse. One might think of paraphilia as types of foreplay or as playacting as an end in itself. Fetishism, cross-dressing, and S&M are the most common heterosexual male paraphilia. The first almost always accompanies one or both of the other two. Fetishism, cross-dressing, and masochism are the most common male paraphilia, in that order. Sadism is a much less common form of paraphilia. Bestiality, necrophilia, and pedophilia are very rare forms.

While women are often somewhat interested in masochism (sexual and otherwise), they have their own paraphilia. Kleptomania, or a compulsion to steal, is the most common. When affordable, compulsive shopping takes the place of kleptomania. Anorexia, bulimia, tearing out their hair, and self-burning or -cutting are other female paraphilia. Men externalize; women internalize.

Since almost all of my clients were heterosexual men, I will talk about them. I have read a great deal about and heard a number of professional psychiatrists in the field talk about male paraphilia, and of course I have seen an abundance of it firsthand. This is what I have learned. The behaviors we call paraphilia become established at an early age, around eight. At some time before that age, unresolved childhood traumas occur that the man seeks to unconsciously and symbolically revisit in adulthood. Examples of these traumas are repressed memories of episodes of a lack of paternal rearing or of conflicted or overprotective mothering. The child may be the ongoing recipient of this anxiety. The child may also, in the absence of a healthy family environment, become sexually ambivalent as an adult. By revisiting these circumstances, the person is unconsciously or symbolically confronting and trying to overcome the childhood trauma.

I must emphasize that the anxiety being addressed by acting out a fantasy with me relates to childhood traumas that are relatively mild, by adult standards. Severe trauma, such as abuse, is more likely to manifest itself in overtly antisocial behaviour, such as substance abuse or criminal behavior.

It is also important to realize something else about the clients who wanted to be put in corsets, diapers, or straitjackets, or to be tortured or treated as slaves: most of them were accomplished members of society. Many were wealthy. Many were educated professionals. Many were happily married, with well-adjusted children. They were often articulate and charming. Some were quite shy as well.

Despite having so much going for them, these men went to a dominatrix. Some paid thousands of dollars yearly for my services. The desire to act out with a dominatrix was powerful. It seems that an inadequate father figure is the key to creating this desire. Absence of paternal rearing because of having a detached father or no father at all may lead to the male child not establishing independence from his mother early enough. His subconscious is haunted by his helplessness, rage, and humiliation early in life as a result of not connecting with more than one parent. This feeling of powerlessness then haunts him as an adult, subconsciously. He feels compelled to revisit the powerful female in order to confront this demon and resolve it to his satisfaction—or at least to prove to himself he can cope with it, or that he has the courage to confront that trauma. His ego needs that reassurance.

I offer but one example that is easy to relate to. Women may remind him of the nurse at the doctor's office or hospital, or of a female doctor, echoing episodes from early childhood when an experience with such women terrified him. Seeing and interacting with women as an adult can tap this now-subconscious memory. In his dealings with women, he navigates toward more detailed reconstructions of these experiences. When the dominatrix offers him a long list of scenes or props, he will choose those that he connects with that experience; he relives the experience. He has now confronted some of his demons. He is reassured. But that demon will return and need to be confronted again.

His subconscious conjures up images of his childhood, but they are vague. Symbols of powerful women remind him subconsciously of what is haunting him. Big women; women in uniforms; women in exotic clothing, such as latex and boots; women wielding whips; and women in positions of authority, such as a nurse restraining him, a policewoman handcuffing him, or a socially superior woman making him her slave: any of these can become the attraction. The dominatrix can be any of these in response to the man's request. She can adjust her behavior to suit his fantasy. She can be his torturer, the mother figure making him cross-dress, and the object of his physical worship. The way she looks at him and treats him brings out the feelings he felt as a child—strong feelings that are difficult to forget.

I am often asked if I consider these men to be perverts or mentally ill. As I have said, many of them are in leadership or advanced professional positions, active in the community, and good sons, husbands, and fathers. My answer to the question and the answer of most mental-health professionals as well is that the acting out of their fantasies is only a perversion when it interferes with their daily lives, even if these fantasies are a major preoccupation of their daily thinking. In short, these fantasies are okay if they can control their behavior. Almost all of my clients could.

Let me tell you about one typical client of the Bondage Bungalow. He would usually visit for an evening midweek and stay over every second weekend. He would be a prisoner in my dungeon and do slave work around the house and grounds. This was only a small part of his life. He had a full professional career and was a productive volunteer outside work. He was thought of by his family as a good son. He was never in trouble with the law. He was personable and polite but could act as leader when the occasion called for it.

His visits improved him, gave him an outlet. His dreams came true; he was no longer repressed. Without this outlet, he might have been less productive and less happy. He had the sex life of a normal bachelor. He did not want children and did not want to marry at that time. And why would he want a family? In most people's eyes, he was an object of envy. I might add, however, that he has since married—happily. And, you may be surprised to learn, he no longer visits me or any other dominatrix. He says he no longer feels the need. He has revisited that dark corner of his childhood enough to know it can't hurt him anymore.

One might ask if, on the other hand, if the men who visited me but were married or had girlfriends were thus cheating. I think it is fair to say they were, at least if they did not tell their partners (I actually had some couples as clients). Such men told me they were too embarrassed to act out their fantasies with their wives or girlfriends. Also, they did not have the privacy to act out at home with their partners if there were children or others living there. And, of course, they did not have my dungeon, classroom, bondage gear, or cross-dresser's wardrobe.

I provided my clients with escapist recreation. Like other recreation, like sports and games, it had therapeutic value. The clients were better off acting out their fantasies in a safe and sympathetic environment. Needless repression brings needless unhappiness.

Who They Are

My clientele comprised about 85 percent heterosexual men, 5 percent bisexual or gay, 5 percent women, and 5 percent couples. They represented quite a cross-section of professions. I would say doctors, lawyers, engineers, and accountants made up about 15 percent of my clientele. Those who were in sales or insurance amounted to about 25 percent. About 10 percent were corporate executives, and 10 percent had their own businesses. Some were retired. The remainder came from a list of occupations as long as my arm. (I should probably clarify that I had no way to knowing if any of these people were telling the truth about their professions.) There was no easy link to be made between what the clients did for a living and their desire to submit to a dominatrix.

About 30 percent of my clients were primarily interested in cross-dressing, 30 percent in fetishistic behavior, 30 percent in masochistic behavior, 5 percent in sadistic behavior, and 5 percent in other activities. When I say "interested" they may just have wanted to watch shows or participate in scenarios. Some would do both on different occasions.

Some of these orientations would overlap. For example, half of the cross-dressers were also fetishists, as were half of the masochists. In a masochistic script, it was important for the dom to be, say, in leather garments or wear a mask. A large proportion of the cross-dressers also liked to engage in masochistic behavior related to being dressed in female garments. About a third of the clients were interested in all of these activities: fetishes, cross-dressing, and masochism. Many liked a wide variety of activities. And as you have seen, some sought very intricate and detailed role-playing.

As I noted above, only about 5 percent of my clients were sadistic. I have read that actual sadism is rare among men and that for every male sadist there are twenty male masochists. When they acted out their fantasies with female employees playing the submissive role, these sadists were often were much less severe than we permitted them to be, or even than they said they wanted to be. It seems to me that overwhelmingly, except for a few high-profile psychopaths, men do not wish to be physically cruel to women. It seems to me that wife-beaters and rapists are not sadists in the sense of wanting to engage in S&M scenarios. If they were, houses such as mine would make a fortune, as the fees would by necessity be much higher for women to cooperate in such scenarios. Oddly, a much larger proportion of my female clientele were sadistic than were the males. They were often wives or secretaries who were seeking instruction on how to dominate their husbands or bosses, and some just sought the outlet of having power over others.

Men over fifty years of age were more inclined to fetishism and cross-dressing. Younger men were more into masochism. In terms of affluence, I could only guess at the true extent of my clients' wealth by their speech and what they told me of their formal education. It seems that affluence and social position are not reliable indicators of what someone might choose to do in a place like the Bondage Bungalow. However, since my fees were much above what one would pay for, say, a massage of any type, I generally was visited by more affluent members of society.

Culturally most of my clients were white Canadians or Americans. Very few were Asian, Latino, or black. I attribute this both to the economic challenges facing immigrants and people of color and to the more traditional cultures of new arrivals to North America or first-generation Americans and Canadians. Also, the Bondage Bungalow was in an upscale community just north of Toronto. Most of the residents for a number of miles in all directions were typical of the cultural profile of my clients. Keep in mind that the ethnic makeup of Toronto and surrounding areas has been changing for many years so that today a Toronto dominatrix's clientele is more ethnically diverse.

Some of my clients were older men (over sixty). They were mostly quite healthy and still physically active, and most said they were retired. They usually were able to visit during the day on weekdays, when we were less busy, and they would sometimes stay and chat. Some had practiced their predilections for years and were anxious to try my facility. Others, now that they had the time and perhaps could afford it, were anxious to experiment with yearnings they had harbored secretly all their adult lives. Some were widowers who were now looking for a different type of companionship. We even had a few women around sixty years of age who wanted to explore other sides of their natures. Elderly clients were generally a pleasure to deal with. Usually they did not want any heavy restraint and rarely any pain at all. Mostly they wanted to be scolded or humiliated. As I mentioned above, a larger percentage of the elderly clients were into cross-dressing than were the younger ones. They were always given extra attention, and they seemed to appreciate this a great deal and would often give generous tips.

Some of my clients were obese. They were often very shy and self-conscious. Many called a number of times before even coming in for a tour and consultation. It was very important that we did nothing to injure their self-esteem. It was equally important to be careful for their safety. For example, when they were restrained, they were never made to stand because of the potential strain on their hearts and the increased danger of falling. We had a special bondage table capable of accommodating larger and heavier clients, and the restraints were always fastened loosely. In their sessions, they were usually passive, for obvious reasons, so the skills of the mistress were called upon to keep the session lively and interesting. A favorite scene for a few of these men was forced feeding, sometimes while restrained. Some others liked to be restrained spread-eagled and tickled for a prolonged period. Some like to be whipped. But never would we refer to their size or to the extra precautions we were taking.

Disabled clients were few; they had enough restraint in their lives. Interestingly, of the few disabled clients I did have, still fewer wanted to play a dominant role, which might have provided their lives with balance. I think the main reason we had so few disabled clients was simply the logistics of coming to the house, and perhaps the expense. Those we did have as clients liked the idea of restraint, though this was hardly necessary to exercise control. It seems that deprivation of power at the hands of a dominatrix, however little one has normally, remains a great attraction for many.

Female Clients

As I said, about 5 percent of my clients were female. This does not include women who came with their husbands, boyfriends, or bosses. As far as I could tell, none of them were practicing lesbians, but rarely did they want a male present at their sessions.

My female clients generally requested scenes of elegant S&M, where they could dominate or be dominated in a safe, private, and nonjudgmental environment. For every ten submissive men there is only about one truly dominant woman. Similarly, submissive women have trouble finding good dominant men, though unfortunately there is no shortage of abusive men.

In my house, women, like men, could safely explore their fantasies. I have no doubt that if the incomes of women were equal to men's, up to a third of my clients would have been female. In their initial consultations, my clients usually told me they did not feel free, in their normal lives, to express themselves honestly. Often they were afraid to engage in bondage or other power games with their mates. Most of my female clients were married.

Most frequently they enjoyed being in bondage and preferred the examination and torture chamber to all other rooms. They never asked for classroom fantasies or to be cross-dressed. Very rarely did they want to play the dominant role. They wanted the mistress to help them rediscover their capacity to relax and enjoy the sensation of powerlessness. By coming to me, they avoided dealing with a man's ego or the all-too-frequent frustration they felt over their mates' inability to deal with their complex erotic needs.

Men could go to prostitutes or massage parlors, but most of my female clients felt safe surrendering power only in clean, luxurious, and upscale establishments like mine. Interestingly enough, a large proportion of them were European, which I think may reflect a more open-minded outlook among women from that continent. For many my house was the only place, they said, where they could act out and discuss their fantasies.

Susan was one such client. She enjoyed having each limb put in a leather restraint and being put spread-eagled into the swing or on the examination table while naked. Once in position, she enjoyed being tickled and teased with various implements, but we made it clear that we would not masturbate her in any way. Nipple clamps while in bondage were another favorite. Often we would drip hot wax over her helpless body and laugh while she moaned. This emphasis on her helplessness and the punishment and teasing, combined with being under observation, was the big turn-on for her. Like most of the women clients, she was not inclined to play a role so much as just have things done to her. Interestingly, she wanted to be dominated by women, though she was not, she said, lesbian. She said she was afraid to have a session with a man.

Some of them preferred not to be restrained and, instead, liked me to put them over my lap, pull their panties down, and spank them with a hairbrush or my bare hand. During their punishment, I would recite a list of imaginary infractions or a read a list they had prepared for me in advance. Perhaps this was their way of dealing with guilt. The "infractions" would often relate to their school days, so I would chastise them for not doing their homework, having sexual fantasies, masturbating, chewing gum in class, smoking, or teasing the boys. Some would seek punishment for being sexually promiscuous, although I never knew whether they were serious.

A select few loved to be in the dominant position and would order my assistants to do tasks or kiss their feet, or they might enjoy just punishing a submissive female. Most of the women who enjoyed this seemed to have an upper-class bearing and a European accent. It seems that the more established class structure in Europe found some expression in my establishment. This was even further emphasized when the female client assumed the role of grand dame and had us do her bidding, having us punished in front of her by each other, or punishing us herself. Some female clients liked being dominant over women, while others asked for male submissives, so I had a huge reservoir of possible scenarios to draw upon. When a female client punished one of my male clients, I got a double fee in the bargain.

One fiftyish, severe-looking woman enjoyed seeing three of us act out a scene in which two of us, dressed in leather, would seize the third, put her in restraints, and leave her alone in a closed room with that client, who would then interrogate and punish her. There were strict rules to be followed, and the assistant could stop the session at any time. In fact, the female client was never very severe, but just enjoyed the power over the slave.

It seems to me that my house and business could have served the needs of women as much as men, if not more. Women put more emphasis on atmosphere and context in their erotic expression than men, though their attraction to power games was less pronounced. Who knows: maybe as women's roles in society continue to evolve, that will change, too.

Chapter 13

THE BIG TRIAL: WHAT A RESULT!

Justice Bogusky made his decisions on August 21, October 9, and October 16.

Let me explain. The trial and hearings before Justice Bogusky began on July 21, 1998, and ended on October 16 of the same year. We were in court for eleven of those seventy-seven days. The trial's first four days were July 21 to July 24. The other court appearances were scattered among the remaining seventy-four days. The last full day of testimony was August 20. On August 21 came the submissions and the ruling on the admissibility as evidence of a videotape the police had seized. Also on that day were the submissions and the ruling on what evidence given by the experts would be allowed—meaning which experts Justice Bogusky considered qualified to be expert witnesses. On October 9, the last day, he made two rulings.

First, he gave his verdict on the charges against me. Then he heard submissions and ruled on a constitutional challenge Alan filed, saying the charges should be stayed—meaning frozen permanently—because of police excesses. The constitutional motion would be considered even if I were found not guilty, because the Crown might appeal the verdict.

August 21, as I have noted, was taken up with the issues of admissibility of evidence—the experts and the videotape. Alan said that even if the judge considered only some of our experts qualified, the declined experts would play well in the media. Remember, the experts were mainly there to add substance to our appeal if we lost, and to inform the public. Alan was realistic and warned me that the judicial system often followed the public, so if the laws were to be changed or clarified, the public first had to get angry at how the judicial system allows police to arbitrarily regulate private behavior without even having to justify such regulation. We were taking the long view.

Alan and Westgate both made lengthy submissions on what the experts could add to the judge's deliberations. Basically, Alan said that the experts established that the activities in my house were not necessarily or even often sexual in nature. Westgate countered that the activities were sexual because they created an erotic atmosphere, which led to masturbation and at least some genital contact. He said that only expert testimony about the specifics of my business was relevant and, according to him, there was none. He also said that most of our experts did not have formal credentials, and their research was not sufficiently scientific or objective to be admissible in court. Alan came back with precedent cases he put before Justice Bogusky in which other judges had determined what constituted an expert and what constituted expert evidence. He said it would be acceptable to the defense if the judge deferred his ruling on the experts until after he had the chance to examine the material. Westgate again said that expert evidence was irrelevant in any event.

But the judge said he didn't need time, nor did he make much, if any, reference to the documents presented to him. I also noticed that during the trial, he made very few notes (as he admitted) during the experts' testimony. The transcripts were not ready until well after he had made his rulings, so he did not have those. And he didn't ask many questions of the experts himself.

The Judge Begins to Rule

So what did he decide, and why? He admitted two of the experts, Granger and Lee. Alan said that the two would be enough to establish what he wanted to establish. The rest he dismissed as too biased, or insufficiently scientific in their research to be used in these deliberations. In my nonlegal opinion, Justice Bogusky was wrong to exclude Baumeister and Hill. They were not known to be activists and participants in the various groups they studied nor were they open advocates for legal reform. They were widely published intellectuals who had done research. In any event, here are Justice Roy Bogusky's own words, from the transcripts:

> If I exclude all the so-called experts on the basis of non-relevancy, the court runs a risk of drawing a negative inference toward the facts or the accused because some of the evidence presented was, although initially entertaining, it ultimately began to progress to the bizarre and ultimately disgusting. To avoid this possibility, I require some assistance in putting a human face on the participants as they are members of our community. In other words, I can use all the help I can get.

Wow! The second issue that day concerned the admissibility of the tape showing me inserting a dildo into a man's anus. Alan had filed a motion to exclude it as evidence. Westgate wanted it admitted as evidence to show that penetration was occurring in the house, which would refute my testimony that dildo insertion was not offered to clients. Alan objected to the tape's admission on the grounds that on it, I was playing with a friend, and not a client. It was one of over fifty tapes seized. The man in the tape was a friend who had helped in the construction of the facility and let me visit his cottage after I was raided. He never paid me, except with this help. However, how were we to prove this? Admission of the tape would be a setback to the defense, but as Alan pointed out repeatedly and made the police admit on the stand, for the tape to be evidence that I was running a bawdy house, it had to be something that I did "frequently and habitually." The judge allowed the tape, with no explanation of how it established any frequency.

Closing Arguments

On August 31, the court convened again to hear closing arguments. The lawyers spoke for about two hours each and agreed that on October 6, the court would meet for the final trial day. At that time, the judge would give his verdict, which was expected by many to be a lengthy written decision, although he also had the option of giving an oral verdict. After the verdict, the judge would rule on the constitutional motion to stay the charges.

Alan recapitulated all his major arguments: the bungalow was intended for role-playing alone. Genital contact was the exception and was not intended to produce orgasm, so therefore the bungalow was not a brothel. He argued again that the tape reflected just one incident, and the frequency of such incidents was not substantiated by the evidence. He pointed to the contradictions in Princess's testimony compared to her cross-examination. He pointed out the pressures to which she had been subjected and reminded the court that (a) she was testifying four years after the fact and (b) her testimony was inconsistent with her written account, done a few months after the raid. He insisted that the testimony of the two experts accepted by the judge established that most of what went on in my bungalow was not specifically sexual and certainly not sex. He pointed out how the police had had twelve weeks to uncover sex for sale in the bungalow and had failed to do so.

Westgate said I was a liar, a "complete and utter stranger to the truth." He said the whole issue of S&M and the other activities being the mainstay of the business was a red herring, and that such activities were a front for sexual services, meaning that we aroused clients by scenarios to facilitate masturbation. He said that the evidence suggested more direct sexual services were for hire, even though the investigation had shown otherwise.

As we rose on August 31 after the lawyers had made closing arguments, I found myself wondering how we would fare with this judge. A few days later, Scott had told me to expect a guilty verdict. It turned out Scott knew people who were familiar with this judge. They told him he was old-school and it was not in his nature to break new legal ground. So he would probably try to skate around ruling on what was and was not legal. However, he said, it was possible that the judge would stay the charges because of excessive police behavior. In any event, he reminded me, history was about to be made. The main issue, he said, was a simple question: What was the crime? If I had run the bungalow without any dildos on the premises, and there were no tape, and the girls had never touched the clients' penises to tie them up, and so on, would I be still be guilty? We know that allowing the clients to masturbate themselves in front of a mistress was legal. But what about the whipping, the spanking, the restraint, the cross-dressing, the diapering, or the foot-tickling? What about riding on their backs? And when are they permitted to get an erection? What about the fact that only a small percentage of the activities *could* have been sexual? I think you get the idea. Society was looking to this judge, in his verdict, to give rules on such matters. Registered massage therapists touch their clients more than we did.

History was also likely to be made on the issue of police power. Did they have the authority to seize seven hundred items, steal the fifty dollars and give it to Princess, rip the place apart, strip-search us, and seek to hold me without bail because they had evidence of incidental genital contact and a sexually arousing atmosphere? Could they get away with that, in Canada, in the late twentieth century? Remember, Charlie Campbell had said I would not likely win a civil suit for lost income and so forth. But Alan believed that Justice Bogusky had a responsibility to prevent the police from getting a conviction by engaging in such behavior. Again, remember, the real damage they did was to the property value, as well as depriving me of my business, my possessions, and a place to live before I had set foot in a courtroom. Would Justice Bogusky accept this? And if so, why? It was going to be interesting, no matter what happened.

Waiting for a Verdict

I spent the five-week adjournment doing my usual phone work from home and looking after the young girl after she came home from school. This was her parents' busy season as gardeners and landscapers. Scott came by a few times and helped me with my memoirs and to make notes on the recent trial days. Most important, I spent some time with my daughter—more about that later.

On the evening of October 8, 1998, the day before the verdict, Scott came to see me that night. He had previously spoken with Alan about arranging bail if I were taken into custody, and other contingency plans. Alan said I would not be given a jail sentence if convicted, and even if he were wrong, I would be set free without bail until the appeal was heard.

Scott told me again that he was almost certain I would be convicted. He had asked Alan for guidelines about what I should and should not say after the verdict, given various possible verdicts. He handed me several cards, on which were written several possible statements for the media. He assured me that he would be in court and would tell me which lines to use if I won, depending again on what the judge said; if we lost, ditto. Scott emphasized to me the importance of repeating the main lines for a given verdict and for the judge's comments. Scott knew that it would be a historic moment, so this was no time to speak off the top of my head or let my feelings of the moment influence me.

The Verdict

October 9, 1998, was verdict day. Running the usual gauntlet of reporters outside the courthouse, I followed Scott's script. I told the reporters that on that day I was entering the courtroom not only to learn my fate, but to find out who had broken what rules and who decides. I told them that I wanted rules in place when I reopened, and I wanted the police to have rules, too. Then I went into the packed courtroom. I was mobbed by media in the parking lot and on my walk into the court. If I weren't the defendant, I wouldn't have gotten a seat.

Then Justice Roy Bogusky came in and gave his verdict. He said he would give an oral judgment. In the transcript, it amounted to just under a thousand words. We had had a previous trial, an appeal, a trip to the Supreme Court, ten days of trial before him, hundreds of exhibits, and extensive media coverage describing it as a landmark case, and this guy spoke for less than ten minutes. When I read the articles the reporters wrote the next day, it seemed to me they were surprised by how he appeared to sidestep important issues such as what constituted sex and what did not.

Here are the essentials of his verdict. He said that the erotica sessions were the heart of the business, that penetration was a regular service, and that he accepted Princess's testimony over mine. He did not comment on the fact that Alan, in his cross-examination, revealed Princess as confused and all over the map, four years after she had worked at the Bungalow. He did not discuss our contention that the evidence that clearly showed how penetration was not only *not* the mainstay of the business, but that it was rarely done, and then only for friends—not as an offered service. But let us hear him in his own words again, right from the transcripts. This is how he began and ended:

> The accused is a dominatrix and, as such, operated a business catering to disciples of S and M. Her house was outfitted with

all the paraphernalia associated with the discipline. Since there appears to be different forms of S and M role playing, certain areas of the house had different visual effects with accompanying articles. The moods created ranged from the satanic, where articles of torture and death were present and in order to stimulate bondage seekers, to the burlesque where a small stage was erected for the cross dressers. If you were to add in female employees dressed in lingerie, which was the case, a strong sexual and erotic mood would be created. The business was well attended by patrons who were primarily male and who had money. The sessions were not cheap … A case against the accused has been made without the Court having to get into the broader question of whether every form of S and M for hire is sex for hire. The facts of this case were not difficult to interpret. Common sense allows no other interpretation for a scenario involving a naked male with a rope around his penis being attended to by a female, even more so when she is wearing lingerie.

After having five weeks to consider the evidence, he comes up with this? In my opinion, the guy was obviously in way over his head. The press printed his remarks and reported their disappointment with his judgment, to put it mildly.

Wait. You think that was bad? He had yet to rule on the constitutional motion to stay the charges. Again, the motion said that police misused the search warrant to put me out of business, rather than just gather evidence and press charges. The motion cited the police for seizing items beyond reasonable bounds, unreasonably barring me from my home, needlessly strip-searching the women, and stealing money out of the petty cash. The motion also mentioned the derisive behavior of the police, such as their mock sword fights with the whips and their boot kissing, as well as the fact that I had been assaulted during the raid. Justice Roy Bogusky said he would reduce my sentence as a way of compensating me. I will soon tell you in some detail what the media said about his ruling on the constitutional motion, but first let's hear some more from him from the transcripts. Remember, the country was watching and listening.

Well I probably should take time to look at all of it, but I think I have a handle on it and I know that a lot of people are here, as I said on other days, trying to make a living and probably want to get out of here as quickly as possible. ... So on that issue [the use of fifteen officers to raid] although as I say in retrospect it appears to be overkill, it was one of those decisions made by the police where they would be damned if they took too many and damned if they took too few and botched the whole search. So a bit of a bad taste there but it is nothing I can hang a remedy onto. ... If you want to get a reaction from a bunch of young bucks present them with some imagery of the male anatomy, including images of penises plus equipment for cross-dressing and you might get a rather strange reaction. The reaction which flowed was almost predictable. ... The number of things taken. There were things taken you must wonder about such as the reason the chandelier would have had to come down. But if I remember the photograph of it, I think it had sort of a look to it. ... The chandelier, as I say, may have had a motif to it that might be relevant on some issue in court.

As he gave his ruling, he seemed to be stumbling about for words and thoughts. And that was how the day ended. I was convicted, and the conviction stood despite the behavior of the authorities.

After the ruling, the lawyers made submissions on sentencing. Westgate wanted a long jail term, and Alan argued for a suspended sentence. The sentencing would be in one week. I was free at least until then.

Afterward, as I exited the courtroom, I saw Scott waiting for me with two other people. The two of them blocked him and me off, so nobody would see him take my cue cards from me and select the one I was to use. He gave me one card that said we were going to appeal, and (if I wanted to say it) that I did not think the judge understood the case. And he gave me another card, of greatest importance. I was to read the two cards and give them back. We had gone over the wording on the numerous cards the evening before. Above all, I was to go out to the microphones and say one twelve-word sentence over and over and to keep coming back to it. I knew that I might have to use this sentence, so I had memorized it and knew why I was saying it. It was meant to resonate across the country, and it did.

The message was that I had not been told why I was convicted. Here is the sentence: "The judge still has not said what I can and cannot do."

There is a bit of a story behind that sentence. Scott had asked Alan the following: If the judge convicted me for the crime (whether that crime were real or imagined), could I claim that he had thereby declared that S&M for money was legal? If so, Scott was going to have me say, "This is a great day for Canada. S&M is now legal. I can work again." But Alan said that if the judge sidestepped the issue, it was not quite fair to say this. Scott and I considered whether we should say it anyway, but we decided that it might put Alan in a difficult position. After the trial, a couple of veteran reporters told me that the judge was simply pushing the matter up to a higher court, and that his rulings were blatant grounds for appeal.

Media Coverage

The media coverage peaked with the verdict and my sentencing. Since most of you know about me through the media, I think I should describe their coverage of me, my legal battles, and the issues raised by those battles from the time of the raid until the day before I was sentenced. By 1998, hundreds of articles had been written about me. At that time, video clips were not available on the Internet. Today, you can type my name into a search engine, read about me, and watch clips about me for years. The coverage of my battles in the media and the public's perceptions are sometimes as interesting to study, as are the battles themselves.

At first, the articles were about the raid. The most famous one ran under the screaming headline "Bondage Bungalow" in one of our three daily papers, the tabloid the *Toronto Sun*. The day after the raid, a major report aired on a major local radio station about the raid and how police would be contacting the clients. The raid was also the lead item on the six o'clock local news. There was a press conference showing items from the house being displayed by a police officer—Norman Miles. The radio talk shows were getting calls about the raid, with most callers asking what the crime was. The next day, the raid was mentioned on page 3 of one of the other local newspapers. It was also in the Sunday papers, because an S&M convention was in town. Later in the month, the raid was mentioned in the papers yet again when the movie *Exit to Eden* was released. Actress Dana Delaney, who played a dominatrix in the movie, was in Toronto to promote it and was quoted as saying, when she was told about the raid, "I thought that was so funny."

The subsequent months brought only occasional articles about and references to the raid in the papers, mainly because I was under my lawyers' instruction to say nothing to the media.

When the first trial was held in October 1995, the coverage was expanded, but none of it showed up on page 1 or as a lead story in the electronic media. The Internet was only in its early stages at that time, but its influence was beginning to grow rapidly. There was some coverage of the first appeal, in August 1996, and again in June 1997 at the Supreme Court of Canada. The coverage really began to grow after Murray replaced Morris. Scott had begun issuing regular press releases on the case using e-mail, which had then become mainstream. Also, a full trial was finally going to happen. The fact that the case was four years old raised media interest even more.

Articles began to appear in which I was interviewed and profiled. The history of the case was given. Journalists did setup pieces for the April 1998 trial, profiling the lawyers and the issues and the kind of testimony that was expected, and this became national coverage. News services in the United States and Britain also picked it up. The reporters attending told me, after my lawyers were removed, that they couldn't remember when they had had such an interesting matter to cover. Before the actual trial, which began in July of 1998, some coverage also appeared of the fund-raiser.

Then there was the trial itself, which made lots of headlines. Here are some examples: "Bedford Case Could Set Legal Precedent." "Dominatrix Trial Begins." "Whips, Chains and Handcuffs, But No Sex." "Cop: Sex Not For Sale at Dominatrix House." "Cop to Bondage Queen: Call Me Master." "Mistress to Cop: Lick My Boots." "Sadomasochism Not Sex, Experts Say." Many of these headlines appeared atop the front pages of the newspapers in large type. The newscasts gave the case a similar emphasis on both radio and television. The coverage was viral on the Internet as well.

After the verdict came a tremendous amount of coverage: "Bondage Madam Found Guilty," "Dominatrix Won't Admit She's Whipped," and so on. It was a great story, but a disappointing ending, given the buildup. Most of the coverage expressed disappointment that the big questions had not been answered and left it at that. But some articles and editorials recognized the importance of the proceedings. I would like to tell you about two of them and quote from them, because they will help you to understand how some informed and influential observers conveyed what they saw to the country.

Thomas Claridge was a veteran court reporter for the *Globe and Mail*, known widely as "Canada's national newspaper." In the courtroom, he sat with Robert Reguly, one of Canada's most respected and widely known journalists. Mr. Reguly had done a major profile of me in *Chatelaine*, one of Canada's best-selling monthly magazines. Claridge's report on the verdict appeared on page 1 of the *Globe and Mail* the next day—toward the bottom, but still prominent. An accompanying photo showed me surrounded by the media's microphones and looking angry. I'm pleased to say that another photograph of me, on an inside page of the news section, showed me coming out of the courthouse with George Callahan (although he is not named), who graciously came to court to offer support, even though he was no longer my lawyer. The October 10 article succinctly covered the important outcomes. It was cutely headlined "What's a poor dominatrix to do? Judge refuses to clarify the rules" and reads, in part:

> Professional dominatrix Terri-Jean Bedford is frustrated. After being found guilty yesterday of running a common bawdy house at her bungalow in the Toronto suburb of Thornhill, Ms. Bedford said: "The judge still hasn't said what I can or can't do." In his ruling, Judge Roy Bogusky of the Ontario Court's Provincial Division sidestepped completely the initial issue between the Crown and defence—whether sadomasochistic acts constitute sexual activity. In brief oral reasons delivered nearly six weeks after the closing submissions on the case Justice Bogusky based his finding on evidence showing that the activity at least occasionally involved Ms. Bedford and her employees touching customers' genitals.

Rosie DiManno was and is a prominent reporter with the *Toronto Star*, Canada's largest-selling newspaper. She covered my trial in 1995 in a manner that was highly critical of the police and Crown. Her reaction to Justice

Roy Bogusky's decisions was beyond highly critical; she was appalled. Her problem seemed to be not so much with the verdict as it was with his ruling on the constitutional motion. Her article appeared on October 11, a few days after the judge had ruled. I will quote most of it for you. It captures how I felt too.

> Conventional newspaper wisdom says that we never attack the judge, only the judgment. So, consider this an exercise in lawyer-imposed semantics. Roy Bogusky's *judgment* is foolish and perverse. ... For the moment let's forget the scads of money this has cost the taxpayer. Remember, the case had already been tossed out once before. But the cops, and the crown, came back. As if Bedford were a crime kingpin or a child molester or a big boil on the rump of the social moral order. All this, yet Bogusky's conviction for running a bawdy house turned on evidence that some clients had been masturbated on the premises. The judge did not rule on whether accepting payment for sadomasochistic fantasies is a criminal act. There are bigger issues to get steamed about here, more reasons to be not just horrified but alarmed. To wit: Guess it's open-season now on sex-trade workers in Ontario, if not just the sadomasochistic sub-genre. Justice Bogusky has made it so. And that's what makes this robed gentleman, you should excuse the expression, both foolish and perverse in his judgment. ... Young bucks! That's how Bogusky described the 15 (!) bully cops who raided Bedford's Thornhill bungalow, where they donned wigs, had mock whip fights, tyrannized the staff. ... Bedford, the learned judge allowed, was 'not well done by.'... But none of this was bad enough, according to the judgment, to have any impact on the case or Bogusky's decision. ... Do you not hear the same tone of condescension and exculpation that once marked the judicial attitude towards domestic violence. ... Bogusky's judgment has undermined the judicial and social progress of the past 20 years— where women may no longer be viewed as rag dolls that could be thrown up against the wall in a fit of rage, or inflatable sex dolls that could be assaulted with impunity. Boys will be boys, my ass.

The Judge Pronounces My Sentence

When we returned for sentencing a week after the verdict, Justice Bogusky's demeanor was greatly changed. Perhaps DiManno's article and other, similar publicity had gotten to him. He had himself been judged and found wanting ... and now he had to sentence me. He said that "in the interest of the taxpayers," he would not send me to jail. He said, "The accused and her associates had gained considerable notoriety from these proceedings" and "any form of custodial sentence would be an additional expense to the public coffers and could provide fertile ground for the notoriety to persist." He looked at me and said, "You have broken the law for money, so your punishment will be in kind." He said he was mitigating my fine because of the behavior of the police. The final sentence: a fine of $3,000, with six months to pay it.

Of course the media ridiculed him for the sentence and his reasons. Again I will quote, from a leading editorial in the *Globe and Mail* a few days after the sentence: "She received only the lightest of punishments, but she should have been given none at all. ... The judge said that her crime ... was 'a serious offence, no matter what other people may say,' but his sentence suggests otherwise. ... The whole affair—the massive police raid, the years of Crown and judicial resources deployed to deal with what should have been a minor nuisance complaint—only highlights the archaic nature of Canada's prostitution laws. It's time for those laws to be overhauled. It's time prostitution was legalized."

When Canada's national paper says my case is grounds for changing the law, I would say we had an impact. But we had lost in court—for the time being. It was time to go to the Ontario Court of Appeal. Surely a higher court, with three judges hearing the appeal, and seeing the reactions to the lower court decisions, would see things differently. Or would they?

Chapter 14

BACK IN BUSINESS

For over three years after the raid, my practice as a dominatrix was limited to visiting a couple of special clients from the Bondage Bungalow days in their homes. I did, on average, only two sessions a month. This income, along with that from the phone jobs as a psychic and tarot-card reader, enabled me to live simply and cheaply. One client paid for his sessions by letting me spend time at his cottage. I was, at the same time, busy with other matters. Scott and I continued working on my book about once a week, and there was often something to do involving my legal battles.

I made a few trips to Windsor to see my daughter, who was in foster care. She was only in her early teens; I knew she felt abandoned by me, and things were not all good with the family she was living with. I wanted to bring her back with me, but this was not the right time. I might be going to jail, and if I didn't, I wanted to reopen by business as a dominatrix. I had opened the Bondage Bungalow mainly because I wanted to make enough money to give her a proper home with her real mother, or at least more financial support. I wanted to try again.

In early 1999, just a few months after the big trial at which I was convicted, I began setting up the new business. One of my supporters knew the owner of a four-story house in downtown Toronto with a couple of vacant floors: the main floor and the basement. The house was designed to house three apartment units, not including the basement. I went to see it and met the owner, who knew who I was from the publicity and said he was rooting for me in my legal battle. I told him I wanted to reopen if I did not have to go to jail.

When I found out I was going to remain free, Scott hired an accountant to ensure proper business organization, recordkeeping, and compliance with all tax and licensing regulations. He and Scott put and kept my financial affairs in order. The accountant's assistance went well beyond that of pure number crunching and business advice, though he had never been a client or a player on the scene. His trust and respect for Scott, combined with his belief in my cause, led him to do more for than he would have for a normal client. Of course, my dominatrix side still wanted to discipline him when I paid him. But then, who doesn't cringe a bit at legal and accounting fees? Everyone should spend some money to obtain professional finance, business, and tax advice, no matter how humble their affairs.

The corporation that we formed, headed by me, leased the premises. The house was going to need major renovations within a few years. The current tenants of the top two floors were students; if, or when, they moved out, I would have those floors. Of course, my rent would then go up. So we had a three-year deal on the house, with an option to extend it a few months. I moved in formally at the beginning of 1999, and was scheduled to move back out at the end of 2001, when the owner wanted to begin renovations. He would just do interim repairs for the next three years. Scott, Albert, Paddy, Roxy, and Phyllis were supportive in a number of ways. So were others I will be telling you about. They all said that even if I did not make money, they wanted me to rise up again and just by having done so make a statement to society. It also meant they had a facility they could use if they wanted. This was a "You whip my back, I'll whip yours" situation, if you will.

The house was on a busy street in downtown Toronto, across the street from a nice park and within walking distance of the central business district and a university. Also in the neighborhood were a large shelter for homeless men, an abortion clinic, a church, and office buildings. So it was as diverse a neighborhood as could be imagined. The house from the outside was a classic old structure in what is called the Georgian style in Canada. Every floor had a large picture window. The house had been designed for a business on the main floor and apartments on the upper two floors.

On my first tour of the house, I was pleasantly surprised by the view of many of the rooms from the end of the main hall. I imagined I could keep an eye on my clients while they were at work or play with one of my mistresses, without having to disturb a session by opening a door. The high ceilings gave the illusion of more space. There were five rooms on the main floor, totaling less square footage than the Bondage Bungalow, but something I could work with. Then, when I stepped into the basement, I knew I had found my dungeon. Diffused light came through a window with steel bars in the far corner of the room. A thick wooden beam stood in the middle of the room, and strong wooden beams spanned the ceiling. What a perfect foundation for a dungeon! In all, my business would have six rooms, excluding the bathroom. The basement would be the dungeon, and the other five could be theme rooms, with one doubling as an office. There was no kitchen.

My plan was to use the main floor exclusively for reception, cross-dressers, and infantiles. S&M sessions would happen in the dungeon. At night I would sleep on a couch on the main floor, and I could keep my clothes with those of the cross-dressers, though not for their use. When the upper floors became available, I would move up there and take in a couple of clients who wanted to be live-in slaves; I would charge them a stiff monthly fee. It would be good value for both parties.

But in the early days, until the upstairs floors became available, the main focus of the operation was serving cross-dressers. I called it the Millicent Farnsworth Sissy Maid Academy, and I advertised it without identifying myself as the proprietor. I advertised the dungeon separately. I don't have to tell you about the clients and sessions; my job was much the same as it had been in the Bondage Bungalow in Thornhill: anything but dull, and a lot of hard work. The police still had my clothes and equipment—over seven hundred items—so I gradually built up my inventory over the first several months with new acquisitions. I went to a lot of yard sales and secondhand stores, and I continued to receive donations from my supporters. Also, I had stored some things they hadn't taken in the raid with a supporter, and now I got them back.

During the last year and a half at the second house, I had five live-in clients for varying lengths of time. They essentially rented part of the premises from me. I also had three nonresident men who were regulars at the house. These three all have the distinction today of being members of The Dozen. I am going to tell you about all eight of these men for two reasons. For one thing, they all helped me keep going and live the life you are now reading about. For another, they were simply very interesting people.

First, I'll list the five who lived there.

- The man I called Sexy Suzy was not a big man, but he was a martial-arts expert who had served in the US Navy and Merchant Marines. After his discharge, he had lived in various places in the United States, mainly working as a truck driver. He was a capable car mechanic, cleaner, and cook; he even knew how to sew. A regular with many doms in the United States, he became known as the Texas Devil Dog. His favorite scene was stealing women's underwear and getting caught. His punishment was to wear the underwear and serve as a sissy maid, and when he was too mouthy, I made him wear a ball gag that was locked in place. When the doms were bored, they would sometimes punish and verbally humiliate him. He slept in a coffin locked in chains. He was the perfect slave at first, but after a time, he had to leave, because he was becoming less obedient. He was with me for about a year, and for him it was a prolonged vacation. He has gone back to the United States, and I still hear from him occasionally.

- The man I called Mary was also a trucker who took an extended work leave to be my slave. He was with me for a couple of months. Lucky for me, his fetish was domestic servitude. His big turn-on was to clean and wash, sweep and vacuum, and so forth while the doms ignored him or yelled at him for doing a poor job. The girls loved him, because he would iron their clothes, polish their boots, help them dress, and hold their ashtrays while they smoked. Of course, he ran errands and took messages when ordered.

- The man I called Gaby was a disabled Vietnam veteran in his fifties confined to a wheelchair. He was also a diabetic. He paid me a generous rent to live there and, of course, could do no chores except sometimes answering the phone or performing other office-type work. He stayed six months. He was not at all demanding, and I personally attended to him each day, by which I mean we did a session. His fantasy was to be my secretary, following my orders and wearing what

I wanted him to wear. He was always sissied up to the nines, usually in a French maid's uniform. He told me that his veteran's allowance, combined with an inheritance, allowed him to fulfill his fantasies; plus, he had all the time in the world. Unfortunately his health began to deteriorate, and he had to return to a veteran's hospital in the United States. He was a remarkably mellow and patient man, and we all learned much from him.

- The man I called Isabella was a young, nearly blind, well-educated European gentleman who put "Doctor" before his name. I am not sure if he was really a doctor of any type; he was quite deceitful in that way. Like Gaby, he had a guaranteed income and paid me for a combination of accommodation and role-playing. He was not there at the same time as Gaby or Suzy, so I had space for him. But having him there proved to be a mistake; for what he was paying, he demanded too much of our time for role-playing and keeping him company. So after a couple of months, I had had enough and made arrangements for him to leave, which took some time.

- The man I called Prissy was a traumatized Vietnam veteran. He did not have any permanent injuries, but he was receiving a military pension, so he did not have to work. Like Gaby, he was in his fifties, and he loved playing the role of slave to a dominatrix. He also insisted on being punished quite severely on a regular basis and humiliated from time to time. I used him as a subject when training my girls. Prissy was with me when we closed, and he accompanied me to my new residence, which was nothing like what we were leaving. There were no role-play facilities in the new place, yet for some months, Prissy still served as my slave in return for very little; he also helped me pay the rent. Then he too went back to the United States with the onset of winter that year. Must be nice!

I helped these men realize their dreams for a time. They wanted to be feminized, to be slaves to a dominant woman, and they were. When those roles lost their appeal, at least in the setting in which they were offered, or when they had to leave, as in Gaby's case, they were free to do so—they were free slaves. The slaves were freer than me!

Then there were three others who did not live there. I will now tell you why they are among The Dozen.

- Cathy Maid was a manual worker in the Canadian Armed Forces. A dedicated cross-dresser, he had never been married. He was of medium height and build, so he looked very good in women's clothing. He took great pride in being able to "pass" when he came on a ninety-minute bus ride from out of town and then walked the streets of Toronto to my house. He was an excellent advertisement for my services, so he went public with me, appearing in ads and before the cameras for some of my court appearances, where he was identified as my slave. He was a regular for most of the three years in my second house, and on the two days per week he was there, he performed domestic duties and sometimes helped the other cross-dressers in and out of their clothing. For some cross-dressers, it is a big thrill to have another cross-dresser help them into corsets, do up their garters, and so forth. Cathy Maid appeared as my spanking victim in some of the videos we used on our website. This unfailingly loyal friend moved to my new residence with me when I left the house. Of course, the move also meant that he was able to attend many cross-dressing events here in Toronto during weeknights. He is also an avid science-fiction fan, and he has a wonderful time using his cross-dressing skills to impersonate characters from sci-fi movies and television at sci-fi conventions. Cathy Maid is number eight of The Dozen.

- Another major presence, the trucker Baby Betty, is an infantile, and he has called me "Mommy" from the first day he came to my second house until today. His resourcefulness at finding secondhand furniture and so forth has been a great help to me. He is very capable of handling responsibility. He has assisted me and others dear to me so often and in so many ways I can hardly believe it. He is still doing so. Heaven is made for such people. Baby Betty is number nine of The Dozen.

- The last of these three pillars in my life is The Geek. He was referred to me when a dom who knew him outside the scene mentioned that I needed some work on my website, which is The Geek's specialty. He was not a participant in any of the activities at my house or involved in any of the lifestyles at all. Nonetheless he has been one of my key supporters. He designs and maintains my website. He helps me on all Internet related matters. He has been a valuable reader of my manuscripts. He and Scott have teamed well on many things. The Geek is number ten of The Dozen.

Aside from Art, and Scott and Albert to some extent, none of my supporters have been rich or even financially secure. But they were many, and they were loyal and hardworking and believed in what they were doing. The lawyers worked mainly without being paid fees. So did the activists. Money may talk, but so do other things.

I Get the Third Floor

When the third floor in my building became available, my resident clients began to move in, and now I also had more living space for myself. My daughter was able to live there as well; we were finally reunited. That alone made it worth the effort. Having her there with her mother was also a great source of joy to The Dozen, who became devoted to her as well. I want so much to tell you about my daughter's story, but only when the time is right.

I Get the Fourth Floor

When the fourth floor became available, I occupied the entire premises. I was able to do something I had wanted to do for some time: advertise my facility as the Bondage Hotel. The Internet was by this time in full swing, so I offered accommodation along with sessions and guided tours of Toronto and even Niagara Falls. These new services were potentially quite profitable, and maintaining them was less of a chore than booking and conducting several low-cost sessions each day. Needless to say, we continued to do both. I had special brochures printed, and I advertised the hotel on the window at the front of the house. We even had a media blitz, inviting journalists to visit for a special media day. Even today, when you search for me on the Internet, you see pictures taken that week, most notably one with me sitting on the throne in full leather with a couple of clients at my feet.

An interesting anecdote arose out of the publicity. Professor Hill, an expert at my trial (although not according to the honorable judges), was on an airplane that week. Complementary copies of the *Globe and Mail* had been given out, and when Professor Hill returned from the lavatory, he saw over the shoulders of many passengers that almost all of them reading the paper were looking at an article about me and my bondage hotel written by the noted female columnist Jan Wong. It was her regular weekly column, "Lunch with Jan Wong."

The hotel was very popular with couples as well as individual men. It featured a suite consisting of one half of the top floor, with private bathroom. In the middle of the room was a heavy bed with strong wooden posts and wooden beams across the top. It was a special bondage bed, with metal rings to attach chains and so on. Two could bounce around on it, and the special mattress and frame would hardly shake. The bed was also available for use by non-overnight clients. It was quite something to see.

Naturally, I wanted to protect my business. When the fourth floor became available, I would be much more in the public eye, because I was going to invite the press to tour my facility as a way of advertising for more business and telling the world, in a memorable way, that I was a force to be reckoned with. Also, since I knew I had to vacate in about a year anyway, if the house didn't urgently need the renovations before that time, I wanted to get another raid over with and make a big splash about it. Alan said he would represent me, and once again, as a backup, Scott had lined up Paula Roachman, who advised Klippenstein, to join Alan if I were charged. It was a different police force and a different time, and, as I said, I still wanted vindication. Here I was, doing what I had done before, openly publicizing it, and about to ramp it up for a year or so. So just after the media blitz, Alan wrote two nearly identical letters to the police, to different officers, so any claim that it had not been received would not be believed.

Copies of the letters were sent to the media, who then followed up with the police. Sergeants Belza and Knapper of 51 Division of the Toronto police got the letter. When asked about the legality of the facility by the media, one of the officers was quoted as saying, "Nothing illegal so far. But I'm assuming that sooner or later we'll probably get a complaint ... at this point she has not broken the law." Alan's letters of July 27, 2001, confronted them with their comments. Alan then said, "To assist you in making this determination (if anything illegal is going on), I am listing the activities taking place at the establishment, as well as the activities which are not permitted." He basically listed what we did and did not do at the Bondage Bungalow, with one exception. He wrote that clients would not be allowed to masturbate themselves in the presence of staff, which we had allowed at the bungalow. This meant that, at least to the public, if the police did not lay charges now, they were condoning the activities in my house.

The officers did not respond to the letters in writing or by speaking to the media about it, with the exception I noted above, despite many calls from reporters. One of them called Alan a week or so after getting his letter and said they would speak to Alan first if there were any complaints. Of course, doms are always complaining to the police about each other as a way of competing for business, claiming the other doms are selling sex, and so forth. So the complaints the police would act on would have been something like an assault complaint and the like.

The police never bothered me at all in those three years.

Decision to Close

Three years after I moved in, the owner of the property wanted to renovate the premises to make all three floors residential apartments. Renovating was actually a hobby of his, and he was looking forward to it. He had been an excellent landlord and had frankly shown considerable courage in having me as his tenant. From my perspective, his timing was good.

For one thing, I wasn't making any money. Remember, my girls generally took about half the revenue as their share, and I had to pay the rent, utilities, and my own living expenses, among other things. Remember, also, that I had lived at the Bondage Bungalow as an extra tenant and had not paid the full market rent. Here, I did. An event that harmed my profits was the September 11 terrorist attack. Much of my business had come from the United States, but after the attacks, the border was closed, travel was more difficult, and many people were afraid. The economy suffered in the aftermath of the attack as well.

Another pressure came from the landlord's insurance company. They charged him commercial rates because of the business that I, one of his tenants, was in. The insurance alone cost over $1,000 per month. Some months I made money, but most months I did not. The members of The Dozen who had made a commitment honored it and made up the shortfall as needed. The temporary nature of the pressure made it easily manageable to them. Also, the building was genuinely falling apart. Repairs or replacement were needed more and more frequently, especially to the roof, floors, and wiring. I finally moved out in May 2002.

But it was mostly my doctor who decided that the timing of the closure was good. Several months before I closed, I began to feel ill and unable to function normally. I was having severe back pain and was terribly weak and fatigued. Just a few months before I closed, I received his diagnosis.

Chapter 15

HIGHER COURTS

The appeal process involves the applicant submitting a thirty-page factum (a summary of what is being appealed and why), accompanied by a brief of authorities (copies of extracts from relevant precedent cases and other relevant documents). The Crown then submits its response factum and brief. Sometimes the applicant will also submit a very short reply to the Crown's response. A hearing is held some months later at the Ontario Court of Appeal, usually in front of three judges, as I noted earlier. They hear oral submissions by the lawyers and question them. The judges then usually issue a written decision, with one judge usually signing as the author. Sometimes they make an oral decision on the spot. If the other two judges agree with the decision, they just sign to that effect; if they dissent in any way, they add and sign comments attributable to them alone. The decision of two judges carries the day. If all three were to decide against me, getting a further appeal heard was unlikely. If only two did, I could probably get a hearing before the Supreme Court of Canada. If the Crown lost, they could automatically get a Supreme Court hearing because they had won at trial.

I was convicted in October 1998. In October 1999, my appeal was filed. A written decision was issued by the Ontario Court of Appeal in March 2000.

Mounting the appeal had obstacles. An obvious one was cost. Alan had to act through a lawyer who had his own practice, so disbursements were incurred by a private law firm and had to be paid by me and my supporters.

These disbursements, as well as the costs of photocopying, faxing, and the like, amounted to less than $1,000, so that was not a major problem. The major cost was that of trial transcripts. We had to produce three sets of certified trial transcripts for the court, one for the Crown, and one for ourselves. These five sets cost almost $8,000. Finally there is the cost of the lawyers' hours, which I estimate to be about 150. You can do the math on that one if you have some grasp of typical hourly rates for lawyers. Fortunately my lawyers worked on my case without fee. Albert, who promised me he would pay the disbursement and transcript costs of an appeal, did just that. Scott was also there with his checkbook, as usual. The members of The Dozen who were then on board never wavered. In fact, they grew more supportive as time went by, as you will see.

Alan was assisted in preparing the appeal by Paul Burstein, of the firm Burstein and Payne. A regular presence on television, he had acted as defense counsel in a number of high-profile criminal cases and was an expert at conducting appeals. He has since become the President of the Criminal Lawyers' Association of Ontario. Of course, Alan had his students assisting him as well. There were five arguments advanced in the appeal, which consisted of a thirty-page factum, the hundreds of pages of the brief, and the 1,400 pages of trial transcripts. The appeal cited five ways Justice Bogusky, had erred.

- He did not properly apply evidence that the premises were "habitually and frequently" used for acts of prostitution, with which the Crown tried to prove that the bungalow was a bawdy house.

- He did not apply Princess's evidence accurately. He used her responses to the Crown, but not her self-correction when Alan got her to change her testimony in cross-examination.

- He wrongly excluded the expert testimony of five of the experts and gave only brief and inadequate reasons for doing so.

- He erred in admitting the videotape as evidence and then proceeded to make exaggerated and inaccurate use of it as evidence.

- He erred in not granting a stay of the charges on the basis that the police had broken the law in the raid, and in their actions preceding and following it.

The Crown's rather predictable response to these arguments was to simply repeat what the judge had said and to say that he was right. Man, are those guys overpaid or what?

The Appeal Hearing

About two months after the filings, the appeal was heard by the Ontario Court of Appeal. I was there for it. To me the discussion seemed very technical, and it seemed to me that the judges interrupted lawyers for both sides too much. They asked Alan many questions and gave him a rough time at the beginning, but as the day went on, they seemed to be more and more interested in what he had to say. They took more notes and listened with greater interest as the day wore on. They questioned him less often. The media were there in front of the courthouse in full force, taking plenty of pictures and questioning me and Alan.

It was a dramatic moment. Would the Court of Appeal overrule Justice Bogusky? Would they recognize that the laws were too broad and their application too arbitrary? In the weeks leading up to the hearing, Scott had ensured that the media were aware of the impending proceedings. Prior to the day of the appeal hearing, a number of journalists visited me at my new facility (more on that later), giving a great deal of coverage to both the case and the facility. They ran pictures of me with clients in bondage, brief explanations of what the case was about, and even a lighthearted article called "Dominating the Oscars" with a menacing picture of me and my picks for the Oscars, the nominations for which had been released that week.

One reporter spent a few hours with me as I ran my business. She seemed different and in some way more thoughtful than most of the other reporters. We chatted when I wasn't on the phone or with a client. She had no photographer with her. She told me her name, of which I only caught "Margaret," and she was from the *Globe and Mail*. I had never heard of her. Scott came by that evening, and I briefly mentioned that a lady from the *Globe and Mail* named Margaret had come by. He said "Margaret Wente?" That reminded me of her last name. Scott told me she was a significant visitor, as her opinions of people carried great weight with establishment types. In the coming days, Margaret profiled me in her column and offered a very positive opinion of me. Some years later, she repeated the column in a book of her collected articles called *An Accidental Canadian*.

The Appeal Decision

The appeal decision was released in March 2000. The three Justices were Finlayson, Labrosse, and Osborne. Justice Finlayson wrote the decision, and the other two signed an agreement. His decision was in support of the trial judge. I asked a few lawyers to read it, and they were appalled. Alan said it meant that a stripper could be deemed a prostitute. George Callahan said it was scary. Other lawyers were even more alarmed. A vague law applied too broadly was made even broader by the decision. It was such a poorly considered decision, and so biased, that subsequent bawdy-house trials never relied on it or even mentioned it. I was shown a couple of articles from legal journals that condemned the decision in no uncertain terms. To my knowledge, nothing positive has ever been said or written about the decision. I cannot for the life of me understand what world Finlayson was living in, or why the other two judges went along with such an irresponsible decision. Subsequent events, as you will see, validated this criticism.

The day the decision came out, I released a short statement to the media, expressing my disappointment with it. It appeared to me, and to Scott, that the full implications of this legal disaster should be conveyed to the public. So he and I prepared a full written response to the Court of Appeal and released it a couple of weeks later. Some reporters called to thank me, but the letter attracted little reaction overall. I am going to reprint it here in full, with very few changes. It remains the single most important statement of what my mission as an activist is.

An Open Letter from the Bondage Bungalow Dominatrix: I Would Rather Live in a Democracy.

I am writing this letter in response to so many requests for my comments on what has happened recently in the Bondage Bungalow matter. In March 2000, the Ontario Court of Appeal released its decision on the Bondage Bungalow appeal. I was appealing my conviction and fine from my 1998 trial. I was convicted of running a common bawdy house. I did not then and do not now believe I am guilty, or that a proper trial was held. Once again, there was no sex and no grounds for calling the Bondage Bungalow a bawdy house. But most important of all was that the trial judge did not tell me, as a dominatrix, what I could and could not do.

For all these reasons, I appealed. I did not proceed without verifying with a number of lawyers that my appeal had solid grounds, and lining up Alan Young and Paul Burstein, two major figures in the legal profession who felt so strongly that I was innocent and that the matter was mishandled by the authorities, that they represented me without fee. Public opinion was certainly sympathetic. Suspicion of the authorities arose because they went to such lengths for such a minor victimless charge, yet refused to clarify the issues.

My appeal did not succeed. The disgraceful behavior of the authorities continues to go unpunished, the findings of a badly flawed trial go uncorrected, and I still do not know why I was convicted. My lawyers cannot explain it to me, either. Democratic countries have rules that people can ask about and get answers. I would rather not have the rules being secret, like in my conviction, for reasons we are still not given. I would rather live in a democracy.

I tried an experiment. I asked some of the reporters who have followed this case for all its years a couple of questions. For instance, is bondage and tickling for money legal if there is no genital contact? For instance, if a man with his pants on gets an erection while kissing my boots, am I breaking the law? The reporters said that they are no clearer on this after my trial or my appeal. Five trips to court! Are not the authorities paid to be clear about what someone does wrong, or right—when there is a trial? I would rather live in a democracy.

Have you at any time seen or heard a Crown attorney or policy officer interviewed on this case? Even after the recent decision? In all the media coverage so much as a quote? People in the media tell me that no police officer or Crown attorney *can* tell them what I can and cannot do as a dominatrix. They do not want to answer questions *on a case they won*. In a democracy, the police and prosecutors account for their actions to the people. I would rather live in a democracy.

Just before my 1998 trial, the Crown dropped the charges on the four other defendants but not my charges. They waited years to do this. They only called one as a witness. All five of us went all the way up to the Supreme Court and were going to fight at trial in full agreement that we were not guilty. Then they told me that I had to dismiss my lawyers because of conflict, since they had represented persons who might be called as witnesses. I am told this is often done as a pressure tactic when the accused dares to fight back. Some fair trial. Some justice. I would rather live in a democracy.

The editors of the *Globe and Mail*, overtly sympathetic to me, in a March 27 editorial ridiculed at length the law and the authorities in this matter. I think the editors, writing for the second time about my matter (they wrote a similar editorial after my 1998 trial), make it very clear that under the prostitution laws, everyone can be guilty of everything and nobody guilty of nothing at the same time. When the very law under which we were charged is incomprehensible to authorities and serious media, how can a citizen know what is legal? In other recent cases in Canada, even in Ontario, judges have thrown out bawdy-house charges because the law is so vague that they deemed it unfair. But not in my case, even though everyone is wondering which of the many things I did were legal and which were not. I would rather live in a democracy.

The decision itself has disturbed—profoundly disturbed—most of the lawyers who have read it. Some of them said it is "scary." I am told that the way the decision "defines" a lewd act is so broad that even a stripper who has no physical contact with a customer can be deemed a prostitute. The decision can be used as a precedent for calling almost anything "arousing." The decision means, I am told, that unelected authorities can decide what is lewd arbitrarily. In totalitarian countries, the authorities decide what entertainment people may find enjoyable and not arousing. I would rather live in a democracy.

The decision itself has disturbed most of the lawyers who have read it in that it ignores facts of the trial. Point 27 of the decision discusses how often clients had orgasms in the Bondage Bungalow by themselves and quotes percentages testified to at trial. However, the transcripts—on pages 554–55, among others—and my appeal factum make it very clear that the testimony cited and relied upon so heavily in the appeal decision was, under cross-examination, retracted to much lower percentages, and the circumstances surrounding such activity were clarified to mean other than what the appeal decision relied upon. And other evidence crucial to establishing the preponderant activities in the bungalow was not cited in the decision despite being raised in the factum to establish that this was a role-playing facility. The decision thus overtly cited flawed and incomplete information and relied on it for analysis. There were uses of inaccurate information, arbitrarily and selectively applied, in what was supposed to be an impartial process. I would rather live in a democracy.

The decision also appalled almost all the lawyers who read it, because it so briefly excused the use of the search warrant, which was given for the police to seize evidence, to take almost everything in the house and put me out of business. The decision said that a violation of rights under the Charter is meant to be cited only in the "clearest of cases" and that this, according to the decision, was not one of the clearest of cases. As the media has so often reported, the police took over seven hundred items, including my clothes of any description, the dictionary, a chandelier, and furniture, as well as bondage gear and the like. How is a chandelier used for prostitution? They tried to hold me without bail, knowing my trial might be a year away. They prevented me from returning to the bungalow, which was my home. They called a press conference to publicize the raid and the officer who called it was reduced in rank and removed from public relations shortly after. The decision acknowledged that the trial judge said the raid involved overkill and called my treatment shabby, but what remedy did I get? A reduced sentence? No! The sentence was pretty standard for the triviality of such a victimless "offence" and for my record. No relief at sentencing, despite what the authorities might say. The authorities made the rules as they went along. The appeal decision let them get away with it. What more did they have to do to me to make it the clearest of cases of abusing a search warrant? I would rather live in a democracy.

The decision surprised most of the lawyers when it indicated that expert testimony was not relevant to the outcome of the trial. If ever there were a trial where expert opinion was needed, this was it. There were many activities in the bungalow, something not recognized in the appeal decision. The appeal decision said that what went on in my house was at issue, but not which activities were sexual or aroused sexual gratification, whatever that means. I think I have a right to know. My lawyers, after this decision, cannot give me a clear answer. I think I have a right to know what I did right and what I did wrong, but I don't know. I would rather live in a democracy.

Crown attorneys and the courts are backlogged and overworked. They love to make deals and plea bargain. They also often drop charges when a costly prosecution will only result in a small punishment, especially when the crime is victimless. But in my case, they spared no expense. Then they had the nerve to whine about how I changed lawyers. They changed lawyers three times. And in 1998 they had my lawyers disqualified when they could have dropped the charges on the others and avoided the conflict issue many months before trial. They whined about how I was dragging this out, yet did not drop the charges even after the case was originally thrown out, or after I was only appealing a small fine. The media has ridiculed them for spending so much on my matter. And at the end, what has been achieved? They are not even commenting in the media. Taxpayers have been plundered by corrupt and incompetent bureaucrats who want to answer to nobody. The really frightening thing is that they came after us even harder because we were innocent and because we fought back. I would rather live in a democracy.

I am asked why I fight. First of all, all five defendants fought. Not one, not one of the five, offered to plead guilty. All of us stood up even though it meant getting lawyers, missing work, public exposure, and other possible retaliation and harassment by the authorities. All of us believed we were innocent. We prevailed in that four of us were not convicted, and that means that those other four who would have had a conviction recorded against them did not get convicted. Even then I felt that it was important to fight. Since there was no sex in the bungalow, this was an excellent opportunity to test, in the courts and in public, the questions that are still being asked and will continue to be asked. There was also one little noticed but very major outcome. Peter Westgate, the Crown attorney at my 1998 trial, who replaced James McKeachie as Crown attorney (as always, with no explanation why) said he would not be citing any of the acts that went on in my bungalow as indecent, because community standards on this matter are too hard to define. Repeat: there were no indecent acts in the Bondage Bungalow. During the trial, this was clearly and repeatedly reinforced. The Crown's narrowing of the case to a charge of prostitution and not indecency was in itself a huge success for us.

I want to thank some people from the bottom of my heart. We have had twelve lawyers on our side, some in an advisory capacity and some formally representing us. They were paid a fraction of what they should have been paid, if they were paid at all. There were also many nonlawyers who assisted us in ways too numerous and occasions too often to even begin to list. These many professional people reaffirmed the belief of all the defendants that they were innocent and had been wronged in a number of ways and had to stand up against the authorities. Please read the names of the most prominent of my lawyers as I now list them. The consensus has been that I have had tremendous representation. Let us recognize their talent and dedication to their profession: Alan Young, Murray Klippenstein, George Callahan, Paul Burstein, Leah Daniels, Morris Manning and Theresa Simone.

What next? I will try to take this to the Supreme Court, but it may well be that the answer lies with our elected officials. The courts do not seem to be effective guardians of our freedom to engage in consenting adult behavior. I will be continuing, with others, to fight for reform of the bawdy-house laws and against the manner in which the authorities abuse this legislation. I believe that our elected officials can be persuaded to protect those, like myself, who are prosecuted without clear reasons.

And what about me? Believe it or not, I am not frightened or unhappy.

I have friends, family, representatives, and allies. We are thinking ahead and are realistic. I will continue to practice as a dominatrix and try to remain within the law in whatever way I can. I just wish I had some rules. I want to obey the law, but how can I when they won't tell me the rules? We may have to do this over again. We shouldn't have to. I would rather live in a democracy.

Corbett Steps Up

The media gave little coverage to the decision and made no attempts to interview Alan or me after its release. There were no references to my open letter. In my own mind, I thought this marked the end of my legal battle. However, Scott, as always, was working behind the scenes.

Before the release of the appeal decision in March 2001, I attended a most interesting meeting. One of Scott's old-school acquaintances was a very highly regarded constitutional and civil-liberties lawyer. Scott had briefed him on the case because he wanted another perspective on whether a civil suit or constitutional challenge would be in order, considering the changes to the legal landscape that had occurred in the five years since I was raided. Apparently judges were now treating issues of seizure and other police excesses more seriously, and were judging the matter of what constituted a bawdy house differently and more thoughtfully than Justice Bogusky had. So Scott thought that if the Ontario Court of Appeal did not overturn my conviction, the Supreme Court of Canada might consent to hear the case.

Scott's old-school acquaintance is now a judge - Justice David L. Corbett. David has quite a legal pedigree. He graduated from one of Canada's most prestigious private schools, and then one of Canada's most prestigious universities, and then one of Canada's most prestigious law schools. He went on to practice at one of Canada's most prestigious law firms before becoming a partner in a smaller firm, which allowed him to focus on the issues that were most personally meaningful to him. David became one of Canada's most famous openly gay lawyers and rose to national attention with cases affecting the gay community, as well as other civil-liberty issues. Shortly after representing me, he became the first openly gay judge in Ontario history. He has been on the bench now for eight years.

Scott brought David to see me shortly before the appeal decision was released. We talked for two hours. David was very sympathetic and patient; clearly here was a superior mind. He had a great interest in the case. When the appeal decision was handed down against me, he agreed immediately to seek leave to appeal. When someone is convicted, as in my case, and also loses an appeal, particularly with none of the three appeal judges dissenting, it is rare that the Supreme Court will hear a further appeal. However, David thought this might be one of those instances. He said change was due, and that this case was an opportunity for the Supreme Court to make some badly needed changes. David said he would work the case without fee, and just asked that we cover disbursements. The differences between David's writing on the case at that time versus Justice Bogusky and Justice Finlayson in my matter remain to me one of the most interesting things about my story.

David worked on the case with his very able partner Lucy McSweeney and articling student Timothy Banks. Timothy has gone on to a very successful law career. They put in over 180 hours preparing their factum and brief of authorities. They were all very committed to the issues at stake. They were extremely professional in keeping me informed at every stage and advising me along the way. Since David did most of the work and oversaw the team, I will refer to him only as I tell you about what happened, beginning with the factum.

To this day, I regard David's factum as—in my humble opinion—the most impressive document of any kind to arise out of my legal battles. I quote from it at some length because I believe doing so will help you understand what was at issue and why it mattered, and not just to me.

David chose not to take issue with the appeal decision on the video, the experts, or the question of whether acts of prostitution were habitual and frequent in my establishment. Rather, he focused on the other two issues: whether the manner of seizure warranted a stay of proceedings and the interpretation of prostitution in the decision. He did this because he was seeking leave to appeal and could introduce the other three matters during the proceedings. He said this was the most effective approach in getting heard when we had lost the first two rounds. Furthermore, he said that the two matters he was raising were of national importance and more likely to be seen by the Supreme Court as deserving a hearing for that reason.

On the first issue, David pointed out that the search warrant was obtained to stop a "morals offence" but was used for other purposes. Here is part of what he wrote:

> The officer in charge admitted that the objective was, in part, to prevent Bedford from continuing her business and living in her home. The officer in charge ordered the removal of all of Bedford's possessions despite having a comprehensive videotape of each room in the house and despite the fact that there was nothing illegal *per se* about any of her possessions. The officer in charge also made an improper return. In a number of cases, the officer made no attempt to indicate the quantity of items seized nor did he describe some items with any particularity. Further, the officer also misstated the quantities in cases where they were listed. The officer admitted that there was no explanation for many of these errors. The manner in which the warrant was obtained and the serious errors and omissions in the return destroyed even the "illusion of judicial control" over the process of search and seizure. ... Bedford submits that the function of a search and seizure is to secure evidence of the commission of a crime. In this case, the police officer in charge knew that the law was uncertain. He had no direct evidence that prostitution was occurring at Bedford's residence. ... The officer in charge knew or ought to have known that the scale of the planned seizure would be a *de facto* judgment of Bedford, since it would serve to put her out of business and out of her home. It is inappropriate for the police to use the important and powerful investigative tool of a search warrant for the purpose of closing down a business: such conduct constitutes judgment by the police before a trial and is a clear abuse of process and the state police power.

On the second issue, David concluded his analysis of Justice Finlayson's approach toward the prostitution charge with the following:

> Bedford submits that the Ontario Court of Appeal has adopted a broad definition of prostitution, which goes further than the Quebec Court of Appeal, and which does not comport with this

court's (The Supreme Court's) analysis of the term "indecent" in the same Criminal Code provision. The Applicant submits that this is a dangerous precedent, which will guide law enforcement officials, and could lead to an over-broad application of subsection 210(1) of the Criminal Code (keeping a bawdy house), which is inconsistent with the principle of strict construction in statutory interpretation. In the alternative, Bedford submits that this honorable court should ... declare that subsection of 210(1) of the Criminal Code is void for vagueness.

David laid some important groundwork for what was to come. The Crown's factum in response was as bad as David's was good. They peppered it with words like "assplay" and "cock and ball torture," and didn't even bother to take issue with David's arguments. David pointed this out in his reply, saying, "The Respondent has spent almost 14 pages out of a 19-page memorandum ... restating the facts of this case. For the most part these facts are not in dispute for the purposes of this appeal." David also pointed out a number of blatant errors and reminded the court that although it had not been made an issue in his factum, the Crown repeated some of Princess's testimony without mentioning that she had corrected it in cross-examination, just like Finlayson.

Legal Battles Over ... For Now

Two months after David filed his reply, I held another fund-raiser. Even though I had supporters to pay for David's disbursements, I felt I should try to raise funds, as I had done for my trial. We had another event at Buddies in Bad Times. We again got good publicity, but not as much as the first bash, perhaps because there just wasn't the interest that we had inspired for the trial, so people had less incentive to sell the event or attend it. The poor publicity may have been why this event was not as well attended. There are a few other possible reasons for this. We held this fund-raiser on the Thanksgiving holiday weekend, which in Canada is in October. The venue was not available on any other weekend within the timeframe when the event would have to be staged.

However, I had important reasons to proceed with the bash. Some students were doing a documentary on me (which they never finished), and from it I was supposed to get photos and films that could be used for publicity when I did finally publish my book. Also, it was a chance for the lawyers and me to tell the public that the battle was still in progress.

At the second fund-raiser, David's factum was given to members of the press. Several of the lawyers involved met for the first time, notably Alan and David. The first panel discussion was just Alan and David giving their perspectives on the case. Their panel was hosted by Pierre Cloutier, a paralegal. In addition to helping with this event, he assisted me when I was rebuilding my business and with other legal matters, usually at no charge. I am grateful to him, very grateful.

The fund-raiser also included a panel of experts, legal and otherwise. Brenda Cossman, a law professor at the University of Toronto, gave a primer on the issues. Shannon Bell spoke about the trial, and Julie Fraser, who had been at the 1998 trial as a researcher and was now a professor at the University of Windsor, spoke about her research on power in relationships. The experts also answered questions. The audience only numbered about thirty people, but they were actively listening and asking questions. A few even made statements for the film students' cameras, which recorded the event. The media actually gave the event decent coverage, meaning they told the public that the case was not over yet.

In January 2001, the Supreme Court issued a statement saying they would not hear the case. Timothy Banks called to tell me as soon as his office was advised. I was only mildly disappointed. It was, and is, the practice of the Court not to give reasons for such refusal. The media gave brief reports of the fact. I sent a note to David thanking him and asking him to convey my gratitude to his colleagues.

With the conclusion of the case, I was now able to pick up my possessions at the York Regional Police warehouse, where they had been held for over six years. I had invited the press, so there were film crews and photographers to record the event. I arrived with a moving truck and a couple of my slave clients came to help—cross-dressed, of course. I posed for pictures holding up some items the police had seized, including my bondage equipment and my Webster's Dictionary. The pictures of the cross-dressed men with the police officer were priceless. Maybe we should have busted them for running an uncommon bawdy house. Needless to say, the equipment came in handy in my new dungeon. It would now be very fully equipped, and I acquired some new clients who were curious to see what had been taken by the police.

It took quite a while to match the items returned with our list of what had been seized and then crosscheck it against the faulty inventory given to us in the disclosure after the raid. Some items were never returned but, frankly, some of these would have been a burden to store, so I did not press the matter. It was sad but funny to see some of what they had seized, including the infamous chandelier. Justice Bogusky said at trial that he could imagine some motif where that could be involved when he excused the extent and motive of the seizure of the contents of the Bondage Bungalow. I wonder if he realized that this was about the smallest chandelier you could buy—so small I could pick it up with my baby finger. But in any event, some justice was done, and I got publicity for my business. Four years earlier, the police had called a press conference to show what they took, and now I called one to show me getting it back.

I then paid my $3,000 fine, and I thought this was the end of my legal battles. I promised my fellow activists that I would appear at events or in the media to help them in their battles to change the laws. But my new facility was now up and running and very much in the public eye, and it took almost all my time. I put my plans for the book on hold for that reason, but also because many things were happening on the home front that I will tell you about later.

No legal developments occurred for a few years. Then Alan called. He said my legal battles were not over. The time was right to go back to court, where we would take our case to a new level. We did, and this time, we would serve the ball. This time, our story would rise above the national level. This time, it would be reported all over the world, and would take Canada and the world by surprise.

Chapter 16

Dominatrix Lineup

What is a dominatrix? Who becomes a dominatrix? What do dominatrices look like? Why do they do it? What does it do to them, or for them? What kind of life do they have outside the craft? Do they like what they do for a living? (Do you?) None of these questions have simple answers. You know about me. But what about the twenty-five women I hired as doms or doms-in-training and the many I know in the business? Some of the answers may surprise you.

The stereotypical image of the dominatrix is a woman in a fright wig, a leather corset, and thigh-high boots carrying a whip or riding crop, whipping a man in bondage or having him grovel at her feet. But as we have seen, the dom plays numerous, sometimes complex roles. As I have also explained, the dominatrix's job is to help a man regress to a childhood or feminine state and subconsciously revisit some trauma from childhood, buried unrecognizably beneath layers and decades of memory.

A dominatrix is an actress and a therapist. She helps a man escape from his normal self through play and the invocation of feelings and emotions outside of his normal experience. She follows the client's script, yet at the same time adds to it meaningfully. But again the question arises: who is drawn to this type of activity, and why?

The gals who seek work in this field, like the clients, come from an endless variety of backgrounds. Some were abused as children, some not. Some grew up rich, some poor. Some are educated, some not; some mentally healthy, some not; some tall, some short; some pretty, some ugly; some fat, some thin; most young, but not all. Some are members of visible minorities. Some are religious. Some need the money; some don't. Some do it full time; some don't. Some do it for many years; some do not. Some love doing it; some don't.

One prevailing factor I have always had to deal with is the lure of money. Many of the gals I have known would far rather be a dominatrix than a prostitute, but there is much more money to be made selling sex. Some of the girls I have hired left my employ because I would not allow them to offer sex to clients, even outside my establishments. The fact remains that most men prefer and seem to need straight sex, or find fantasy role-playing too awkward or embarrassing. Plenty of massage parlors offer men sex or at least masturbation by a woman, and escort services allow men to meet women for sex. Look at the yellow pages of the phonebook of any big city, or even smaller ones, and you will see endless ads for escort services and massages by nonregistered masseuses, but very few for services such as mine. Although the backgrounds of doms are highly varied, the common thread running through most of them is that they did not want to be prostitutes. I say most, because a few did both—again, mainly following the money.

Another factor was that most of the gals who were serious about the craft were intrigued by its complexities. For example, they liked learning about costumes, settings, performing, and being adored or feared by men. Not all of them could persevere in the business, but many were attracted to it for these reasons. There was the lure of better money and more interesting work than awaited them as waitresses, maids, or store clerks. Thus, as you will see, many of the gals who were studying for careers in the arts or journalism found their way into my houses. They all had their stories.

Now I'll tell you about some of them and how they fared, but first some preliminary remarks.

I will refer to the doms who were defendants at the trial by their stage names. I will also refer to one of the doms who worked for me downtown by her stage name, because she asked me to do so. I will refer to the others with pseudonyms, such as Mistress L. Just as I respect the privacy of my clients, so, too, do I respect the privacy of my employees, associates, and supporters, unless they explicitly wish otherwise.

The girls I hired were of two types: the professional mistresses and the amateurs. I will refer to the professionals by a pseudonym, such as Mistress

A. I will refer to the amateurs as, for example, Amateur A. The professionals relied on being a dominatrix or submissive as their main or sole source of income. They had spent years learning their craft. They had reputations and loyal clienteles. They were not prostitutes, or at least not supposed to be. The amateurs were hired on the basis that they would have to be trained. They usually did sessions as assistants to the professionals. The clients loved the attention of two women at the same time and willingly paid a slightly higher fee without complaint. Also, the sessions went better, because with a team of two doms, the banter was easier to maintain, with more variety in what the client saw, heard, and felt.

The Amateurs

You already know about Princess, one of the employees at the Bondage Bungalow in Thornhill. She was a journalism student working her way through school. She came from a middle-class South American family, but she had no accent and was totally fluent in English. She had no experience in the field and had never even heard of it. She responded to my ad for mistresses out of curiosity. When I told her what was involved and how much she was likely to earn, she was sold on the job, even after I told her all about the downside: long hours of idleness, cleaning, making and answering phone calls, and so on. She said she was industrious and begged—literally begged—for the job. She brought her homework for the downtime, and she often did it in the mock classroom when she was not busy with her duties. She turned out to be dedicated and a very hard worker indeed, and had the raid not happened, she might have become very skilled and successful in the field. She often stayed over, flopping on a couch, and could be relied upon to oversee overnight clients. She was short and thin, but I have found that for some men, being dominated by a small woman is more enticing than by a large one. She was developing good performance skills and techniques. She could be a submissive in one session and dominant in another. She was an extrovert and could maintain a flow of words. Most men prefer a dom who talks constantly, adding an element of humiliation and intimidation, which of course requires much talking. A greatly skilled dom never finds herself at a loss for words, and such a flow came naturally to Princess—although she also knew when to be silent, which may well be the ultimate verbal skill.

You were also introduced to Mistress Morgan. Her hometown was a small Ontario city several hours' drive from Toronto. She was studying the fine arts at university; she was an accomplished musical soloist and had some acting training. She had a dominating appearance, reveling in her strong physique, and a natural aura of refinement and superiority surrounded her. Her physical strength when spanking a client or tying him into a corset was a real turn-on for many of them. For several weeks, she stayed at the bungalow, and she and Princess did scenes together, with Morgan as dominant and Princess submissive. They were a great team and would have become famous as such if the police had managed to arrest them in session, as the police had planned. Morgan loved flogging men in bondage and interrogating them. She also loved putting men in corsets and straitjackets. She would sometimes serenade them on her musical instrument when they were in bondage and, say, had nipple clamps tormenting them, and then further punish them for not applauding her. A few clients became obsessed with Morgan and saw her repeatedly for the few months she was with me. Morgan did not stay with the craft after the raid, for a variety of reasons. But she told me that if she could have afforded it and her family situation would have been different, she would have loved to make her living that way.

Judy, another defendant, you heard about before. She was the bungalow's receptionist; most of her time was spent answering the phones. Many clients told me that they found her telephone voice chilling and enthralling. She certainly brought them in. But if, when they met her, they realized it was she to whom they had spoken on the phone, they were shocked. She looked like a plump librarian: glasses, no makeup, and the outfit of a mother about to pick her kids up at school. Judy was not into S&M or any of the other activities at the bungalow. But she was proficient at helping in sessions in a limited capacity. She also liked the paperwork, which certainly endeared her to me.

Amateur A was at that time was a married mother of about forty years old. She and her husband first came to the bungalow as clients; they had been having problems in their marriage. She asked me if she could work there, and for a few hours per week, she did so for most of the time I was open. This job was a labor of love for her, and sometimes she would come over when clients asked for her specifically. In makeup, she looked quite refined. She specialized in bondage, discipline, and humiliation. She did not like to work with cross-dressers or infantiles. Often clients did not specify what type of bondage and discipline they wanted, so she would guide them into her preferred script, which seemed to satisfy most of them. She liked to put her clients' hands and feet into chains, whip them, and order them to crawl, kiss her feet, and beg for mercy, although she was never too severe. She would do that for almost an hour, yet the clients never seemed to mind.

Amateur B was a very attractive natural blonde who kept her hair short, which suited her. She was quiet and not a natural performer, but I hired her as a favor to someone I knew. Because she was between jobs, she needed the money and was willing to work with me. She did not like being a dominatrix and didn't even like to be referred to as one, but she had the look. The clients were attracted to her at first, of course. She looked great in a rubber corset and thigh-high boots with spiked heels, but her performance skills were poor, and she was not a great learner. As I said, she did not enjoy what she did, and despite her efforts to hide that fact, it was not lost on the clients. She was only with me a couple of months and has never since worked as a dom, as far as I know.

I had a few amateurs working for me when I reopened in downtown Toronto. Amateur C was about twenty. I took her in off the streets. She was pure potential but couldn't get her life together. She dressed in punk goth clothes but had a great natural look, with long, blonde hair and a great figure. She only needed to apply a bit of makeup, do something with her hair, and wear even every-day clothes, and she would have been a knockout. She was always late for work and even kept clients waiting while she changed for her sessions. She usually wore a tartan schoolgirl uniform for the clients and played the part of a naughty schoolgirl. She was not a prostitute when away from me. She was drug-free. She was enrolled at a local community college and was an aspiring poet, artist, songwriter, and dominatrix. However, she was weak on the aspiration part. Wealthy clients asked for her. She had great verbal and acting skills and, when assisting a pro, was very effective. She could even handle some sessions on her own and be effective as a dominant or submissive. But the potential of most of her talents was never fully realized. The pros and the clients eventually couldn't handle her, and I had to let this diamond in the rough go.

Amateur D was more disciplined. She was a tall, slender girl in her early twenties with long, blonde hair. She wore glasses and had the look of an intimidating librarian. She was quiet and reserved on the outside, but a real tiger in the dungeon. She loved to learn and experiment, and the pros liked working with her. She looked great in leather and other fetish wear. She loved dominating men and projected that love while in session, which is so important to the submissive. She worked for me part time while she did two other things. One was studying journalism at a local community college. She was also a newscaster, doing the naked news on a cable television station. It was a joy to have her, and when I closed, we were both very sad our time together had to end. I have lost touch with her, but I have no doubt that success is in her future in whatever direction she takes.

Amateur E was a university student who also had a part-time job in a retail store. She generally worked for me about two evenings a week and was always at our Saturday-night fetish parties. She was a blonde of Scandinavian background with a robust figure. Her own fetish was corsets, and she loved being put into them or putting cross-dressers in them. She loved the sissy-maid side of the business but was very eager to learn all aspects of the dominatrix trade. She was also a switch, meaning she would also play the submissive. She was one of those rare gals who genuinely enjoyed all the roles she played. When I closed, she moved on to other houses and continues to be a part-time dominatrix. She has blossomed into the role and has a loyal following of regular clients, but when I told her I was closing, she said she was losing a family.

Amateur F was a friend of E. She was from fortunate family circumstances, so her work for me was out of a genuine desire to learn the trade. She could have been a model. She was of Mediterranean extraction, and tall, with exquisite, bewitching features and long, dark hair. She was a student of graphic arts, very much drawn to the fashion aspect of the dominatrix trade. She had a limited role in the dungeon: a strict dom who acted like a mannequin, giving the submissive the constant impression she was disgusted and impatient with him. This was a big part of many clients' fantasies: a superior and impatient dominatrix who seems to genuinely want their slave to suffer. She was the perfect assistant to the pros. She had a great fetish wardrobe of her own that she loved to wear and show off.

Amateur G was a beautiful little redhead of about thirty who couldn't have weighed more than one hundred pounds soaking wet. She loved to be tied up and spanked by women. She was truly a submissive lesbian and assisted the pros in their sessions acting as a naughty schoolgirl. It was critical to her that her private life was protected, so she did not allow herself to be photographed, because she had another job as an office executive at a popular conservative magazine. A raid on the house might have ruined her career, but she couldn't stay away: prim and proper by day, naughty by night.

Amateurs H and I were stylists by trade, but wanted to make more money more quickly. They were both gorgeous. Both were perfectly proportioned. H was blonde, and I had straight black hair. They were well-spoken and knew how to dress and make the most of their looks. I played a big role at my second fund-raiser and asked the legal panel questions that showed she was intelligent as well as articulate. She was committed to my legal fight and offered to help in any way, although there was little to be done at that time. H and I worked part time as a team. They were very good at role-playing, and I considered giving them more time, but they were not interested. I soon found out why. I noticed an ad in the escorts section of the local paper that clearly identified them. They advertised for outcalls as a duo, which was one way to ensure safety. They had been taking calls at my place and even when in session with clients. One client finally told me they were also offering him sex outside of my place. With all I had been through, I had to let them go. They were following the money first and foremost.

The Professionals

One of the interesting things about the pros is that they tended to be specialists, with the exception of Mistress A, who was a professional actress. Mistress B was a specialist in adult babies. Mistresses C and D were male cross-dressers. Mistresses E and F were pure submissives. The others were truly dominant—what the average person would expect a dominatrix to act like.

Specialist Pros

Mistress A worked part time, but I consider her a specialist professional because she actually was a professional actress. She was a tall, slender blonde in her midtwenties. She would engage in any role a client wished, and she revelled in exhibiting her creativity and performance skills to truly become the person the client had paid to be with. She loved devising elaborate scripts, which she would suggest to clients when interviewing them and finding out what their general interests were. She was very popular with clients, who asked for her again and again. However, her availability was almost always a problem. She was in shows most nights, so she had to restrict her sessions at my house to afternoons. She was with me most of the time my downtown house was at full capacity. I learned a lot from her.

Mistress B was only with me for the last three months that I was open. She was a tall, fat, busty woman in her late thirties. She was a specialist in adult babies. She had an extensive Victorian wardrobe, wore her hair in a bun, and played the dominant mother role superbly. She had her own website and worked out of her home. I regret that I didn't get to know her better.

Mistress C was a transvestite. He was a middle-aged man with a private income who indulged his desire to playact as a woman full time. He knew more about cross-dressing than I did. He was raised on a plantation in the southern United States, which he inherited and sold when he retired in his thirties. He donated clothes to my business and was always on hand to work with the cross-dressers who came to me, yet refused to accept payment. He performed at my fund-raisers. He was a big hit at our fetish parties, too. He enjoyed hanging out at my establishment, with my blessing. He taught the novices much about the trade, and he loved sitting around with the girls. I don't think I ever saw him dressed as a man, or even without a wig and makeup. He cried when I told him I was closing.

Mistress D was also a transvestite—a Jane Mansfield look-alike. He was only in my employ for a short time. He was transgendered, meaning he wanted to become a woman. He was taking hormones as a step toward a sex-change operation. Interestingly enough, he loved to perform in gay bars. However, he was very opinionated and mouthy, and was not always welcomed where he went. Very often cross-dressers asked for him the way they asked for Mistress C. He had a lot of issues.

Mistress E was a pure submissive who wouldn't even participate in sessions where she was to assist the pros by being dominant. She was in her early twenties, of medium height, a bit busty, and a bit plump. She was university educated and came from a solid middle-class family. She had a great attitude, was a hard worker, and was eager to learn and to help in any way she could.

She was a great hit at fetish parties, which she would spend in restraints and fetish clothing. She loved to have some of the other girls dominate her when there were not clients for her. They liked her very much and so accommodated her, and when the dungeon was available I allowed them to play. She couldn't get enough time in bondage and loved to be tickled, be spanked, and have her nipples tortured. She was a genuine player. She has remained in the business to this day, advertising as a submissive.

Mistress F was also a pure submissive. She had an extreme fetish for bondage and loved to be tied up or kept in a straitjacket for hours on end. She had her own collection of straitjackets and restraints given to her by a client who had gotten them from an old mental hospital. She kept some of her equipment at my place. She loved to have clients, men or women, torture her while she was restrained. She loved to scream, so she had to have a gag placed in her mouth—a safe gag, of course. It was pleasing to see such enthusiasm for her craft, which she practiced on her own time with friends as well. She is still in the business today.

Classic Pros

Mistress G was an established dominatrix from downtown Toronto who worked part time at my bungalow in Thornhill for a few weeks. She was the only pro I had there, aside from myself. She worked at a couple of dungeons downtown part time as well, and at one time had her own. She practiced her specialty, heavy S&M, with some of her established clients when they came to my place. Heavy S&M means that she whipped hard, spanked hard, applied nipple clamps, administered electric shocks, and cut clients to draw blood. I did not allow her to do most of what she did downtown at my bungalow, even if the clients requested it. The problem with her was that even though she agreed to my terms, she was still too rough with some clients—too genuinely dominant and sadistic. I had hired her despite her reputation in the S&M community for unnecessary roughness. I had to let her go or run the risk of complaints of assault.

I ended up training Mistress H for her next employer. She was with me for the last six months I was open. She was in her late twenties and married to a man who made a very good living. They were both very active on the fetish scene. She was short and thin, an eager learner, a good listener, and very much liked by the other girls. She modeled at my second fund-raiser, which was well before she came to work for me. She had just lost her regular job, and she and her husband agreed that she should try being a dominatrix. In fact, she told me he was thrilled with the idea of her dominating other men as well. This is not uncommon among submissive men—the fantasy, or reality, of knowing that they are just one of the victims of a cruel woman. As a dom, she did a range of sessions, but specialized in bondage and discipline. She loved to dress in leather and boots. Many submissive men actually prefer a small dom. I think this is because being helpless for a small woman increases the element of humiliation, which is part of what these men are seeking.

Mistress I had a European accent, which many men found irresistible. She did not work for me. She rented my dungeon and had her own small but loyal clientele. She was tall and thin, but muscular: the perfect natural physique for a classic dominatrix. In her wig, makeup, full leather, and boots with heels, she was stunning. Her clients brought her gifts because she required them to. She said they also tipped her well. She was in her midthirties, with a daughter just beginning school, so she had to work in the afternoons and would then pick her daughter up from school. She had a babysitter who could start on short notice and whom she paid very well, so she managed to schedule some evening and weekend work as well. Mistress I was an expert in hardware: she knew how to use chains, harnesses, straitjackets, restraining benches, and so forth to their maximum effect while maintaining the client's safety. When I closed, I lost touch with her. I have not seen any ads that I can say identify her. If she has left the business, it is a huge loss for the business and the art.

I met Mistress J through The Geek, who was the webmaster for both of us. She was a college graduate and had worked in an administrative capacity on and off. She was about thirty when she worked for me. She also worked on an occasional basis at other houses and did some outcalls and saw some clients in her home, where she had a small dungeon. She generally worked for me a couple of times a week during the time I fully occupied the house in Toronto. She was the total pro, but was not willing to take the risk and responsibility of running a dungeon full-time. She could do everything I could do and just as well—sometimes even better. She could be counted on to run my place when I had to be away. She was well liked by the girls, and they respected her authority when she was in charge. She ran fetish nights in clubs. She was a true dominant. Her own preference was hard-core S&M, especially flogging and caning. This type of thing cannot be entrusted to amateurs. She knew that I set limits even below the limits of some client requests—that is, no serious injuries, and leaving no marks on anyone other than long-established clients. A real pro, she worked within the guidelines I set.

Finally Contessa Cintra, a very tall and heavily built woman with longish blonde hair. She was absolutely stunning in leather or fetish wear, of which she had a large collection. People often remark on her resemblance to Marilyn Monroe. She was about thirty when she came to work for me downtown, and she was a sensation. She was an intimidating presence and a very strict dominatrix. She used her size and strength to great effect and loved to wrestle with clients. Some smaller men love to be outwrestled by a powerful woman. She loved to administer heavy, but safe, punishment and to humiliate those who submitted to her. She was also a great colleague and a great role model for the younger girls in every respect. She was honest, punctual, loyal, and hardworking. She was also willing to teach, and the amateurs who assisted her in sessions or watched her sessions learned from the best. She was also a well-known stage performer, and her acts included singing and doing Marilyn Monroe impersonations. She was the first inductee into the Canadian Burlesque Hall of Fame. She began as a burlesque performer, and when she sported an S&M look onstage, she got the strongest audience responses. She gradually worked more and more as a dominatrix and to this day combines three vocations: dominatrix, burlesque performer, and maker and distributor of antique and fetish clothing.

So there are most of the dominatrices who worked for me. Once again, I cannot begin to tell you how personable most of them were or how much most of us liked each other. Nor can I begin to tell you about the camaraderie in both my houses. There were, of course, conflicts and disagreements. Some of the younger ones in particular had to learn about accepting responsibility and about the value of money and loyalty. But that is to be expected from college students just venturing into the work world. They have to mature and gain experience; they need to realize that they have a lot to learn. They have to come to a job for more than just its enjoyable aspects; they need to be stimulated by the challenges posed by the negative aspects of the job. They have to learn how to be considerate of others. This is true of almost any job, but for a dominatrix, it is just the start. It is one of the most awkward and challenging occupations you can imagine: nobody deals with hurt feelings the way the dominatrix does.

You may have been wondering, and I posed the question earlier: what effect does being a dominatrix have on a woman's life? In my experience, almost none, at least in the case of the amateurs. Whom they date, whom they marry, whether they have children, and how they act with their partners in the bedroom: none of these factors are usually changed by the experience of being a dominatrix.

That is sometimes not the case, however, for the professionals. Many were never meant for a conventional life. Their work is their life. I call them lifestyle dominatrices. They don't want a husband or children. Most of them like being obsessively and sexually dominant (though a few like being submissive) in their private lives as well. However, many professionals can keep their personal and professional lives separate, and the difference between their personas off the job versus on the job is a big surprise to people who get to know them. "I can't believe how normal she is" is a common refrain.

Finally, there is me. What happened after I closed my house brought big changes in my lifestyle, and not just because of my declining health. Remember, I was a mother. Then I became a grandmother.

Chapter 17

STAYING ALIVE

Finally, I can bring you up to date on my private life during the time I operated the houses and fought these legal battles. Let's start with my daughter.

Janet

My daughter and I were reunited in stages, beginning in 1999 when she came to Toronto and then when she moved in with me in 2001. Whatever my struggles were, whether it was getting sober or running the Bondage Bungalow, my main motivation was my daughter. I didn't really raise her and only got to see her growing up when I was able to visit her. You may recall that I had left her in foster homes under the supervision of the Children's Aid Society, visiting and sending money as my circumstances allowed. When I was raided in Windsor, she was placed in a foster home in Windsor, one of three kids. The other two were their natural children. They got a government allowance for taking care of her, and what I gave them was on the sly. I did everything I could to send money to and make it worthwhile for the family who were her guardians to do well by her. There were times when I could think of no other reason to live.

At this point, I should give my daughter a name, or at least a pseudonym. She must make a life, and it should be, if she wishes, outside the shadow of my reputation. I'll call her Janet. In 1999, when she was sixteen, she was thrown out of the home. She was going through a period of teenage rebellion, and her guardians were not equipped to cope with both her and the other two children. In addition, I was not sending them as much money as I had when I was running my business. I was barely surviving on my own.

I had no place for her to stay. I could not afford to move back to Windsor and would have no possessions and no prospects when I got there. Janet was too inexperienced to make it on her own. I had no money to send her. What was I to do? The answer came from the usual source: The Dozen. I believe they saved her life. Those on board did everything that was needed, or that I could have asked.

Camilla

One of the women who had worked on my matters with one of the lawyers had remained in touch with me after the case had been decided. She is number eleven of The Dozen. I will call her Camilla. Camilla came from a secure background. After a failed marriage, she led the normal life of a single working woman with a good career. In addition to her contributions to my legal battle, she provided support to me personally as someone I could talk to and trust. She had met Janet during one of Janet's few visits to Toronto, and Camilla became a second mother to Janet. When Camilla heard what was going on in Windsor, she went there with Scott and spent an entire day gathering Janet and her belongings and arranging Janet's transfer to a school in Toronto. That same day, they brought Janet to Toronto and moved her into the spare room of Camilla's home. Janet was in the middle of high school at that time, and Camilla made it clear she expected Janet to finish high school. Janet was in school the next week. Of course, Scott pulled his wallet out as soon as he heard what was happening.

Miracle of miracles! I had had to give up my child. Then I had found out my child was in trouble, and there was nothing I could do. Then almost all was made right. I say "almost all" because for all to be made right, I would have had to rescue Janet and take her home myself. But at the time she was rescued, my notoriety was already a problem for her in Windsor. Just imagine how bad I felt just before Camilla intervened.

I wish I could tell you more about Camilla. What she has done for me and my daughter is only the tip of an iceberg of goodness. I again lament the need to protect privacy. I would hold this woman up to the world as a role model. She is the sister I always wanted, in addition to being a second mother to Janet. My baby was safe.

Janet had not attended a school with high standards in Windsor and did not do well in her Toronto school. But she was very popular with both the girls and boys, and this did much to raise her esteem and confidence. Like any teenager, she was at times a trial to Camilla, but Camilla said it had always been her wish to have a daughter. Janet also came to visit me regularly, and I visited her at Camilla's. So overall, it was a happy time for all three of us.

About two and a half years later, the situation changed. Camilla's mother, who was elderly and in rapidly declining health, needed Camilla to move in with her. She said she would be delighted to have Janet as well, which would mean more care for Camilla's mother and less pressure on Camilla. It was a house with plenty of room, and over a period of about six months, the house was cleared out to make room for Janet and Camilla.

However, when moving day arrived, Janet surprised us all, declaring her intention to drop out of school and move in with some friends. She did not want to leave her new neighborhood and friends and was spooked by the idea of living with a very old person. We had no time to debate this last-minute decision. Camilla was hurt, but just told her mother that Janet needed to stay in the old neighborhood, which was at the opposite end of Toronto, to work and finish school. Camilla was also going through some health issues and was grateful to get the move over with, rest, and unpack, move in gradually and start looking after her mother. Remember that Camilla was working full time. These competing pressures made it easier to resist dwelling on Janet's rapid decision not to accompany her. Also, having a teenager there might have proved stressful to the elderly lady. Camilla's mother was moved to a nursing home two years after Camilla moved in, and about a year after that, her Alzheimer's disease had progressed to the point where she no longer even recognized Camilla. She died a few years later, and in the final, terrible crisis, Camilla was able to call upon Janet to be at the hospital for days at a time to help.

Reunited

I was gradually acquiring space in my second facility, so Janet was able to move in with me in 2001. We were finally reunited! For a time, we operated the facility together, and I gradually trained her in the business. She proved to be a very good dominatrix, especially in the dungeon, able to bring considerable focus to the work. Also, she only worked as an assistant to me or another professional mistress when in session, at least at first, so her role was limited and she learned gradually, which is the way to do it. She looked great in the dom costumes. She had a youthful, athletic figure perfect for a dom of her height—meaning not too thin, yet not what someone would call fat.

While Janet made progress in the dungeon, she was difficult otherwise. Part of it was the usual rebellion against parental authority. She was generally popular with the other girls, but she did not have a good work ethic and was often moody. I will certainly admit that my skills as a mother to a teenage daughter in an awkward setting had something to do with it. There was also the lack of a stable, loving home and normal family in which to grow up. I think we all did the best we could, but I just wish we had been able to do better.

You may be wondering how I felt about bringing my daughter into the business. At the time, I asked myself the same question. If your daughter is considering a career as a dominatrix, or you are considering it for her, I think the following questions are key: What is she giving up? What is she risking? What is she gaining? In the case of my daughter, as with the many other fine young women I have told you about, she is making money. Again, follow the money; money talks. If, on the side, a young woman can double the weekly income from her full-time job by working an additional four hours doing something that intrigues her, why not? What does she lose? Maybe the four hours and other time surrounding it for travel and waiting around. Does she lose her dignity? No; quite the opposite. Is she at risk? Less than working in a factory or going into the military. Rarely has a dom been assaulted by a client. What risk is there of disease? None, since no sex occurs. I think you get the idea. I think you might also consider that doms are probably subject to less sexual harassment than secretaries.

(Then there is the parallel question of whether your daughter should become a prostitute and sell sex. As you will see later in this book, the arguments are much more complicated in that arena, but I will just say at this point that the potential risks and rewards are elevated if the present archaic laws are allowed to remain in place. That being said, girls are having sex all over the place anyway. They should not be penalized if they are paid for it and are taking measures for their health and safety).

One of the advantages of being a dominatrix is that you come into contact with rich and cultivated men. Stories circulate of men falling in love with their doms, and when their means permit it, they may even want to marry their doms, or keep them in luxury or do other things for them. (Later on, I will tell you about the final member of The Dozen, who, to some extent, was just such a man for me.) Janet met such a man. Her trade as a dominatrix made her very popular with the guys she met at parties and rock concerts. She had a couple of boyfriends in the time she was living with me. Then she met a South American musician whom I will call Ricardo. She was smitten with him, and vice versa. Interestingly, he was not at all interested in her as a dom. In fact, he was mildly disapproving of what I did. In his home country, an establishment such as mine was unheard of. Ricardo had an accent, but his English was quite good. He had inherited money, so he could travel the world and perform and study music. This kind of guy would be attractive to most young women, don't you think? He took Janet to South America to meet his established and fairly conservative family. Not long after that, he took her for another visit to South America, where they were married. So my daughter and I were separated again, just before I closed the bondage hotel.

My Health Fails

About a year before I closed the bondage hotel, which closed in the spring of 2002, I was clearly in declining health and could ignore the symptoms no longer, although I could still function. I had had health issues before, due very much to a hard life and my own lack of personal responsibility. I had been a sickly child, born anemic, and had been hospitalized for malnutrition twice before my second birthday. A bout of the mumps almost killed me. I suffered from heatstroke as a child and would often pass out where I stood. In grade school, my gym teacher pointed out that my hips were displaced and that I needed corrective shoes, which I did not get, so the condition was never corrected. And, of course, my adoptive mother beat me. I was always getting whipped by the belt or hit over the head and across the body. She knocked me off my feet once with a soup ladle, and my ears rang for a week. For years I thought she would kill me any moment in a fit of rage. In my teens, I underwent a knee operation for a bone disease and had to wear a cast for several weeks. It was in the winter and, as luck would have it, my crutches slipped from under me, and I took a ghastly fall down a flight of icy concrete stairs in my cast, enduring more pain and suffering than I had originally bargained for.

As a teenager, I also suffered from horrible periods and PMS. I just wasn't myself at these times, so they decided to put me on the Pill. One day, I when I was angry and depressed, I swallowed two packages of birth-control pills. Nothing happened at the time, but it may be related to the fact that later in life I had problems with my reproductive organs.

I was a teenage drug addict and alcoholic prostitute by the time I was seventeen, when I contracted my first venereal disease, followed by more later. For two years, I did a lot of cocaine. I knew about condoms but often had sex without them. AIDS was not a widely known risk at that time. I was injecting drugs intravenously and sharing needles. One time I had an appendicitis attack that was mistaken for VD by an extremely judgmental nurse. Lucky for me, an ER doctor caught it just in time. As far as the nurse was concerned, I could lie there moaning in agony.

Another time, I had pelvic inflammatory disease, which can be fatal. I was admitted into the emergency room with toxic shock syndrome. Finally, they found out what was actually wrong, and I spent a week at death's door on intravenous antibiotics. One time a guy kicked me in the back with a steel-toed boot, and I was too strung out on drugs and alcohol to bother with an X-ray, so the broken bones didn't heal properly. Late nights in the bar drinking and smoking my brains out didn't help, either. I could go on, but I think you get the idea. My life as a prostitute and the crowds I hung out with combined into a prescription for disaster.

My health was a ticking time bomb. It was almost a miracle the bomb didn't go off more often or more severely. By rights I should have been dead long before 2001, when my symptoms became too severe to ignore. Late that year, my doctor sent me to a couple of specialists. Many tests were run, and early in 2002 I was diagnosed with four major health problems.

I had hepatitis A, B and C. I still have hepatitis C. The first two strains of hepatitis, A and B, were cured by a series of injections. Hepatitis C, on the other hand, is a killer—a slow killer. Seldom cured, it is a virus that is most commonly transmitted via blood through sharing or using infected needles, or by blood transfusions with tainted blood. In Canada there was a major class-action lawsuit against the Red Cross by people with hepatitis C who could demonstrate they had received transfusions with tainted blood. Millions of dollars were paid out to these people, whose lives had been shortened. I was told, however, that it was pointless for me to file a claim, because I had accumulated so many other risk factors in the 1980s, when the bad donated blood had been given in transfusions.

Hepatitis C scars the liver gradually. Twenty, thirty, forty, or even fifty years can pass before the hepatitis causes liver cancer. Until then the liver is called cirrhotic. In 2002 I was already at the highest level of cirrhosis, level four. Remarkably, since then, my tests have shown that the disease has not progressed. Unfortunately, the scarring never heals. The cure for hepatitis C is chemotherapy with interferon and similar drugs, but you have to have the right genotype for it to be effective. I don't have the right genotype, but nonetheless underwent three rounds of chemotherapy from 2002 to 2007. I had to lose sixty pounds to be eligible for the treatments. They did not cure my hepatitis C, but they did mean much suffering from the nausea and exhaustion that often accompanies chemotherapy, and they did retard the progress of the virus somewhat. New treatments are always under development, and I am hopeful, but under no illusions. It is probably too late. There are times when I am frightened.

I also had and have spinal issues: specifically, spinal stenosis and degenerative disc disease. Stenosis means degeneration of the spine, which narrows the nerve channels, causing numbness in the legs and pain—sometimes great pain—in the lower spine. Degenerative disc disease is an uneven deterioration of the spinal discs beyond what most people with routine back pain experience.

As if that weren't enough, I also suffer from fibromyalgia. I have had it since early in life, but of course with age, it gets worse. The disease may have as many as eighty symptoms, the most common of which include aching, burning, touch sensitivity, and bruiselike swelling. The moving parts of the body are the areas most likely to be impacted.

With all these issues, I cannot take conventional painkillers or herbal remedies. In the first place, my liver specialist forbids them, and alcohol as well. Second, as a former drug addict, I am aware of how dangerously addictive painkillers can be. Fortunately, I am a licensed medical marijuana user, under the supervision of my doctor and Professor Young, who fought so valiantly for government permission to use medical marijuana. Some days I can barely move. Nonetheless it is important that I go to a local community center with a swimming pool and do stretching exercises in the water as often as I can, along with daily stretching and strengthening exercises at home. I try very hard to keep my weight down for both the liver and back issues. I have learned to live with a lot of pain.

Almost all my life, I have suffered pain and indignity. I wonder what it is like to live free from worry and pain. How ironic it is that I became a celebrity by inflicting pain and humiliation for money.

Moving On

After I closed my facility, I moved in with three trusted clients who offered to help support me and role play as my slaves. Two of them, Cathy Maid and Prissy, were residents of the bondage hotel. The other was a client who had mentioned to me that he was looking for a place to live. We moved from downtown to lower midtown, in a section of Toronto called the Annex. The rent was a bit high, but it was manageable, because the location was convenient to shopping and other amenities, so no car was needed, and because four of us shared the rent. For the two years of the lease, we lived there quietly. The guys got on well. We fixed up the basement as a minidungeon. Despite my poor health, I still did sessions with the boys. They knew how tough it was for me, so they asked for very little of my time and offered to do anything for me. Other members of The Dozen also provided any help requested. Scott, of course, was there with his checkbook, as were Camilla and Albert. Here I was, at the bottom of my fortunes, broke, sick, and without prospects, and they were always there for me. After a time, I also received welfare, since I was unable to work, so I no longer depended on the charity of friends. I maintained my website, but the public no longer showed much interest in me.

Scott came by weekly to continue work on the book, and by 2006, I thought I might want to finish and publish it.

I Become a Grandmother

Meanwhile Janet and Ricardo, who had settled in his family's home in South America in 2001, came back to Toronto late in 2002 for a prolonged visit. Janet was pregnant, and they wanted to have their baby in Canada, so that it would be a Canadian citizen and born in a good hospital. Good medical care for a newborn, especially if there were any complications, was hard to get in the area where they lived in South America. The plan was to go back there when the baby's health was assured and he or she was a few months old. Ricardo found a modest apartment for the stay.

A couple of months later, I, along with Camilla, Scott, and a friend of the young couple, spent most of the night in the waiting room in the downtown Toronto hospital. Finally, at just after four in the morning, a boy was born without complications. At first I was relieved of the fear of a difficult birth or the baby being in ill health, although there was no unusual likelihood of any of these. Then my emotions changed to elation. It finally hit me that I was a grandmother! I knew it was not a good time or the best circumstances for the baby to come along, but on the whole, it was great night for us all. For a few months, Janet, Ricardo, and their son were a happy, if poor, family. Ricardo did not have a permit but had some work, both performing music and doing manual labor. As I have mentioned, he had some family money, and he and Janet were careful with their spending. He was not worried about being deported, since they were planning to return to South America anyway.

Ricardo left a few weeks before Janet and the baby; they moved in with me until it was time for them to rejoin Ricardo. So, for a few precious weeks, I had my child and grandchild and nothing to do but look after the baby while my daughter shopped for groceries, did the laundry, and arranged for their trip to South America. How I wished those weeks could have gone on forever. Now not only was my daughter about to leave, again, but my only grandchild as well. I did not even know if I would live to see them again. After they left, I was very sad for some time, but Janet's e-mails telling about how good things were in her new homeland made me very happy. A friend of Janet and Ricardo's from near Toronto visited his family in South America once a year. She told me details of their life, which helped to reassure me. It seemed things were going well for them.

Another Move

Early in 2006, I moved again. Prissy had left in 2005; the place was too costly for the three of us, and I didn't want to advertise for another roommate. So I took another step back and down. I was going to lose my little dungeon in the basement. I dismantled the equipment, which was then put into storage by a loyal client with a crawlspace in his basement. We rented the basement of a two-story house converted to a three-bedroom apartment on the top floor, an office on the main floor, and a two-bedroom apartment in the basement. We moved into the basement to save on rent. I slept in one of the bedrooms, and one of the guys had a bedroom as well. Cathy Maid did not in the least mind sleeping on the couch. We had to go to sleep early each night, because Cathy Maid had a job in food service, for which he would leave at four a.m. five mornings a week. So the other guy and I went to our rooms at nine each evening. During the days, when I did not have doctor appointments or when I was not too sick to go out, I went to the community center for the swimming and the exercise room.

Legally Disabled

In 2005 I had applied for disability benefits. The experience was a real eye-opener. Both the federal and provincial governments turned me down, because I was, according to them, fit to work. This angered me, because I had observed people in much better condition than me receiving CPP (Canada Pension Plan) disability benefits and working as well. I saw no hope of reversing the decision, but my accountant, advised me never to assume anything. With his help, I sent a short letter to a federal tribunal requesting permission to appeal the decision.

Permission to appeal was granted. The accountant asked someone he knew who had experience in this sort of thing, and whom I will call Walter, to represent me in the matter. The appeal tribunal office was very accommodating. They paid all our expenses, including a generous stipend for my meals for that day. My appeal was heard in a hotel near the airport. Walter made a lengthy presentation, with exhibits, to the panel of three. Then he and I answered numerous questions. From the way they looked at me, I suspected the panel may have recognized me from my publicity of a few years before, but they never indicated it. Walter pointed out case precedents and explained in great detail why I could not do various types of work. He pointed out that I was receiving welfare and provincial disability support payments. Then the panel's CPP representative said that the disability unit of the CPP maintained its position that I was able to "do some work." Surprisingly, the panel did not seem taken aback at his lack of a presentation or a response to Walter's. I was told that the decision would be sent to me in about two months.

I won the appeal. The panel was emphatic that I was disabled. Everyone is capable of doing some kind of work, of course, under the right circumstances, but the issue was whether I could support myself. They said I could not. This was, I suppose, another legal victory for me—and I hadn't had many to date. The CPP could have appealed the panel's decision, but they didn't. As it turned out, a bit of a scandal arose over the improper denial of CPP benefits to people, and it was reported in the national media about a year after my appeal. I am told that many years before, the CPP had been in trouble for giving disability pensions too liberally. That must be why the CPP representative at the hearing said so little and why that did not surprise the panel. My appeal was part of a bigger problem.

I only qualified for the minimum pension, because I had only paid into the plan for a few years before I had to stop working. One condition of the pension was that I was allowed to earn $4,000 without being penalized. The pension also automatically qualified me to receive a "top-up" from the provincial plan—the Ontario Disability Support Plan (ODSP). In a complicated system designed to encourage recipients to work, I was supposed to report my earnings; that amount would then be "clawed back" (subtracted) from my next check, but restored to the subsequent check, along with an increase in payment.

So, since 2006, I have had a livable income, at least enough to pay my share of the rent and feed myself. This is still the case as I write these words. I have been doing some bookkeeping of sorts and some phone work for a business in the neighborhood, from home. As a dominatrix, I play with the odd loyal old client, but they know I am not well, and they do not ask for much of my time. I have also taken up painting. Most of my paintings are of outdoor scenes, flower arrangements, and animals. My daughter also has a flair for art, so maybe it's something she inherited from me. Some of the people who have seen my paintings have expressed surprise that I didn't paint S&M scenes. It had never occurred to me to do so. I also took up photography, and again, the outdoors proved to be the target of my art. I also love to sing and will sometimes do a medley of songs for friends.

The Hurricane

But back to 2006, when word came of a hurricane in South America. Hardest hit was the region where my daughter and her new family lived. I was almost frantic with worry; about two days passed before we got word that they were safe. I was also worried that the region would erupt in violence, which in fact happened later.

Janet had written to me that business of all types was a bit slow there and that, despite a very low cost of living, they were having trouble making ends meet. Her mother-in-law was ill, and some decisions had to be made. I knew that by sending some Canadian dollars down there, I could help them get by, but their long-term prospects would never improve. The decision was made for Janet and the child to return to Canada, with its free schools and medical care. Also, for a mother with a child, welfare was available. Both mother and child were, of course, Canadian citizens, but Janet's husband, Ricardo, was not, so he would have to get a work permit to come to Canada. Also, his mother needed him. So Janet returned with only her son. Basically, her marriage was over.

She moved in with us in the basement apartment. Fortunately it was a large basement apartment. My two roommates accepted this temporary arrangement. For a few months, while Janet looked for a job and an apartment, I was a babysitter. At first the boy spoke no English, but he learned. In fact he no longer speaks or understands much of his first language. A church ran a day-care center just down the street; each day I would take him there for preschool and pick him up later if Janet was out. Except for the crowding, it was a happy household. Everyone loved the boy, and Janet was, of course, well-liked by the guys, despite being twenty years or so younger than they were. Of course, my schedule left me no chance to work on my book. My little bit of phone work, paperwork for the business, and my family duties took most of my energy. Where do kids find all *their* energy?

Michelle

Also in 2006, I got a call from an older gentleman who said he had always wanted to meet me and engage my services. I told him I was no longer in business, but when he told me his story, I told him to visit me, with no fee. He was a very successful retired corporate executive, the former CEO of the Canadian division of a multinational corporation, the name of which you would almost certainly recognize. He had been retired for several years. Recently he had had to put his wife in a nursing home because she was suffering from Alzheimer's disease. He hired companions to sit with her during the day, and he visited almost daily, but she no longer recognized him and could barely even speak anymore. He had children, but they had moved away.

So he was alone, and he told me there was now no longer any reason for him not to live out his fantasies. So we struck a bargain that still holds today. He takes me up to his summer cottage north of Toronto for long weekends when we both can get away. About once a week, he takes me to his house, where I do my laundry. On the way home, he takes me to the supermarket. When we are in his home or cottage, I am his dominatrix. I have his preferred equipment at his home, and we take it with us when we go to the cottage. His slave name is Michelle; I dress him in women's clothing and punish him. Of course, his age is making itself shown, so I am never too severe, but he can take a lot of pain. Nonetheless, I am careful.

We also play during our long weekends at his cottage. I get to go for what, for me, are long walks when the day is nice and I am up to it. Sometimes I swim in the lake a bit; sometimes we cook on the barbecue or have a small bonfire—great treats for me, when you consider how I live and have lived. I have met some of his neighbors; if any of them recognized me, they did not let on. He tells them that I accompany him to do some of the driving, which I really don't, and to do chores around the cottage and generally ensure he does not strain himself. He describes me as if I were his servant. If only they could see what goes on behind closed doors!

Obviously, his driving me to the grocery store and the laundromat has been a great help. He has also been helpful sharing his executive experience with Scott, advising him on how to advise me. He has reviewed the drafts of this book and made some very perceptive comments. And he has given me an opportunity to be a dominatrix again, which of course I enjoy. As I have said before, I think it is always so wonderful when men can safely act out their fantasies without being persecuted for doing so. Think of all the barriers that had been in his way before: a wife and children, a demanding career, community obligations, and so forth. He could have been blackmailed or arrested as a found-in at a bawdy house, and it would have been devastating if his wife or children even knew he was acting out S&M or cross-dressing fantasies. Remember as well that, say, thirty years ago, few if any practicing dominatrices were available. Prostitutes were not equipped for the kind of role-playing he sought. It is therefore with pleasure that I tell you that Michelle is number twelve of The Dozen.

Janet on Her Own

Early in 2007, I was a babysitting grandma most of the time, doing my exercises and resting to cope with my pain and stiffness. And, of course, some weekends Michelle took me up to his cottage. In time Janet found a job and a place and moved away. Her boy is in school now, and Janet is doing the single-mother thing—not an easy job, but it is great to see how she has matured. She and her son still visit me almost every weekend, and he often sleeps over with his grandma. One day, my grandson, you will read this memoir, and if I am not around when that time comes, I want you to know that my time with you and being together again with your mother have been more important to me than anything in the world. Wishes sometimes come true.

Aunty

One day Scott came to me with a request for help. I told him that I would help him in any way I could; I owed him so much.

Scott was his ninety-year-old great aunt's guardian, and he had just moved her into a nursing home. He told me he could afford little of the help she badly needed beyond standard care. She was blind, partially deaf, and totally nonambulatory. He knew that my time was fairly flexible, so he asked if I would sit with her for a few hours a couple of times a week as a companion and help her with things like getting her a drink, taking her for walks in her wheelchair, and helping her make phone calls. He told me that in all likelihood, she had just a few months to live. Two other part-time paid companions kept her company when I was not with her.

I had never looked after an elderly person. I had never even visited a nursing home. However, I had the time and wanted to give it a try to help out, as Scott had done so much for me. I told him I would make no promises, because of my condition, but would try. There are always new things to learn and interesting people to meet, and it's nice to do something different. Plus, in some ways, I was suited to the work. As a professional dominatrix, I am a good listener and I have a lot of patience.

At first glance, his aunt looked like the stereotype of a classic matriarch. Her hair was white as and soft as snow; her peaches-and-cream complexion showed hardly a wrinkle. I could still see traces of beauty that time could not erase. She sat still in her wheelchair, her little legs and tiny feet dangling several inches above the footrests. Scott introduced us. I immediately took her hand and told her not to worry and that I would be there for her. I had to work to remember to speak loudly, or at least clearly, and directly at her.

She grabbed my hand, kissed it, and said "Thank you, darling," in a distinct European accent that reminded me of Zsa Zsa Gabor.

Aunty had lived twice my life in years. Her life had been just as active as mine—which, as you know, has been anything but dull. She was the youngest of twelve children, and she had come to Canada alone when barely a teenager because her family in Europe was too poor to keep her, and some of her sisters had already migrated. Her mother had died shortly after she was born.

She and her late husband had worked hard most of their lives, yet she had little left, having lived so long. She was street smart and clever, and she loved to talk. Indeed, there was little else she could do. She asked me many questions about my life. I only told her that I was a manual worker, but that because of a back injury, I was living off a disability pension, so I was free to spend time with her. I added that it was a nice change of scenery for me for a couple of days a week. She never learned who I really was.

Sitting with Aunty gave me the opportunity to listen to a fascinating, bittersweet life story. In return I told her jokes and funny stories that made her laugh and forget her troubles.

She never ceased to surprise me. One day she was sitting silently in her wheelchair when, suddenly, she asked me if I "sucked cock." Those exact words! She said if you want to keep a man or take another woman's man, that's how you do it.

When I stopped laughing, I said, "I'll tell you if you tell me."

She laughed back and said for her the answer was no, because that "would make me a whore." Of course I told her I agreed with her. Many times, though, I was tempted to tell her who and what I really was.

You may wonder if, over the years, I have been recognized when out in public. Didn't I have to give my name and show identification to the staff of Aunty's nursing home? I did give my name and show my identification. Terri-Jean is my middle name. So all my identification lists my formal first name, and it was by that name that Aunty, the staff at the home, and her other companions knew me. I wore a different wig than people were used to seeing me wearing when photographed or on television. I also wore glasses. I had special glasses for this purpose, with plain lenses that did not change my vision, but made my face look much different than usual. Nonetheless, a few people looked at me as if they recognized me, but nobody said they did.

The nursing home itself provided me with a getaway from home. The facility hosted activities, although Aunty did not attend very many. I got to meet many health-care professionals, social workers, and other staff of this large facility. When I started caring for Aunty, it was wintertime, but when the warm weather came, we spent many hours outside. She enjoyed sitting in the sun and feeling the breeze. It was so sad that she could not see. I learned about life in such a place: how slow and unhurried things often had to be, and the importance of both routine and variety. I also saw how families coped, or didn't cope, with the challenge of aging loved ones.

When Aunty became ill and was taken to the hospital for the last time, all three of us who were her companions followed. We were with her as much as possible in those final two weeks as she slowly died. Her will to live was incredible to see. I will always consider it an honor and a privilege to have been with such an extraordinary lady in her final months. Scott asked me to stay away from the funeral, and rightly so. His privacy had to be protected, and it would have been awkward for him if I were recognized and perhaps pointed out. This was bound to happen with a large number of people assembled.

And Up to Now

In 2007 Scott took me to a lawyer who came highly recommended to him. I think this was the first time I ever consulted with a lawyer for anything other than a legal battle. This was Sender Herschorn. Sender is a well established Toronto lawyer whose practice includes family and criminal law. Sender has worked with me on my will and made many arrangements and representations related to the book you are reading. He has read and advised on my manuscripts. He is also a source of advice and assistance to my daughter when needed. Sender has been wonderful.

As you will soon see, my legal battles resumed. They began around the time I was helping with Aunty and, although a constant preoccupation, they have not demanded more than an average of a couple of days per week, when I was up to being involved. I have continued to live quietly in shared accommodation and have done what I can to fight my afflictions. Some weekends I have spent at Michelle's cottage. I have been painting and done some photography. I have done and am doing a bit of part-time phone work and paperwork for a local business. As I mentioned, my liver disease is very advanced but at the moment not progressing significantly. I don't hold false hopes, but sometimes I pray.

I put my memoirs on hold again in 2006 because I was once again going to court to fight our terrible laws, and I did not want to tell my story before that was at least partly over. You are, of course, reading my memoirs. So now let me tell you about my last legal battle.

Chapter 18

CONSTITUTIONAL CHALLENGE

In 2006 Alan told me he was ready to proceed with a motion to strike down Canada's prostitution laws. You may recall that Alan saw his mission as a lawyer and law professor as getting government out of the private lives of consenting adults. He believes that laws such as Canada's prostitution laws and marijuana laws are bad as well as underenforced. They are bad because their existence does more harm than good. For example, marijuana was one of Canada's largest export crops, yet the mere possession of it, let alone the sale of it, was illegal. Its use is widespread. In the United States, hundreds of thousands of marijuana users were in jail for mere possession.

It's much the same for prostitution, whatever that is. For now let's say it's a woman having intercourse, performing oral sex, or doing a rub and tug in a massage parlor. In the United States, again, hundreds of thousands are in jail for prostitution-related offenses. All for consenting behavior among adults.

Canada's prostitution laws were and are a fiasco. I won't get into the technical details any more than I have to, at least for now. Believe it or not, prostitution has always been legal in Canada. That applies no matter what your definition of prostitution is. Not only that, but there is no clear definition of what sex is or what a prostitute is. In the appeal of my conviction, Justice Finlayson basically said it was whatever the local cop deemed it was. S&M might or might not be sex. Cross-dressing might or might not be sex. But again, prostitution is not illegal. So the authorities here control the terms of prostitution using three laws.

- The first law forbids communication for the purposes of prostitution. This basically means you cannot exchange words that might lead to sex for money. So if I ask a man to have sex with me and afterward he leaves an envelope with money without being prompted by me (not even telepathy is allowed), I am not a criminal.

- The second law says anyone sharing in the proceeds of prostitution is a criminal. So if I had a man drive me to the place where the sex occurred and act as security during the act, paid him out of the proceeds of the found envelope, and never communicated with my sex partner for money for the act, my chauffeur and bodyguard is not a criminal.

- The third law says you may not run a common bawdy house. This refers to an establishment where prostitution or indecent acts habitually and frequently occur. So to remain in compliance with the law I have to have this noncommercial sex in different places. As for indecent acts, that is set by something called community standards. So the local cop could arbitrarily deem something indecent and deem a place a bawdy house. The bottom line is, as you will see, that the law was "impermissibly vague." You remember my open letter, of course. You find out the rules after you break them.

But what can one do? In my trials and the subsequent appeals, the judges had plenty of opportunity to show that the authorities must not be arbitrary and that the laws had to be more specific. In my first trial, Judge O'Hara quashed the case because the charges were vague. Other judges had cited my case to acquit others under the bawdy-house laws. Parliamentary committees, academic papers, coalitions, and even individual members of Parliament had spoken against the laws, yet there seemed to be no widespread support for changing them. No political party could see themselves gaining votes by defining what private behavior should be regulated by the government and how.

Canada elected a new government early in 2006. The Conservative Party, led by the new prime minister, Stephen Harper, replaced the Liberal Party. The

Conservatives were more right-wing than the previous government. Part of that was a more "law and order" agenda, basically meaning "stiffer penalties" for offenders. Some of the new Conservative Party members of Parliament were religious Christians, for whom it would likely be distasteful to engage in any debate in which they would have to justify regulating people's sex lives while in the next breath touting less government involvement in society. So organized crime, pimps, underage prostitutes, tax evasion, spread of disease, violence against women in the sex trade, and all the other negatives of the current situation would go on as before. (Remember also, however, that the Liberals had had many years to remedy this legal mess and did nothing).

In my open letter, I had written that the courts may not be the place to change the situation, but I may have been wrong. Alan told me that things had changed. Over the previous ten years, statistics and other evidence had become available that showed that the current laws were unconstitutional. In Canada we have a kind of rulebook for lawmakers called the Charter of Rights and Freedoms. It is similar to the US Constitution. When a law is on the books, it can be challenged as unconstitutional and therefore illegal itself.

Alan explained to me when he was considering mounting the challenge that it was not just the fact that the laws were vague and arbitrarily enforced. He said they were also discriminatory against women, caused more harm than good, and worked against the ends they were supposed to promote. But, I asked, didn't you need to be charged and become a defendant in order to challenge the validity of the law? Alan said no, although that is usually how citizens raise the issue of constitutionality. He was planning to sue the government of Canada for having the laws and thereby have a judge strike them down. I will tell you more about the specific arguments later.

He said the process required plaintiffs, ordinary citizens, who would come forward and argue that they had been, and continued to be, negatively impacted by the laws. He wanted me to be one of them, because of my notoriety and because the press was always asking him about me more than any of his other cases, despite the fact I had been out of the public eye for a few years at this point. He said my notoriety would greatly increase all types of support he would need, and that I was an ideal plaintiff from a technical legal standpoint. He said that the fact that my last name began with the letter B would give additional public impact, since alphabetically I would be the first plaintiff: Bedford versus Canada.

However, I did have some reservations. I have always maintained that a dominatrix was not a prostitute. But I had been a prostitute, and the term *prostitute* needed defining. I knew I would be called upon to explain this confusion, but I felt it was imperative that I participate despite the old dominatrix-versus-prostitute subissue. I have told you my story as a prostitute. I am probably going to die prematurely because of the way in which the law now forces prostitutes to live. I know what the girls go through and that the existing laws are a large cause.

I was too ill to do very much, and I was certainly no lawyer. But if I could lend my signature, name, and face to this and speak to it occasionally, I was going to do it. There were also the two other plaintiffs. All of you owe them a debt of gratitude, whatever your views on the issues are.

Valerie Scott had worked in the sex trade since the early 1980s; in recent years, she has worked as an activist, campaigning for the rights of sex workers. She had served as the executive director of Sex Professionals of Canada (SPOC) and had been regularly communicating to the federal government that violence against sex-trade workers on the streets had been escalating. To combat this violence, she posts a "bad date" list on the SPOC website, so that sex-trade workers on the streets can obtain information about customers who may pose a risk to their physical safety. Val wanted to resume work in the sex trade by opening a secure and safe indoor location, but did not do so because of the criminal prohibition on bawdy houses.

Amy Lebovitch had been a sex trade worker since 1997. She had worked on the streets but then chose to work from her home. By working from her home, she believed she had increased her physical security, but was concerned about the legal consequences of working indoors. She was also concerned that her live-in partner would be charged with living on the avails of a prostitute. Amy was well-educated and came from an affluent family. Despite these advantages, she was a free spirit, and an ordinary lifestyle were not for her. She was in her thirties when she came forward.

The laws had not changed in well over twenty years, and their enforcement was erratic, to say the least. It was obvious for other reasons as well that the time was ripe for such a challenge. Canada had been shocked by the mass murders of women in western Canada by serial killer Robert Pickton, a farmer who picked up street prostitutes, killed them on his farm, and fed their bodies to his pigs. It is possible he killed over fifty women. But that was just the most sensational case. From 1991 to 2001, seventy-three prostitutes were murdered while working the streets. Take note: those are the ones confirmed by investigations. What about those not reported? Significant findings had also emerged in new research that had not been made available to the courts that made prostitution rulings in the past. The new information confirmed that the laws worked counter to their objectives—that they caused more harm than safety. Alan was going to argue this fact, and also that the victims were disproportionately women. So he had his evidence and his arguments lined up.

The specific legal arguments for striking down Canada's prostitution laws centered on the fact that it was impossible for sex-trade workers, whose occupation is not illegal and who are overwhelmingly women, to pursue this lawful trade in a safe and secure environment. They are not permitted a secure premises, security guards, or even accountants. Their landlords can be charged. This means that a large underground industry arises, inviting the interference of pimps and organized crime, and these women are afraid to report it when they are abused by their pimps or crime bosses. If a prostitute goes to the police, she fears being charged, especially if she is the perfect recruit for prostitution: a young, female illegal immigrant who has been put to work in brothels and massage parlors and does not even know whom she is working for. Raids on these establishments are regular, and new ones open up as soon as old ones close. The point is that the prostitution laws are not constitutional, because they negatively impact a segment of society in a discriminatory manner.

The legal battle that followed was over a period of over four years and is not over yet.

- The challenge was filed and announced in March 2007.

- Affidavits were filed by the three plaintiffs and the experts in the ensuing months.

- Early in the process, there were also hearings in front of a judge by various groups who wanted to be interveners. Interveners are parties to the proceedings in that they get to provide evidence and arguments to the judge.

- Cross-examination of the experts behind closed doors went on from mid-2007 to mid-2009. No judge was present during testimony, but transcripts were produced.

- In the fall of 2009, nine days of arguments by the lawyers and interveners were held before a judge.

- In the fall of 2010, almost a full year after the last day in court, the judge, Judge Himel, released her decision.

- The appeal of the decision is to be heard in June 2011, and the decision of the appeal court will probably be released several months later.

- It is uncertain at this writing how long the stay on Judge Himel's decision will be extended.

Launching the Challenge

In March 2007, Alan called a press conference to announce the challenge. Val and I were there. Amy chose and has chosen to avoid being photographed. This has enabled her to act unrecognized in whatever she chooses to do—a wise choice in her situation. Val and I had long ago had our pictures published and did not have the same decision to make. However, Amy has spoken on the radio and given interviews over the phone to reporters.

There was a small turnout at the press conference, but the major Canadian press services were there, along with the television networks. But what could they report? They gave the basics of the challenge in their stories, usually showing or quoting Alan. They printed glib headlines like "Dominatrix Out to Whip Hooker Laws." Then they gave a picture or clip of Val or me speaking about it as well as the backgrounds of Val, Amy, and me. Most of the pictures were of me because of my prior publicity and because it was apparently more of an attention-grabber to show or talk about a dominatrix going to court than a prostitute. Canada's attorney general made no attempt to comment.

But after the press conference, there was nothing for the press to report. The experts' hearings were not attended by the media. There was no requirement to open them to the public. So for eighteen months, no personalities or images fed the media, and we disappeared below the radar.

Interveners

In 2009, as the date for open court approached, four parties sought intervener status. The government of Ontario sought and obtained intervener status at the hearings. However, Judge Himel did not give that status to the other three groups seeking to intervene in the case after hearing their requests and Alan's argument against granting them this status. She felt that the input from these groups would be covered by the expert testimony. These three groups were the Christian Legal Fellowship, REAL Women of Canada, and the Catholic Civil Rights League. All three of them wanted our motion to be defeated. They appealed to the Ontario Court of Appeal, which reversed Judge Himel's decision and granted them intervener status. These groups are basically religious groups, although REAL Women of Canada is more of an antifeminist group. They believed that if we won, it would send a signal to Canadians that you can always make a living as a last resort by selling your body. This was the third time the Ontario Court of Appeal ruled against me.

Our Team and Theirs

The lawyers on our side throughout the case made quite a lineup. Alan represented me and headed the team for the plaintiffs. He was assisted by two lawyers. Ron Marzel represented Amy, and Stacey Nichols represented Val. Ron was a partner in a small legal firm that provided a broad range of legal services to businesses. But he had diversified as a lawyer and worked with Alan on the issue of the availability of medical marijuana, and had risen to prominence with his work on that issue. Now he was again rising to prominence by representing our matter with Alan. Of course, Ron had a practice to be concerned about, and was not being paid to be a member of our team. Nonetheless he worked with the media, reviewed all materials, and worked with Alan on the submissions to ensure his client's interests and wishes were properly represented and protected. Stacey Nichols, Val's lawyer, served her client in a similar way. Stacey was not a veteran lawyer, but she was a heavyweight already. For one thing, she was a former Crown attorney. She had represented clients involved in issues ranging from fraud and civil actions to mental-health cases before courts and tribunals. As if that weren't enough, she had been involved with other constitutional challenges and was a partner in a thriving practice. What a team! Alan had plenty of backup if the need arose.

And what a team there was helping the team. The three lawyers were assisted by a group of law students from York University's Osgoode Hall Law School. This would be a big feather in their caps for the remainder of their careers. They coordinated the vetting of experts, did research, prepared and proofread documents, and did whatever else needed doing.

Two lawyers and numerous assistants headed up the opposition by the attorney general: Gail Sinclair and Michael Morris. As I have said before, lawyers have a job to do, and theirs was not an easy one. They fought the motion by bringing experts of their own and by vigorously cross-examining the three plaintiffs and our experts. They attacked evidence, arguments, and credibility. If they were to lose, it was not because of lack of skill, hard work, or resources. They were nobody's fool.

Hearings behind Closed Doors

After the affidavits were submitted, we began a process, lasting about eighteen months, of cross-examining the witnesses: the three plaintiffs and experts of both sides. Curiously enough, most of the meetings were held in the Trudeau Room, in a government building. Pierre Trudeau had been Canada's prime minister during most of the years from 1968 to 1984. One of his famous quotes was the "The state has no business in the bedrooms of the nation."

On our side, twenty-one witnesses tendered affidavit evidence for the application. Collectively we described and outlined the nature and frequency of physical and psychological violence experienced by sex-trade workers in Canada. Of the twenty-one witnesses, eleven had worked or were working in the sex trade. Of these eleven, four were then working for groups or associations that provided assistance to sex-trade workers. Eight witnesses had academic postings at various universities across Canada, and most had conducted formal research into issues relating to violence against sex-trade workers. One witness was a journalist, and another was a member of Parliament. All of them maintained that the current legal regime significantly contributed to the risk of violence experienced by women who entered the sex trade. The Crown countered with thirty-two witnesses of their own. Not all witnesses were cross-examined. Alan's team simply did not want to waste their time on witnesses whose evidence they saw as irrelevant.

There were no examinations in chief (the questioning of your own witness under oath), only affidavits that the witnesses defended in cross-examination. They then answered questions from the lawyer for the side they were appearing for. This is called reexamination. These sessions were usually held in a boardroom in a downtown Toronto office building. There were only ten people in the room at most. A court reporter also attended to produce the transcripts. Because of my medical condition, it was difficult to sit for full days or even a few hours; some days I had to stay home. At one point, in the late summer of 2009, I was so ill I could attend no sessions at all for two months. However, overall, I attended about two-thirds of the sessions and, when there, I read the affidavits as well. The court record amounted to tens of thousands of pages of transcripts and exhibits, all now available on a disk to all parties involved in the proceedings. It was no wonder the judge needed almost a year to write her decision. Over the eighteen-month period, I would say sessions were held an average of two days a week. Of course, preparation and follow-up were done on the off-days.

My role was basically to be a member of the team and do support work. I went to the airport to meet some of the witnesses, put a couple of them up at my place, and escorted them to the hearing room when I was well enough, and sometimes when I wasn't. I would sit in on most of the cross-examinations of the witnesses I escorted when I was able. Michelle, of The Dozen, my loyal sissy slave, took me to the airport in his luxury car to pick up experts and take them to their accommodations. Sometimes he would ask for permission to speak, and the experts would be surprised at how articulate he was. He was usually cross-dressed for the occasion. The experts found all this to be quite a hoot. During this time, I got to know some very prominent intellectuals and other types of people. On several occasions, Alan, an expert, and I would go for a working dinner, with me mostly listening to them discuss what needed to be done for the coming cross-examination. It was so reassuring, almost shocking, to see how much support we had for our application, and the quality of that support. I did not meet some of them, such as Libby Davies, the member of Parliament, who had been advocating reform of the laws. I hope to meet her someday.

To sit in on those sessions was to observe some stunning contrasts. Our experts gave statistics and evidence that stood the test of cross-examination. They debunked the myths about the harm that would arise if prostitution were legalized. They accurately portrayed the experiences in other countries where the laws were more liberal. They established that things were getting worse for women in the sex trade under the current laws and that governments were fighting—to the limited extent they were fighting—a losing war. Our experts were on point in that they addressed the legal points on which the application turned and, unlike the opposition's experts, they didn't just spout platitudes. Our experts were effective when cross-examined, whereas theirs were easily dismantled by Alan in cross-examination.

This raised an interesting question: why would the Crown bother spending so much time and money to produce so much that was irrelevant? You may remember that Scott was well connected in surprising places. He called some of his contacts in the government, who very willingly filled him in. The Crown had been instructed from Ottawa to make our case go away. If delay would do it, they were to delay. If prolonging proceedings would do it, they were to prolong. If winning would do it, they were to win. But above all, they were to make it go away from the public view—especially when the government in Ottawa held a minority.

In Canada the usual course is for the political party with the most seats in our Parliament's lower house, the House of Commons, to govern the country. The party may have a majority of the seats or only a plurality of seats, in which case it needs the support of some members of the opposition parties to remain in office. Stephen Harper's Conservatives, as I mentioned earlier, came into office about a year before we filed our application. They had a reputation for having a kiss-up and kick-down management style, as well as the priorities I also mentioned earlier. So rather than speak to the government about the merits of the motion, the Crown just listened to the order, clicked their heels, and attacked us any way they could. Failure was not an option. So they made it a massive undertaking by piling on the material and prolonging the process. If nothing else, the sheer volume of material would discourage judges from wading in.

Of course, Val, Amy, and I had also submitted affidavits, so we were cross-examined as well. Val answered many questions about SPOC and dealt with the Crown's expected attempts to show that it was never totally safe to be a prostitute. Val was calm and often responded by challenging the relevance of the Crown's questions. Amy, being younger and less seasoned, found the experience stressful. She was sometimes on the verge of tears, but managed to relax as the session went on. Val and Amy spent about four or five hours each in session.

I Am Questioned

My turn came in the summer of 2008. Some members of the media were there outside the boardroom; they photographed me and asked me questions. They wanted to sit in on my cross-examination. They had not attended any of the others; the question had simply not come up. Alan and the other lawyers discussed it for over an hour while I gave interviews. In the end they decided, mainly at Alan's request, not to admit the media to this session or any other, because media presence might inhibit testimony from witnesses. Much of that testimony would cover topics like abuse the witness may have suffered, and they might struggle even harder to be forthcoming if they knew their testimony would be in the press and mainstream media with their name disclosed.

My testimony lasted about four hours, with a late lunch break. I was not nervous. I had been through this type of thing before, in court and the press. I wanted to tell my story because I believed in what we were doing. Alan had prepared me for this day, but it was hardly necessary: the affidavits and cross-examination of the plaintiffs was more of a formality than anything else. I went in knowing that nothing any of us—Val, Amy, or me—were likely to say in the session would alter the final decision. The experts, the hard evidence, and the legal arguments were what mattered. Nonetheless, when they cross-examined me, they tried to establish that my life as a prostitute caused or contributed to my other problems and tried to elicit information about my daughter's participation in the dominatrix trade. I was talkative and frequently digressed, which tried the patience of all the lawyers, including my own. But I had nothing to hide. My life was an open book, and when asked, I read that book to them. The transcript of the session runs to about eighty pages. Sure enough, the judge barely referred to the cross-examinations of the plaintiffs in her decision, but the transcripts proved valuable to me as notes for the writing of this book.

Judge Himel

The closed-door sessions had ended, and now, in the fall of 2009, it was time to go to open court, where the lawyers would make their submissions and the judge could question them. Much would depend on the judge. Justice Himel had overseen the administrative aspects of the case; her ruling on the interveners had been overturned by the Ontario Court of Appeal. She was going to remain on the case itself, and not just oversee its administration: she would make the decision.

Scott again got on the phone and was pleased with what he heard. He found out that Himel was no Bogusky or Finlayson. She was a very energetic judge who paid close attention to proceedings and was unafraid of making decisions. Perhaps the higher court's reversal of her first decision, on the intervener question, would give her some incentive to give them a decision they would have trouble reversing. But Scott said she had a reputation of being very rigorous. She wouldn't just make a decision because of a sense of right or wrong or to settle a score among insiders. Our application had to stand the test of the legal system. So, all in all, I concluded that she was likely to be fair.

I was also glad the judge was a woman. It just seemed to me that you almost had to be a woman to pass judgment on a matter like this. How could a man understand what it was like to be a prostitute? Plus, she might know other women who had been prostitutes. Maybe she had had experience with such issues before becoming a judge or while she was a judge. Also, female lawyers are more likely to do family law and criminal law than the males.

Whatever her background, this matter was about to become Judge Himel's to decide. And when she did, the world was shocked.

Chapter 19

Constitutional Decision

Open Court

I was in court again, but this time I was there by my own choosing. This time I was expecting to win. It felt good.

It was so reassuring to see that the media remained so interested in me and my doings. For a total of nine days in October and November 2009, in a courtroom in downtown Toronto, with the media there, Judge Susan Himel heard from Alan, Ron, Stacey, Gail, Michael, Shelley, and three other lawyers representing the three interveners. Many boxes of transcripts, affidavits, and other evidence were wheeled in. I sat at a table behind Alan and his legal team and assistants, the ever-present students. About five assistants had come with the government lawyers. Also present were a court reporter to produce transcripts, a court clerk, and of course the judge. At the back were seated between twenty and thirty spectators each day, consisting of media, legal students following the case, the interveners themselves, and other interested citizens.

Scott and The Geek had ensured that the media would be there. We sent out a press release describing the reasons for the hearing and explaining that this was the culmination of over two years of activity behind closed doors. On the first day, I was met in front of the building by cameras and microphones. I was wearing a very fashionable leather suit and black dress boots with spike heels and black leather gloves. The photographers got plenty of pictures and splashed them throughout the papers and television. Of course they made sure they described what I was wearing and mentioned that I had brought my riding crop. But in addition to amusing the public, the media made efforts to inform them as well. In the ensuing eight days, the reporters shifted their coverage away from me and reported what was said by the lawyers and the judge.

The lawyers for the two governments and the interveners argued against the challenge on the grounds that prostitution was bad both for society and for the members of the trade. They also attacked the standing of Val and my application, saying we were not valid plaintiffs since we were not currently working in the trade.

Alan argued that the merits of prostitution as a trade for individuals or society were not on trial. He repeated the argument that the laws were unconstitutional for the reasons I have told you about before. He attacked the relevance of the testimony of the Crown's experts and suggested they were more activists and advocates than experts. He said their evidence was unsupportable and went into considerable detail to show why.

Clearly the judge was having difficulty with the cases being made by the governments and interveners. She constantly interrupted them and asked them to clarify how their points were relevant to the application, whereas when Alan or our other lawyers spoke, she rarely interrupted and made extensive notes. She extended the hearing from the six days scheduled to another three days in November. She appeared to make every effort to ensure that all arguments got a hearing.

When Alan made his summation, I was practically reduced to tears. I had never heard him speak so eloquently. Without wasting a word, he hit so many points squarely that to me, at least, there hardly seemed to be anything left in the way of opposition to our application.

The media coverage moved off the front pages, and there were no more new images to produce. But the essentials were still reported nationally, and the topic was raised in editorials and letters to the editor as well as on radio talk shows. The consensus seemed to be clearly in favor of our application; there was general agreement that the laws needed overhauling, and considerable debate on what the new laws should seek to achieve.

I went to most of the court sessions. I wanted to go to all of them, but some days I just wasn't well enough. When I did go after that first day, I dressed conservatively. The images were no longer important; a major public trial was under way, and the stage belonged to the judge, the lawyers, and the issues.

Decision

Judge Himel had six months to reach a decision from the date she began hearing the case, with the option of extending her decision preparation for up to another six months. The due date was September 30, 2010. Finally, on September 28, 2010, her decision was released. We were advised of the release a few days before.

Alan wanted Val, Amy, and me to accompany him to the courthouse to receive an envelope with a copy of the decision, after which we would have a press conference at a nearby community center. Scott was there with us, and he had the Geek on alert. When Scott had the decision, they would do a press release and update my website. I would be at the press conference. Scott and I discussed what I would say in the event of different outcomes, just as before. I was ready. I was confident. I was nervous.

We gathered at the courthouse. Alan, Laura (Alan's wife), Val, Ron, Stacey, some of the students, Scott, and I were there. I was dressed just like on the first court day: leather, boots, gloves, and riding crop. Alan was handed the envelope and stepped away to read it without distraction. He kept his back to us and faced a wall to concentrate while scanning the decision, which was 131 pages. Waiting for him to tell us what the judge had decided was pure suspense.

When he turned around and spoke, it would set the landscape for me for years to come. If we won, it probably meant I would be at the center of a high-profile national legal battle touching the deepest nerves of millions of people. If we lost, my legal battles would probably be very much over and my story a bit less interesting. The others standing with me were also biting their nails, so to speak. And outside the courtroom, the impact that would or would not be felt was about to become known in just seconds.

After about two minutes, he turned around. He came up to us ... and was smiling. He told us we had won! We had won big! Judge Himel agreed with us on just about everything! She had struck down the three main laws against prostitution in Canada. What a moment, and not just for me, or us, but for everyone in Canada. The laws were only struck down in Ontario, but nationally the path was clear.

I wasn't just happy. It was the happiest day of my life.

Scott had already been hustling some television reporters, who were there to cover another story, and in minutes we had microphones in our faces, and the cameras were rolling. Scott got a copy of the decision and headed home to go to work on the publicity. By phone he told me that within two hours, the story had gone viral. I was getting calls from all sorts of media requesting interviews. I gave Scott the contact info and got him to schedule my appearances. Then our group walked to the community center, where the press conference was scheduled for one hour after the release of the decision. With my spike heels, it was a slow walk, and the students had to make sure I didn't fall. I got lots of looks on the street. An obvious dominatrix surrounded by cameras and a small crowd, making her way down busy downtown streets! You had to see it to believe it.

At the press conference, Alan briefed the media, and Val spoke about how women and society would benefit from an overhaul of the laws. I read a statement saying that the onus was now on the prime minister to ensure that Parliament finally acted on the will of the people, and on today's invalidation of the laws, to ensure that clear, fair laws were passed that respected people's freedoms and protected them. I pointed out that nothing could be worse than the laws the judge had struck down. I invoked the prime minister's name specifically, because he had a reputation for running a tight ship, and without his intervention, nothing was likely to be done. It would also more likely that the media would follow up if it were the PM who was called upon to take a position. There would also be media pressure on him, and he would be characterized as cowardly, if the government appealed, as was expected, and he merely said that the matter was before the courts on appeal. The press conference got a lot of coverage.

All over the papers and on television the next day was a picture or clip of me holding up my riding crop and yelling "Hurray!" There were also pictures of Val and Alan. There was even a cartoon of Judge Himel dressed as a dominatrix with a whip, standing by a copy of the Canadian Constitution, which she had presumably shredded with the whip. Of course the media mentioned the reasons for Judge Himel's decision, but they were obscured by the wider debate on the merits of legalizing prostitution. Of course the things I fought for, like clear laws which defined prostitution, were lost in the shuffle. But that was okay. The main thing was that the debate was on.

The decision included a stay. That meant that for thirty days after the September 28 release date, the old laws remained in effect in order to allow the authorities to prepare for what might happen when the old laws expired. The federal government, however, only needed a few hours to announce that they were going to appeal. In less time than what was required to get and read the decision, they made up their minds. Great government! Great prime minister! It didn't take the government of Ontario much longer. Monkey see, monkey do, right, Mr. Premier? ("Premier" is the title given to what amounts to the prime ministers of the Canadian provinces.) At least the premier was in a position where he could claim he had read the decision.

So the days ahead looked as if they were going to be interesting. The media said that the matter would probably be before the court for years. Fair enough; my previous cases had been before the courts for years. But what about the stay? Would that be extended?

What the Judge Wrote

Before I tell you what happened next, let's, at last, look at just what Judge Himel said. In her 131-page decision, she noted that she had examined 25,000 pages of material encased in 88 volumes. She took almost a year to prepare her decision. So this was not a whimsical ruling by a lower court judge. This was a meticulous and learned analysis.

She pointed out what her decision was *not* about. It was not about the good and bad of prostitution, or even what prostitution was. It was also not about whether prostitution was illegal. It was not. The decision was about whether three provisions in the Criminal Code were constitutional. With that in mind, she went into a great deal of detail about what might make laws unconstitutional. Finally, she put her decision into context. She distinguished what her role was and what Parliament's role was, and put it squarely to our political leaders that they had some work to do.

She analyzed the evidence given by the witnesses, particularly the experts. She analyzed the affidavits and transcripts of the cross-examinations of dozens of expert witnesses. In addition, she analyzed, in the context of this case, what Parliamentary committees and working groups and other committees had published prior to this case. She commented extensively on the experience of other countries in dealing with prostitution, thereby answering squarely most of the comments on this topic made subsequently by those who had not read the decision. And finally, she commented at great length on what other judges had to say about the arguments used by our side and by our opponents. According to learned commentators, she was writing as much for higher courts as anyone else.

She found that our application was right. The laws against communicating for the purposes of prostitution, living off the avails of prostitution, and keeping a common bawdy house were unconstitutional for a number of reasons. For one thing, they did not achieve their objectives but in fact worked in the opposite direction. She agreed that the laws prevented prostitutes from protecting themselves, and that the laws protected the perpetrators of violence against women more than they inhibited such violence. She agreed that indoor prostitution was safer than street prostitution. She agreed that the current prostitution laws were only minimally enforced. She agreed that the laws were too broad, leading to unelected officials distinguishing right from wrong. She agreed that striking down the laws would not lead to a dramatic increase in prostitution. She pointed out that numerous other laws are already on the books to combat the worst aspects of the sex trade. In her own words: "The conclusion I have reached is that three provisions of the Criminal Code that seek to address facets of prostitution … are not in accord with fundamental justice and must be struck down."

She went to great length to point out that Alan was right to say that the Crown's witnesses were advocates more than experts, and that the Crown was often off point in arguing against our application. She further noted that the arguments against the application were also more rhetorical than relevant. She seemed to be validating my testimony. The government, lacking a winning strategy, had resorted to delay and attrition: months of useless evidence and arguments to delay a judgment. As a taxpayer, the judge may have been angry, but could not say so. It was one thing for the general public to comment without knowing what they were talking about. It was quite something else for government lawyers to keep talking when they had nothing to say. Have I mentioned that these guys were overpaid?

I Speak Out

For the next three days, I did interviews for television, radio, and print media. Alan was with me for some of those. I would say I did about twenty interviews from home over the phone. Alan also did some interviews on his own, as did Val. Our other lawyers also did some media. The government lawyers were unseen and unheard. The lawyers for the interveners also were interviewed. Of course, activists of all types, discussion panels, and editorial writers jumped in. After those three days, I was so exhausted I slept for most of the next three days.

Then Scott came over and said another open letter was appropriate—a formal statement of where I stood on the decision, what should happen next, and my reaction to the governments' decisions to appeal. Together we worked up a new open letter and released it to all the media on our contact list. Here it is.

> It has been just over a week since the Canadian judicial decision striking down our laws restricting prostitution, a legal occupation. I am one of the three plaintiffs. The proceedings lasted almost 3 years, with thousands of pages of evidence, many weeks of closed testimony from dozens of experts, and 9 days of public argument. The 131-page decision took the judge almost a year to prepare. But the federal government announced an appeal within hours of its release.
>
> Politics, not prostitution, is the world's oldest profession. It was in all probability the prime minister, without even having the time to read the decision, who decided to appeal it. His justice minister is a transient name and face between cabinet shuffles. His party never draws a breath unless he signs off first. It must have been the prime minister's decision.
>
> The appeal process may take years. If the government wins each appeal, prostitution will remain legal, yet the law will criminalize those who are involved. The prime minister will have preserved a status quo that nobody understands, that few obey, that is

rewarding organized crime, that responds to stiffer penalties with more recruits, and that puts the vulnerable at risk. All this while he has a comprehensive constitutional judicial ruling as proof that the laws need to change. I am not even talking about which direction that change should take. I am simply talking about Parliament finally getting around to making decisions.

The people want Parliament to act. If the status quo remains intact, Canada will become a laughingstock. The polls on this that I have read or heard reports about generally indicate that 75 percent of the people asked approved of the judge's decision. The rest are split between not approving and having no position. Almost everyone dislikes the status quo, whatever their views on prostitution. Some charges have already been dropped.

I have also read and listened very carefully to the views of those who were opposed to the judge's action in striking down the laws. To me it seemed that few of those people have read the decision. And if they did read it, they failed to tell their readers or listeners that every objection to striking the laws that we have heard these last days received a detailed analysis in the decision. The judge explained why the current laws are wrong—no matter what your values or your views on prostitution.

The judge relied on proof. The government legal team, despite their vast budget, did not have the evidence that the laws were constitutional. Professor Young and his team of students and experts had the evidence that the laws were unconstitutional. I think that we all understand that the word "unconstitutional" is a code word for "wrong."

Those who think that a judge should not have been the one to decide the issue of whether the laws are constitutional should remember that the prime minister has just enlisted more judges via appeal. He had the alternative of not doing so and instead taking his position before Parliament and the people. I am not as concerned about what the specifics of his position may turn out to be as I am about his willingness to keep things the way they are—even as an interim measure. That is bad government.

Extending the Stay

The government lawyers asked Alan to agree to have the stay extended until all appeals had been heard. Alan agreed to extend the stay for an additional thirty days but added that there would be no further stays unless a quick hearing date was given for the appeal. He did not have to do this, but he recognized the importance of the changes taking place and, while demanding a timetable, wanted to be as responsible as possible. He needed my approval, and I had no problem with his thinking on this.

After a couple of weeks, the Crown filed a motion to extend the stay until after all appeals had been heard. This was not a surprise. The motion would be heard by the Ontario Court of Appeal. The judge was Alvin Rosenberg. He heard the case with only a couple of weeks left in the sixty days and made his decision a week later. He extended the stay until April 29, 2011. But would the Court of Appeal be able issue a decision on either the stay or the appeal of Judge Himel's decision by that time? As 2011 began, the Court of Appeal said it would hear the case for two weeks in June 2011, and it would be heard by six judges. I repeat: six judges. Normally, appeals are heard by three judges. They were obviously not taking the matter lightly.

But what about the stay? It expired almost two months before court convened. Would the Crown go back to court to get another stay? And what if the stay was extended? Would that extension cover the many months the Court of Appeal would need to produce a decision that had occupied the trial judge for almost a year?

The Prime Minister and the Dominatrix

I was at the court for the hearing to extend the stay. I made a point of dressing more conservatively than I had for the media in the past. I felt no need to attract attention by providing images. I carried no riding crop and wore no boots or gloves this time. I told the media there should be no appeal. I pleaded with them to ask Prime Minister Harper whether he had read the decision and what it was about the decision he disliked. And they did!

As it turned out, Mr. Harper was on a visit near Toronto that day, and some reporters told him that I wanted to know if he had read the decision and what he had to say about it. He smiled and said he did not know who I was and had never met me. They laughed at him. He then said he had never been asked to respond to a dominatrix before. They laughed again. He seemed a bit unnerved and spouted the usual clichés about being against prostitution and that it was bad for society.

After that incident, I got some e-mails and phone calls from reporters. They congratulated me and told me they were delighted with this opportunity to embarrass the prime minister. I felt that some response to him was necessary, so I wrote to the prime minister in the way a dominatrix would write to him, and I copied the press. At the end, I included the press release I had issued a week after the decision was released. Here is what I wrote to him.

> Your behavior requires modification. You told the media you have never heard of me even after you have devoted vast resources to appealing a 131-page court decision reached in my favor. If you are being honest, it means you are not up to date on current events. For even claiming not to know of me, you should be punished. You refused to answer the media as to whether you have read the decision. For being evasive, you should be punished. If you have not read the decision, you should be punished. If you have read the decision and believe what you say about the existing laws being good for the country, then you do not care about violence against women. For turning your back on abused women when you can do otherwise, you should be punished. On the other hand, if you have read the decision and realize the current laws are not good for the country, yet insist on appealing the decision to keep the laws intact, it means you are afraid to bring new laws in. For being afraid, you should be punished. Your punishment is to read my statement about your decision to appeal the judge's decision. I issued it a few days after you appealed. Here it is [and my recent open letter followed].

Alas, that is all I can tell you about my legal battles for now, since I must very soon hand in my manuscript. It is now March 2011. I hope that not only the prime minister and the premier of Ontario, but also all those who serve under them, will take a higher road than they have to date. If you are a Canadian, and particularly if you live in Ontario, make sure they do answer for their actions and their lack of action. If you are American, or wherever you are, learn from us here in Canada. Learn that people want to be free and safe. That means our leaders must make the tough decisions, not the easy ones. They must learn not to put themselves first, or else they will have to answer for their positions, or, failing that, learn to live with the blood of innocent people on their hands.

Chapter 20

Final Words

So now you know my story, with all its roles: child removed from her parents, abused foster child, wild teenager, addict, prostitute, dominatrix, legal battler, mother, and grandmother. I have always been on trial, fighting to survive or to vindicate myself. Now I am a sick older woman, often in pain, and I may not have long to live. But at least I have told my story, although there are parts of it of which I am not proud. It has often hurt and shamed me to look back. I had lots of help in writing it, especially toward the end, when my concentration and stamina began to decline, but even with that assistance, it has been a lot of work.

This effort was, all the same, worth it. As I worked on these memoirs, it became more and more clear to me that my life has not been a waste. I have made mistakes, and I have suffered, but it seems to me that when my first legal battle began, I was also making a contribution as a citizen and as a woman. I was fighting for something. At first I was fighting to make a life for myself and my daughter. Then I was fighting to vindicate myself and the others who were charged with me. Then I was fighting for others like me—women who were victims. But in a larger sense, I was fighting, and am now speaking, for all innocent victims.

I think our society is defined by who our victims are and what we do for them. Some are victims of misfortune who did nothing to deserve their suffering, such as those born poor, crippled, or ill. Even those who live wholesome lives are yet stricken with misfortune; bad things happen to good people. I can accept that. What I cannot accept are the needless victims, such as spouses, children, seniors, and animals who suffer neglect or abuse. Ask yourself what we are doing for them. Is it enough? Do our leaders care enough? Are things getting better or worse for them?

Then there are the victims of the abuse of power. There are workers who are taken advantage of. Innocent people are denied adequate protection from businesses that rip them off. Hospitals are too crowded. Jails are too crowded. Schools are too crowded. Public transit is too crowded. All this, yet we see so many enjoying so much luxury and security.

Judge Susan Himel agreed that another member of society, the prostitute, was a victim. But in particular, this type of victim is a victim of the law itself. Her decision was the culmination of literally decades of good works by citizens trying to improve our laws. But our leaders are not grateful for the opportunity they are given to make change. They have not risen to the level of understanding or caring that we require of our leaders if innocent victims are to be treated fairly.

Our leaders must rise and fight for people to get what they deserve, rather than only what they are given or can attain with luck, talent, or hard work. Some victims are not blessed with luck or talent, or are not in a position where their hard work will pay off.

But there is always hope. Never forget that, and never give up. As I told you at the beginning, heroes live among us, not just above us. It has been my distinct privilege to tell you about many of them: the sympathetic police officer and his wife in Windsor; numerous social workers; halfway-house workers; the lawyers; the activists; the media; and, of course, The Dozen. I wonder how many lives they have saved besides mine.

I have survived. I have lived to see my daughter, my grandchild, and others I love on the path to good and happy lives. I have helped others I have not met through my struggles. I am going out a winner.

CPSIA information can be obtained at www.ICGtesting.com
Printed in the USA
LVOW051612270911

248100LV00006B/32/P